Ghislain Lafont, O.S.B.

Imagining the Catholic Church

Structured Communion in the Spirit

Translated by
John J. Burkhard, O.F.M. CONV.

Foreword by
Rembert G. Weakland, O.S.B.

A Michael Glazier Book
THE LITURGICAL PRESS
Collegeville, Minnesota

www.litpress.org

A Michael Glazier Book published by The Liturgical Press

Cover design by David Manahan, O.S.B. Illustration: oil painting, *Church of the Minorities I*, 1924, Lyonel Feininger. Courtesy of Staatsgalerie, Stuttgart, Germany.

This book was first published in French under the title *Imaginer l'Eglise catholique,* © 1995 by les Editions du Cerf, Paris.

1	2	3	4	5	6	7	8

Library of Congress Cataloging-in-Publication Data

Lafont, Ghislain.
    [Imaginer l'Eglise catholique. English]
    Imagining the Catholic Church : structured communion in the spirit / Ghislain Lafont ; translated by John J. Burkhard ; foreword by Rembert G. Weakland.
      p. cm.
    "A Michael Glazier book."
    Includes bibliographical references and index.
    ISBN 0-8146-5946-2 (alk. paper)
    1. Catholic Church—Government. 2. Catholic Church—Doctrines. I. Title.

BX1802 .L34413 2000
282'.09'049—dc21

00-057459

Contents

Part II: Vatican II: Toward a New Form of the Church

Chapter 3: The Status of Truth   69

Foreword

Ghislain Lafont is a French Benedictine who was formerly the superior of the Priory of Chauveroche in the Diocese of Belfort. He has since returned to his home monastery of La Pierre-qui-Vire. During the years I was Primate of the Benedictine Confederation (1967–77), he came to Rome, at my request, to teach theology at the Pontifical Atheneum of Sant' Anselmo. During those years I came to know him personally, admiring his deep monastic roots and convictions and impressed by his reflective and serene approach to every theological issue.

There is a freshness about Father Ghislain's writing that will impress the reader at once. He proceeds not only to present a profound analysis of each problem and its historical roots, but to outline innovative and creative solutions that correspond to the theology of the Church in the documents of Vatican Council II. At the same time, one is surprised by his perceptive understanding of the current post-Enlightenment culture that dominates in our world. Perhaps only a monk, endowed with a certain innocence and insouciance about Church politics, could articulate with such fresh insights—which might appear at first blush to be rather startling—new conclusions to complex issues and to do so with such calm and faith-filled observations. Underneath those solutions—and as creative as they may at times seem to many—lies a well-thought-out theological perspective that can be at first reading very deceptive in its simplicity and profundity. These solutions are presented with tentativeness yet clarity, with modesty yet forcefulness, with serenity yet eagerness, because they have their roots not only in a set of personal theological convictions, but also in a deep love for the Church and a comprehensive knowledge of its history and theology.

Father Ghislain does not think in words, sentences, and paragraphs, but in centuries. For any practical applications of a new ecclesiological approach one must know the history of the present structures. Although Vatican Council II expected that there would also be structural reform in the Church, the bishops knew that this reform or *aggiornamento* could not happen without a good knowledge of where we have come from. Father Ghislain roams the historical territory with ease, describing the present structures and their roots with precision and clarity, pointing out the origins of so much of our structural heritage and thought, and then outlining the direction in which we should be moving in the light of the documents of Vatican Council II. At times his solutions might strike one as audacious, but the more one reflects on them the more one can see where they are leading and the vision of Church they presuppose. The major question he proposes to his readers is really whether the Church after Vatican Council II has found the structures for itself that reflect the theology it tried to put forth in its documents. Father Ghislain shows how structural change can take place if one alters one's thinking about the Church, refocusing one's attention on the new images of the Church that animated the bishops at Vatican Council II.

Father Ghislain's work is solidly based on the documents of Vatican Council II and their perspectives. He does not look back on those documents in a "restorationist" or "revisionist" fashion, but always searches out the vision that inspired them and made them different from previous official documents on Church structure. It is refreshing to see how a theologian, so embedded in the theology of that council, continues to carry forward its thrust; for Father Ghislain is a futurist, not in predicting what will happen, but in pointing out what could happen if we remain faithful to the vision of that council. Father Ghislain is not one to go back and reinterpret the council so that it turns out to be just a blip on the historical screen and the Church can then return to life as "normal." Instead, he seeks to ferret out how Vatican Council II opened up new vistas that correspond more to the needs of our times while remaining faithful to the larger historical tradition of the Church.

In keeping with this perspective, so ingrained in documents of that council, he also keeps before him an ecumenical vision. He sees, like many others in our day and as the Holy Father himself did in *Ut unum sint,* how important it is to seek new, creative, and unifying ways of imagining Church structures, especially with regard to the functioning of the papacy. Like Pope John Paul II, he knows that the future of Church unity depends on such rethinking and re-imagining.

It is a privilege to present to a larger English-speaking audience the creative theological insights of a friend and fellow monk whom I have known and admired for these many years—Father Ghislain Lafont.

Rembert G. Weakland, o.s.b.
Archbishop of Milwaukee, Wisconsin

Translator's Preface

In 1995, I had the opportunity to do some research in France. While there I came across the just released book *Imaginer l'Église Catholique* by Ghislain Lafont. Within the first few pages I sensed that this book was special. After reading it, I decided that it deserved to be translated into English and that I should bring it to the attention of a publisher in the United States. But what was it about the book that convinced me so quickly that it merited a wider audience? And what are the specific strengths of the book?

There are many fine books that approach the Church from various perspectives: history, exegesis, Church office and ministry, ecumenism, current pastoral problems, etc. Each approaches the Church from a valid point of view and adds its piece to the puzzle. In reading Lafont, however, first of all I had a sense of the Church as a whole, and that this comprehensive understanding emerged from a close reading of the Church's history and the current human condition. The general approach and perspectives made sense to me, and the proposals for solutions to particular problems possessed added power because they emerged from a comprehensive understanding of the Church. The Church cannot be contemplated in isolation from history and from the urgency of the human situation today as analyzed by social critics, sociologists, psychologists, literary and artistic figures, politicians, philosophers, as well as theologians. Lafont presented a marvelously integrated study of the factors that contribute to the malaise in the Church many experience, while offering a challenging vision of how to address these issues. The book offered both a study of the Church and a program for addressing underlying ecclesiological problems. From a careful study of the fundamental teachings and accents of Vatican II, Lafont knew his destination, and his analyses made sense because they explained how the council had arrived at its positions in the first place. This approach also helped to address the urgency of the Church's and the world's condition today, since Vatican II had already anticipated many of the cultural and social changes that have become clearer in the years following the council. I call this general approach to a theology of the Church a "Fundamental Ecclesiology."

Perhaps it is fitting that a European theologian, who in his scholarly and teaching career has immersed himself in modern and contemporary philosophy, should present us with such a Fundamental Ecclesiology.[1] Unlike the study of the Church in North America, European theologians have retained the tradition of a Fundamental Ecclesiology, that is, a theology of the Church that continues the discussion with the traditional dialogue partners of theology—philosophy, history, and Scripture—and that seeks to justify the Church in the face of evidence or counterclaims coming from these disciplines. The contemporary European form of Fundamental Ecclesiology, however, is much more sensitive to issues of culture, as a pluricultural and fragmented postcommunist Europe demands. Finally, Fundamental Ecclesiology attempts to come to terms with radical secularization and the problems this phenomenon poses to the Church's self-understanding. In developing countries, the issues of inculturation and liberation loom large. In the United States, where radical secularity is tempered by a continuing toleration for religion, the state of give-and-take increasingly takes the form of culture wars. Europe's experience, on the other hand, is characterized by the exhaustion of institutionalized religion, widespread religious indifference, and painful memories of Christianity's inability to hold in check the forces of disintegration experienced in the First and Second World Wars and in the Holocaust in particular.

Lafont dedicates much attention to his cultural analysis of the Church under the siege of secularism. His analysis takes two forms. First of all, he examines the critical state of Church and world from the perspective of a double "end": the "end of modernity" for society in general and the "end of Christianity." Both have been loudly ballyhooed since the critical decade of the 1960s. But the Church seems to have anticipated that the way things were done and thought about was drawing to an end. Lafont points to Pope John XXIII and Vatican II as having perceived the critical state of Western civilization, and of Christianity as well, before the critiques of the "God-is-dead" movement, or radical secularism, or the widespread disenchantment with existentialism's stress on interiority, etc. Another way of expressing these crises has been to speak of "postmodernity" and "post-Constantinian Christianity." The world and the Christian churches could no longer go about business as usual. Their very foundations were under

---

1. Lafont has laid out the philosophical background in particular to his Fundamental Ecclesiology in his earlier detailed study *God, Time, and Being*, trans. Leonard Maluf (Petersham, Mass.: St. Bede's Publications, 1992). This work appeared in French in 1986 as *Dieu, le temps et l'Être* in the prestigious series *Cogitatio Fidei*, no. 139 (Paris: Les Éditions du Cerf).

attack as represented by new theories of criticism of their respective literature and their founding documents, new views of morality based on a different anthropology and sociology, a chastened view of the Enlightenment
ideal of progress or development, the emergence of a global perspective governing politics and economics, the "new science" that attempted to explain a
far more complex universe and the relativity of its "laws," and the emergence
of a more positive estimation of the pluriformity of the world's religions.

Lafont's view is that Vatican II glimpsed the urgency of the situation
and the consequent need to adopt a new strategy of openness to the world,
a spirit of cooperation with anyone who would serve the human, and an
unflinching dedication to advocating and working for peace. The problem
we experience today is not with the council's insight and assessment, but
with the courage and the imagination necessary to fully implement that vision. The conciliar bishops saw matters in broad strokes and had only a few
practical solutions. Instead, they left more extensive solutions to postconciliar generations. It is more the spirit of Vatican II that is fundamental and
not its precise proposals. But the official Church, and many of the faithful,
have subsequently preferred to limit themselves to maintaining the exact
decisions of the council and no more. To do otherwise, they presume,
would be to betray the council. For Lafont, however, these decisions were
only the beginning and prototypes, as it were, of the vast changes that
would be necessary for the Church to implement its policy of serving humankind and cooperating with the "world," itself a slippery term. Lafont
maintains that we build on these conciliar decisions and extend them according to changing circumstances of the person, of society, and of the universe,
and not that we codify our understanding of them in some calcified form.

Beyond the study of the two "ends" that have emerged in the twentieth century, Lafont examines the two basic forms Western civilization and
the Church assumed in the second millennium. These two forms or world
views give greater specificity to our present experience of something drawing to its "close." They are "modernity" for Western civilization, and "hierarchy" for the Church. Where "hierarchy" emerged from Neoplatonic
thought as represented in Pseudo-Dionysius in particular, "modernity"
emerged from European Enlightenment efforts which were bound up with
the primacy of the individual subject, the superiority of reason over physical matter, the autonomy of freedom over society's traditions and heteron-
omy, and the dichotomy between object and subject making valid
knowledge possible. The Church rejected "modernity," and Western intelli-
gentsia rejected "hierarchy." The Church in particular came to understand
itself as fully independent of society, not interactive and a part of the world
but "other than the world" and superior to it. It had its own "body," the ecclesial one, and no longer constituted the larger, cosmic body of Christ.

Like the state, it, too, was a "perfect society." The ramifications of such a separation have proven harmful not only to the Church but to the world as well.

With the eleventh-century reforms of Gregory VII, the Church increasingly took on a specific figure, the "Gregorian form" which institutionalized "hierarchy" as a principle. No longer were order and structure only necessary for the Church, they became "constitutive" of the Church. Lafont shows how this mentality can be seen in the Catholic Church's repeated refrain regarding the "hierarchical constitution of the Church" in its documents from the last hundred years—not wrong, as far as it goes, but not central or primary either. Thus, when the Neoplatonic, Pseudo-Dionysian thought world permeated ecclesiology under Pope Gregory VII and his successors, hierarchy became synonymous with the clergy. According to Pseudo-Dionysius, truth and value are communicated in a downward movement from above: higher beings communicate reality to lower beings and thereby act as mediators of truth and value which would not come to lower beings without this mediation from above. When the clergy are thought of in this way, they become the depositories of truth and grace. And even here, in the clerical order, the distinction between higher and lower obtains: the pope communicates to those below him, the bishops, who communicate truth to priests. Finally, priests communicate to the religious, who communicate truth to the laity. On these assumptions, the pope is higher than the bishops, bishops are higher than priests, priests are higher than vowed religious, religious are higher than married persons. Truth and holiness always come from mediators who are above in the chain of hierarchies. Nothing, by the way, can go in the inverse direction, so that the clergy cannot learn anything from the religious or the laity. Such an exaggerated emphasis on the dichotomies within Pseudo-Dionysius' understanding of hierarchy created imbalances, discontinuities, and ruptures in the Church's understanding of authority, ministry, and the basic dignity of every baptized person. By the same token, such an understanding of hierarchy meant that the "Church" was superior to the "world," the pope to the secular prince.

Lafont proceeds to examine how this theory of hierarchy is worked out when applied to the areas of revealed truth. Revelation is no longer a matter of the whole Church, the community of believers, but the province of its clerical leaders. The faithful, lay and vowed religious, learn revealed truth from their priests, whose understanding is regulated by the bishops' higher perception of truth. In turn, bishops must obey the teachings of the pope, himself the recipient of divine truth from Christ, whose Vicar he is. Arriving at religious truth is not a matter of adverting to one's experience, sharing and clarifying it, not a matter of personal study or prayerful consideration, not an affair of testing and validating, but of listening to and obeying the Church's authoritative teachers, who cannot be mistaken because they are protected from error by Christ's Spirit of truth. The principle of mediation is clear and determined: the Christian always looks to the person or office that is immediately higher. The whole structure of the "hierarchical Church" rests on this principle.

In addressing the nature of truth as understood by Christianity, Lafont refers to the underlying thought world of Neoplatonism as representing an "epistemology of illumination." He explains that Neoplatonism opted for understanding reality in terms of the One-beyond-everything—the origin and synthesis of reality that, as thoroughly transcendent, cannot be approached directly, cannot be truly named or known in itself, and which brings the multiplicity of reality into an all-embracing unity. Because it cannot be known directly, cannot be the product of deduction or induction, the One-beyond-everything can only be approached by way of the illumination of the mind. Human effort can never make the transcendent "One" present or known. Furthermore, knowledge of the One-beyond-everything is only communicated to individuals who are higher in the social chain. In the Church, this means to the pope and the bishops. What they know about revealed Christian truth comes to them from the divine source of truth and not from human effort, and therefore they cannot be criticized for their understanding of the Christian mystery. But it also means that unity is as high a goal as truth, and that their teaching authority or magisterium is intended to preserve unity among Christians. Error and disunity are two sides of the same reality, the "One"-beyond-everything is also the "True"-in-every-truth. Heresy leads to breaking the unity of the Church, which in turn leads to endangering salvation itself. The gravest sin the ecclesiastical hierarchy needs to guard against is heresy.

Lafont examines this Neoplatonic synthesis from two perspectives. First of all, he asks if this approach was characteristic of the first centuries of the Church and concludes that, although the Church of the patristic period lived in a largely Platonic thought-world, it did not reduce its understanding of the Christian faith to Platonic categories of thought. An attentive reading of Scripture reveals the primacy of narrative, poetry, and rhetoric with respect to language. When we consider the ministry of the bishops, the primacy of preaching and the language of testimony, i.e., mystagogy, emerge. Any authoritative teaching adopted by the bishops was always incorporated in the context of the creeds they formulated, creeds that were intended for confession by the community at worship. The doxological always had priority over the doctrinal, and so dogma needed to be interpreted in the light of the language of confession and testimony. Dogma was not excluded from the vocabulary of faith, but it could never fully capture the richness of the Christian story and the range of symbols and metaphors Christianity employed to narrate the story. In time, and under the dominant influence of Neoplatonic thought forms—and later in modernity's fascination with rationalist explanations—the wide range of Christian language gave way to univocity of definitions and official interpretations.

Secondly, the tenor of late modernity (i.e., the "end of modernity" or postmodernity) no longer values the ideal of the One-beyond-question, the One univocally captured in concepts. Its sympathies lie with pluralism, multiplicity of perspectives, the richness and ambiguity of history, the importance of language. The temper is more "Heraclitean" (stressing the Many) than "Parmenidean" (stressing the One). Are these sympathies to be simply dismissed as erroneous, or do they offer the Church a new moment for evangelizing? Is there something of fundamental value in the contemporary project of arriving at truth by trial and error? Is the person of today frightened off by claims of absolute certainty, or is he or she reassured and attracted by probable claims that are not merely opinions either? Do the underlying paleontological and anthropological views of the gradual emergence of the human species and the development and maturation of the individual person not make the more modest language of confession, testimony, and challenge to the engagement of faith more credible to our generation? The official Church can go a long way in effectively addressing our contemporaries if it adverts to truth as both sapiential and eschatological. What does Lafont mean by these terms?

Truth is eschatological which is open to fuller expression as well as newer expression in the light of humankind's changing self-understanding. Truth is not closed off and self-contained but reflects the genuine historicity of the human being. The person is not the passive recipient of a truth that is superimposed on his or her consciousness. No, the person assists with the emergence of truth. Truth is eschatological because it really emerges out of history. It is not the end-point that dominates history in some predetermined form but the end-point that entices our historicity to realize itself in total freedom. Only open history can be eschatological. Moreover, it achieves its eschatological finality by being sapiential. Lafont means growing in the understanding of truth that is the product of human experience, individually and collectively. Truth is a wisdom *(sapientia)* that humankind shares and grows into. It is practical, meaningful, communally perceived. It is not in competition with reason as speculative, logically rigorous, and discursive.

Given the different accents our contemporaries place on truth—its more limited role in our thought life, its unfulfilled or eschatological character, its pluriformity, its being wrapped up in language and imagery, its symbolic nature, its emergence in shared wisdom, etc.—Lafont draws two

conclusions and elaborates on them in the course of addressing specific ecclesial issues. The first is the need to allow greater room for the exercise of
imagination in the Church. This fact explains the book's title. Our conscious thoughts are the result of the prior process of our imagining reality
and not simply finding it and describing it with pure objectivity. Understanding begins with imagining and advances with the help of our imagination. Conscious understanding participates in the larger thought world
of the symbols that ground, enrich, and extend our encounter with reality.
Some scholars today, e.g., Bernard J. F. Lonergan and Ian G. Barbour, describe this view of understanding as "critical realism." Others, e.g., Robert
N. Bellah, speak of "symbolic realism." Whatever the term employed, many
today realize that the world of our experience cannot be simply captured
by the speculative intellect. Rather, the mind continues to come under the
allure of the imagination, which is not simply reducible to denotation,
definitions, and logical categories. It operates primordially in the realms of
narrative and storytelling, testimony, ritual, metaphor, poetry, rhetoric,
persuasion, and dreaming about new possibilities.

Lafont pinpoints many problems in the Church today as deriving
from our inability to imagine. In the efforts of the Gregorian reform to in-
stitutionalize an "epistemology of illumination" in the office of the magisterium, as well as in the Church's efforts to adapt itself to the
Enlightenment's dominant ethos of rationalism and the ideal of scientific
objectivity, the Church has largely lost its ability to engage the imagination. This fact explains the rather fruitless efforts to interpret rather wood-
enly the documents of Vatican II. The real point of the council—its
spirit—was to free the Church from the increasingly sterile thought-
worlds of Neoplatonic hierarchy and modernity's rationalism. The process
of evangelization that the Church has committed itself to in the postconciliar period can only be realized if the Church returns to the primacy of
religious imagination and its concrete forms of expression. Lafont, in fact,
points to the priority of liturgical reform at the Second Vatican Council,
and the relative success of this effort, as proof of his contention. Ecclesiologically, he points to the primacy of the image of the People of God in the
Dogmatic Constitution on the Church and throughout the council's documents. This image is both the driving force of the council's ecclesiology
and the theological way that the bishops deepened the Church's self-
understanding as the body of Christ. In a word, the People of God image
opens up how we might concretely understand the Church and all humankind as constituting the body of the risen Lord. People of God and body of
Christ are co-determining and co-constitutive images of the Church, and
the tension between the images is essential for preserving both the christological and the pneumatological bases of the Church's life.

Secondly, by returning to the imagination as a source of human thought and by according a greater role to the sapiential dimension of truth, Lafont calls for all in the Church to become involved in the process of addressing the problems found in the Church and indeed in the world. If the "epistemology of illumination" has seen its day, then the council's call for the involvement of the "sense of the faithful" *(sensus fidelium)* and the special contribution to be made by theologians broadly speaking, must play a greater role in the Church's thought life and decision making. From these general perspectives, Lafont is then able to address a broad array of concrete problems especially in the Catholic Church, e.g., episcopal collegiality and the papacy, the importance of synods, reform of the Roman Curia, election of bishops, the state of married life and the sacrament of matrimony, the understanding of sexuality and sexual ethics, the renewal of the diaconate, clerical celibacy, the condition of consecrated life, the role of women in the Church, etc.

Finally, Lafont incorporates the ecclesiology of communion incipient at the council but developed only in the postconciliar period into his understanding of the Church. The "communional" structure imparted by the ever-present and ever-active Spirit highlights the fundamentally charismatic understanding of the Church that necessarily includes institutional forms but without assigning primacy to them. Structure and institutional elements "serve" the communion of the People of God. The Church is both body of Christ and communion in the Spirit, and precisely as such the Spirit calls for structures and institutional forms—always open to the Spirit who is their author—that realize the Spirit's life-giving activity in the Church. Communion in the Spirit is really a communion of charisms. Lafont insists on the need for structures since without them the activity of the Spirit would be merely notional and always run the risk of not becoming historically tangible. Such structures, however, are pluriform and flexible. If this is the case, then Christians must ask themselves which forms or structures will enhance the Spirit's life in the Church. A Church of communion in the Spirit will acknowledge and call forth all of the Spirit's charisms. Yet, for their safeguarding these general charisms also require official recognition in the form of their being appropriately embedded in the structure of the Church. It is not enough to concede in principle the place of charisms in the Church, they must also be fostered and protected.

Ghislain Lafont has placed before the reader a broad spectrum of reflections on the Church. I think most readers will be grateful for the solidity of the foundations Lafont has laid in carefully examining how the Church has emerged in its historical exchange with a wide variety of cultures and thought-worlds. They will also appreciate his explanation of the recent emergence of a more positive assessment of the human imagination and its concomitant rhetorical and narrative forms. Finally, many readers will be grateful for the concreteness and the moderate, though challenging, tone of Lafont's suggestions for change. Most are practical. I hope the book will serve as a point of departure for lively discussion among Catholics, Orthodox, and Protestant Christians of the many suggestions Lafont makes for possible changes in the Church and its relations with other Christians. It is my hope that by making this book available to the English-speaking world the practicableness of Lafont's proposals, made in fidelity to the broad and rich tradition of the Church, will be widely considered.

John J. Burkhard, O.F.M. CONV.
Washington Theological Union

Introduction

Crises in the World and in the Church

Thirty years ago, in the midst of a worldwide crisis, which in the meantime has only been exacerbated, Pope John XXIII dared to ask the following question: "What will the Church *do?* Should the mystical barque of Christ remain tossed about on the waves and allow itself to be dragged along in their wake? Do we not expect the light of a bold *example* rather than simply another new *warning?* What might this light be?"[1]

In the passage quoted, I have underscored the opposition between another *claim* ("warning") and another *deed* ("example"). The Second Vatican Council, convoked by John XXIII, was intended to be a *deed* and not simply a *claim,* an event and not simply an admonition. Without any hint of arrogance, we might say that the council was in fact an event in world history and not only in the history of the Catholic Church. Yes, the council was an event for the other churches and perhaps, too, for all humanity. On the one hand, the council itself benefited from the participation, modest yet real, of the other churches, whose traditions were represented in the course of the discussions. Without losing their own character and maintaining their separation from the church of Rome, these same churches, in their own life as well as in their mutual relations, have not been unaffected by the council but have profited from the reflection which took place there. But Vatican II was also an event in the history of the world to the extent that, despite its apparent age, the body of the Church manifested a surprising suppleness and vitality which became a source of hope for the whole human community. The repercussions of the death of John XXIII, truly a spiritual

---

1. The quotation is from a conversation of John XXIII with Cardinal Tardini, at the end of which the idea of a council came spontaneously to the pope. I take them from an article by Bishop Capovilla, "Profili di Giovanni XXIII," *Echi de Papa Giovanni e della Beata Morosini,* 14 (3) (1993) 28.

event of worldwide proportions, could be considered a symbol of what the dynamism of the council could accomplish among men and women.

After the council, and in order to prolong the event, reforms were undertaken which have had a real impact not only within the Catholic Church but also in the other churches, and perhaps, too, in the world. It might be said, for example, that the Catholic liturgical reforms were not without having indirect effects on the liturgies of the churches of the Reformation. Some of them considered the efforts among Catholics as an invitation to become involved in the reform of their own liturgies and as an inspiration for them in the process of such updating. Moreover, if the liturgical movement continues to move forward and if it develops in particular the awareness of being rooted in human nature itself and in human culture, we might even ask whether the day will eventually come when, thanks both to continuity and transformation, the reform will be in a position to offer an acceptable proposition to a generation of men and women who are at the same time fully secularized and yet thirst for symbols, rites, and myths.

Beyond the example of the liturgy, and others which could be advanced, one might still demand whether, on the institutional level in general, the Catholic Church does not in fact still have a great deal to *do,* if it is to advance the unity of the churches and if it is to provide the world with a witness that will help it survive and to some extent avert human tragedies.

Open Possibilities

Regarding Ecumenism

Since the council, on the level of what is said and written, many theoretical steps have been taken, and eventually, too, there have been many symbolical gestures, viz., the lifting of excommunications, substantial doctrinal agreements, and the common celebration of the liturgy. None of this, however, has reached the level of *effective* reconciliation. To some extent, one could attribute this delay to continuing doctrinal differences, but I think that there is another aspect to these matters: which noncatholic Church would dare to enter into full union with the Catholic Church structured as it is at this moment? Conversely, given a "more agreeable" climate, if the Catholic Church were to present a less worrisome face, and that without renouncing anything deriving from the apostolic tradition, it is possible that the doctrinal differences would appear less insurmountable. If our *deeds* were to change noticeably, maybe our *claims* would be better heard.

Regarding Human Institutions

Human institutions, national and international, today are in fullblown crisis: economic and social crisis, of course, but moral and political crisis as well. We simply don't have any credible models that would permit other nationalities and traditions to develop without at the same time fostering insupportable provincialisms or without provoking murderous confrontations. We don't seem to be able to imagine forms of government that keep equal distance both from rejected totalitarianisms and from the corruptions one encounters in various democracies, to the point that democracy itself as a political form is called into question. Nor do we know how to establish the bases for an international community, where a certain discipline would obtain not simply because of the will of the strongest but which would really open the possibility of engaging, on the international level, the most rudimentary problems of nourishment, lodging, and labor, in the face of which we seem so impotent.

The Catholic Church, itself an international institution, can *claim* many ideas apropos of these subjects, and in fact does not fail to do so and, together with other individuals and well-intentioned organizations, thereby contributes to the growth of an "alternative" mentality. But do the Church's *deeds* measure up to the search today for new models and new inspiration? Do the institutional forms which the Church today presents to the world and the way in which those forms are implemented constitute something attractive and forceful, capable of being regarded and transposed into human political and social life? I don't think it is being disrespectful to suggest the contrary, so that the question today must be the following: What are the conditions which would permit the Church, while remaining faithful in an audacious yet creative way to its own tradition, to help other groups of persons, according to their own conditions and their own insights, make some progress in the same general direction? Reciprocally, in its sincere concern to find its true face in the midst of the human community, how can the Church become more aware of what is being sought elsewhere in society?

Regarding Evangelization

It is also legitimate to ask if a new *deed* isn't also needed to advance what is foremost in the Church's mission, and which is also the foundation of the Church's ecumenical actions and its efforts to establish communion among humans, viz., evangelization. Let us consider a paradox which in the past was perhaps experienced with less intensity than it is today: the contrast between a real "holiness" of the recent Church and what has often seemed to be but a sterile expression of that holiness (outside the Church, the de-Christianizing of society and a certain indifference; within the Church, various degrees of dissatisfaction and estrangement, the crisis of vocations, etc.).

The Christian believes that the gospel is Good News, joyful yet demanding, which not only can save men and women, but which permits

their full personal and social development. Now the Church itself is responsible for the gospel. On the one hand, the Church is entrusted with the
Good News, which it contemplates through the centuries, and it is also the
principal means, though not the only one, by which the Church approaches men and women. On the other hand, this Good News is not simply
a wisdom which can inspire human conduct, but a force for salvation and
transformation with which the faith and the sacraments of the Church are
imbued. For this reason the full reception of the Good News of Jesus
Christ includes not only an attentive listening to the message which the
Church proposes, but even more so the effective entering into the body
which it constitutes and which is the body of Christ.

Today, it is said politely that the Church receives less recognition than
its witness to the Good News of Christ. Often, one hears such expressions
as "Christ, yes; the gospel, yes; the Church, no." In the eyes of Christian
faith, however, the separation of Christ and the gospel from the Church is
an impossibility. Such a division can only harm Christ and the gospel, and
ultimately the salvation and the happiness of men and women today.
*Evangelization absolutely presupposes that the Church regain the confidence
of men and women.*

But why exactly does the Church lack this confidence? Whether believer or not, whoever knows a little about the history of Christianity must
admit that in the past two centuries the Church has shown itself more
faithful to the gospel than at any other period in its history. Of course, one
could always draw up a negative inventory. Nonetheless, and limiting ourselves to the Catholic Church, in what other period could one list popes of
such Christian and apostolic quality as those who have succeeded Pius VII
(elected in 1800) up to John Paul II? What other era can pride itself on
such a commitment to the missions? Unquestionably, these missionaries
arrived in "the colonies" after their conquest, and unquestionably, too, one
could pose questions about their appreciation of foreign cultures, still
these missionaries preached the gospel and were heard. As far as their giving themselves to God and their fellow men and women, their readiness to
die for announcing the gospel, not simply by martyrdom but also by facing
disease and exhaustion, was a sign of the grace of faith and love which
comes only from God and which they knew how to accept. In their countries
of origin, too, they were supported by the prayers and the generosity of
other Christians. We need only mention Pauline Jaricot and the Propaga-
tion of the Faith. The same could also be said of the home missions in the
nineteenth century, so dear, for example, to the Curé of Ars. From the beginning of the twentieth century up to the present, apostolic movements—
fortunately more intelligently informed than their predecessors regarding
human circumstances and the impact of culture—have continued to de-

velop, and the faithful of all walks of life have sought ways of giving witness to Christ before their fellow men and women. Such missionary effort rests upon a real evangelical holiness, and like St. Francis of Assisi in his time, the faces of certain contemporary saints shine forth well beyond the faithful of the Catholic Church, e.g., St. Theresa of the Child Jesus or Charles de Foucauld.

After the missions and holiness, one could point to the areas of knowledge and reflection. The churches—and the Catholic Church in particular—were rather dormant in this regard in the past few centuries. But what a magnificent revival has occurred in the last third of the nineteenth century, continuing up to our day. In all fields, this great moment of knowledge rests upon the wealth of this period. One need only think of systematic theology, spiritual theology, philosophy, and the retrieval of the treasures of biblical, patristic, liturgical, and scholastic sources; research into the methods of interpretation, studies on contemporary culture, a new openness to the human sciences, sometimes intelligently critical of them, as well as openness to the wisdom of all continents, etc.

If we rejoice humbly in the gifts of the Spirit which the Church has received and capitalized on, as rarely before in its history, the believer is still obliged to admit that very little of this vast wealth shines brightly on the world of our contemporaries. This Church, in some respects enjoying good health, is still losing a not insignificant number of its members, is of little interest to many, and is becoming more and more a minority, etc. Even if one were to point to an occasional sign of rejuvenation, passing or lasting, or if one or another person catches the attention of the media and is listened to, still the Church itself can hardly be considered as a herald of the gospel or of humanity. The Church today is aware that it is not the kingdom of God and that its mission is not to enlist all people in its fold. It also has the task of entering into dialogue with others. But how does it measure the *effectiveness* of its dialogue? How can it come to an understanding of the extent of the "de-Christianizing" process (with all the nuances that this complex term entails) which has appeared precisely at the moment that the Church seems to have received impulses fostering the spread of the gospel? Of course, we might accuse those "others" who are outside the Church and who oppose it. We could also say that when God is more clearly revealed, the devil cannot be far behind. Such expressions contain a grain of truth, but still leave the problem unresolved. To the extent that the Church is committed to its mission of evangelization and of dialogue, we still need to ask what appearance the Church will put on in order to surmount such indifference and even such hostility. Next to the fundamental values of holiness and intelligence we have just considered, is there something else necessary which is not happening in the Church and thus obfuscates the true visage of the Church for those who genuinely yearn for wisdom and salvation?

For More Imagination in the Church

In spite of the advances made since Vatican II, I am convinced that something else is not functioning well in the Church's institutions. In a word, there is a certain need "to imagine the Catholic Church today." Such an exercise of imagination would be fruitless, if we did not pursue the deeper causes of the situation. My hypothesis is that in order to understand the crisis in the Catholic Church, we must also try to understand the broader crisis in society which many call "the end of modernity" or "the shipwreck of Western civilization."

During the first centuries of the Christian era, there was a rather felicitous mutual articulation of the gospel and the culture or civilization of the time. This synthesis is called the patristic period or the "undivided Church." Unfortunately, a similar articulation was not possible in the period which followed, the period of human reason, of scientific investigation, of political action, logic, technology, and pragmatic reason. On the side of reason, we were not able to define an authentic autonomy that remained open to the human search for salvation and to revelation as a totally gratuitous offer. On the side of revelation, we were incapable of separating the act of gratuity from the nonessential religious and political means by which it is manifested. A rationalistic modernity was perishing in the crazed demand for total independence, and its technical progress has never been able to assure human societies of the happiness they yearn for. As for the Catholic Church, it turned in on itself and concentrated on its internal life, showing itself increasingly incapable of developing a balanced criticism of an exclusively hierarchical interpretation of its institutional forms. Meanwhile, the churches which emerged from the Reformation have gone in yet another direction, developing an exclusively spiritual and biblical, even anti-institutional, inspiration for its life. But these churches, too, have not resolved the problem of articulating a synthesis between modernity and the faith any better than the Catholic Church's attempts to do so. Thus, we are left with a modernity devoid of any openness to Transcendence and a Christianity too timid to take into account the true depth of the human, with the result that both have become alienated from each other and have precipitated what can be called a "total" crisis: the very crisis we are experiencing today and which the twofold expressions of "the end of modernity" and "the end of Western Christianity" are but the two sides of the same coin.

I sincerely believe that the vague, divided, and individualistic proposals which today are opposed to the deceptive promises of modernity (e.g., the various new Gnosticisms, the New Age movement, recourse to ancient systems of wisdom, etc.) are not serious and durable solutions to the crisis. Such proposals only further juxtapose a vague mysticism, often lacking in grandeur, to the hegemony of a technocracy which no one can live without. But I also do not think that an authoritarian and somewhat irrational reaffirmation of Christian identity is any authentic way of salvation for us. Though I do not want to stand aside from the problems of modernity, I find it more helpful to reflect on the Catholic Church, whose faith entrusts me with the message and the sacraments of salvation, and with undertaking this investigation on several levels.

First, to take up an analysis that is faithful to the secular conflict between modernity and hierarchy. Then, to define more precisely the inspiration underlying the institutional forms which the Catholic Church has chosen to conserve in the face of all opposition in the last millennium. Next, to show how Vatican II, sometimes boldly, sometimes timidly, for the first time in centuries undertook to squarely face the conflict and to begin to reform its institutions. And finally, by taking up attempts made by others in the last fifty years, to engage in an effort of theological imagination that will result in concrete proposals. As we will have occasion to see, these areas will include the questions that have been raised largely in the past few years: the state of marriage and the problem of divorce; the relative autonomy of religious life in the Church; the possibility of taking local initiatives regarding mission, catechesis, and liturgy; the freedom of theology; episcopal collegiality; the reform of the electoral processes for the papacy and the episcopacy; priestly celibacy; the proper extent of the magisterium; the reform of the exercise of papal primacy; etc.

The extent of my proposals should not astonish anyone. The classical solutions given to this manifold of questions depend on the institutional forms which the Church adopted in the course of the Middle Ages. These forms constitute a whole with the Church. When another ecclesiological form appears, new solutions are entirely possible to the extent that they, too, constitute a whole. It is precisely this coherence, at once necessary but not yet fully realized to the extent it should be, that I will try to illustrate.

Such is my intention in this book. I wish to move toward a new investigation in areas still open to *what the Church can do,* as I listed above. It is my sincere hope, too, that thereby I might contribute to a rearticulation of the institutions and the concrete forms of modernity with those of the faith and the Catholic Church. It is my hope that this rearticulation will be reciprocal and beneficial to both parties caught in the grip of the crises of our day.

All Saints Day, 1994

Part I

An Attempt at a Diagnosis
of the Condition

For as long as it has existed, the Church has never been an island. It has developed in the midst of a world of human societies. Sometimes, it almost disappears in their ideologies and their institutions; sometimes it borrows, with or without much reflection, the very models it will transpose ("inculturation"); and sometimes, it exerts an influence over these same ideologies and institutions, by communicating norms, principles, examples, and evangelical values to them ("acculturation"). As the saying would have it, "Church" and "world" have always been "in the same boat." But to navigate the boat today, we must take time to map out the itinerary. To remain faithful to historical truth, I propose first to survey globally the destiny of Western civilization, of which Christianity is not the unique element but only one of its essential components. In a second chapter, I will examine what is particular to the Catholic Church in this more general destiny. And even more precisely, I want to show how, in the first period, the figure of the world, and correspondingly, the Church, conformed to what might be called a "hierarchical" model; whereas, in the second period, this figure emerged as "modern." Modernity developed historically in ever sharper opposition to the hierarchical model and eventually abandoned it in indifference. Undoubtedly, it is the inability of both these figures, each fraught with possibilities for the other, to find points of convergence among the values they represent, that explains the failure (hopefully only relative) of Western civilization up to the present. In the first chapter, I will attempt this objective only schematically. The second objective, relative to the Catholic Church in particular, will be developed at somewhat greater length in the second chapter.

Chapter 1

Hierarchy and Modernity: A Failure of Western Civilization?

The Emergence of the Hierarchical Figure in Western Christianity

Let us assume in principle, or better perhaps as a hypothetical starting point, that our Western civilization was originally constituted by reason of an encounter between the proper contribution of Christian revelation and that of the Mediterranean Hellenistic culture. We need to offer a few explanatory remarks about the one and the other.

The Contribution of Christian Revelation: The Creed

One of the oldest texts of the Christian tradition, the Apostles' Creed, provides us with the fundamental features which the Church brings to the world in its message of salvation.

What is first of all proper to the Church is to move toward a goal: the Church awaits Christ ("He will come again to judge the living and the dead" and "I believe . . . in the forgiveness of sins, the resurrection of the flesh, and life everlasting. Amen"). Here, the idea of an "end" takes on a positive significance: it implies both our earthly time, which the parousia of Christ will bring to completion, and a transformed or transfigured time, when our flesh will enter and dwell in life eternal, once the flesh has been purified of the negative element, called "sins." In the final analysis, the "end" is not so much a concept as an existential act of waiting. It is possible to highlight the positive realism of these affirmations of the Creed concerning the end. While at the same time admitting the presence of evil in the world and the precariousness of this time, such statements claim to have an eschatological meaning, something inconceivable if earthly time and the world were destined for condemnation, destined for destruction. The idea of an end does not necessarily mean an irremediable failure, but rather points toward themes of temporality, purification, and fulfillment. The "question of meaning," so frequently spoken about today, is not insoluble. It even receives in essence the answer it seeks, though perforce obscurely. The reality of an end which is the work of God, who alone knows the moment which the Church waits for in faith ("I believe") opens up the issue of the *beginning*, again the work of God ("I believe in God the Father Almighty, creator of heaven and earth"), so that God too is marked by a spatiotemporal dimension, since God has inaugurated and accompanies this time. But it is also marked by a transtemporal dimension which implies both a "first instant" and a presence of God in time without which it could not exist. Both concepts, creation and completion, in all their complexity, permit us to envision time as history.

The Creed envisions Christ as the very rhythm of this history, Christ ("I believe . . . in Jesus Christ, the only Son, Our Lord") whose divine sonship and whose human life are signified by the two extremes of birth and death–resurrection ("born of the Virgin Mary, crucified under Pontius Pilate . . ."). Then come the Spirit and the Church ("I believe in the Holy Spirit, the holy catholic Church . . ."), which in some sense fill in the interval between Christ's resurrection and his parousia, and so are themselves essential dimensions of this same earthly time. In terms that are no longer those of the Creed, we can say that we pass through creation and completion by covenant. Considered the free contract between God and humanity, the covenant is the principle by which we listen to the Word and discern the way, one open to the vicissitudes, the ruptures, and the repetitions of history. In the horizon of the Creed, evil is more a refusal of the covenant which intervenes formally only with the announcement of its own definitive surpassing in the *forgiveness of sins*. At the very heart of the covenant, revelation envisions redemption by the Word incarnate and the sending of the Spirit, which little by little unveil the trinitarian reality of God and the ultimate vocation of humanity.

The Contribution of Hellenistic Culture:
A Mystical and Hierarchical World

In the Hellenistic world, at that moment when the churches of the first centuries were being established, it is possible to observe a grand quest of wisdom, which, in a wide diversity of schools and practices, was moving toward a convergence in ethics, politics, and religious cult, but also in cosmology and an anthropological vision of the human. At the risk of grossly oversimplifying this culture, one might characterize it by appealing to the two great names which dominated the ancient world and which Western civilization has tried to reconcile and to synthesize ever since, Plato and Aristotle.

Plato

Under the aegis of Plato, particularly in the tradition of the many commentaries on his dialogue *Parmenides*,[1] philosophical reflection assumed the character of a search for religious union with an absolutely transcendent Mystery, beyond all human control, which with antiquity one might name the *One-beyond-everything*. Such a search ineluctably involves a pessimism that is, in the last resort, rather radical regarding the world here below, inhabited by an evil whose origins escape us. There can be no union without purification. This double quest of averting evil and arriving at unity, implicit for all, while more conscious for others, involves a structuring of the world that is *hierarchical*, i.e., both the cosmos and society in the form of the state. This world is marked by mediations which at the same time communicate from on high to beings below this mysterious access to the One, and define the initiatives and actions to be performed in order to find one's way of returning to the original One. These initiatives include, first of all, a cultic life involving a great diversity of forms, and over which priests and initiates alone hold the key. These are able to communicate with the hierarchical worlds beyond the power of humans, utter oracles and offer libations and sacrifices, so that they become the mediators of the needed purification. This explains why antiquity acceded to a certain political submission to "rights" and to those institutions which demarcated men and women into classes, some more elevated in authority, and which assumed hierarchical form beginning with the emperor. The latter, in some way or other closer to the world of the gods, if not himself the source, is at the very least the guarantor and the one responsible for authority. Cult and rights are ultimately in the service of the search for truth, whose guardians are the sages and philosophers, not the sophists and rhetoricians, because these former have some interior experience of the return to the One. Truth is of the essence, since it opens the way for salvation, conceived as the return to knowledge of the One, the foundation of all that is true. A world of mysticism, of ideas, of rights, and of cult emerges, but a world weighed down by evil in the world and among men and women, a world destroyed by wars out of whose ruins arise new forms and where the emblematic figures of the sage, the prince, and the priest can always be found.

Here is found the origin of the primacy of the idea of God who is the One-beyond-everything, and which on the one hand engenders both an

---

1. This explains why I will often refer to the "Parmenidean culture" in my book. This idea has been explained often. Among many possible works, I refer to J. Trouillard, "Le *Parménide* de Platon et son interprétation néo-platonicienne" in *Études platoniciennes* (Neuchâtel, 1973) 9–26, and Eugenio Corsini, *Il trattato "De Divinis nominibus" dello Pseudo-Dionigi e i commenti neoplatonici al Parmenide* (Turin: G. Giappichelli, 1962).

attitude of "mysticism" and creates a ladder of spiritual mediations, and on the other, in an apparent paradox, nourishes an intellectual and political totalitarianism. The mystical form demands a strong political power, because the ruler is thought to declare the truth inaccessible to the vast majority. His power imperatively orders the polis toward its indescribable completion, and for which he alone possesses the key. In principle, this power is not accountable to anyone, because it is exercised by those persons who are capable of true political action by reason of their contemplation and mental lucidity. It might nonetheless permit the community to further survive but not to really live fully. Thus, there is no "separation of powers": they possess both legislative and executive power. Moreover, there is no identifiable border separating the religious and the political domains.[2]

Aristotle

Aristotle's approach to reality is first of all that of a "naturalist," a man of science interested in the things and phenomena that surround him, from the rhythm of procreation of animals to the movements of the celestial spheres, and along the way the mysterious structure of the human, at once body and mind. The unity he sought was that of the physical world here below with the metaphysical world, with celestial space and beyond. The question for Aristotle is to know where the human spirit here below can rest in order to find happiness. His more realistic vision, more down to earth than that of Plato, accords greater attention both to the reality of matter as well as to the possibility of freedom, and all that without losing a religious reference. Without drastically changing the meaning of the word "being" as employed by Plato, Aristotle adds a decidedly different nuance. Being for him is the true ground of knowing which accompanies the steps of knowledge without itself ever being exhausted by it. Truth is seen to possess a certain humility, even in those fields which it has direct access to,

---

2. Upon reflection, one might well ask whether the genius of Platonism was not to have brought paganism to its pure essence. Even if it contained elements that were more or less errant, idolatrous or perverted, every form of paganism implies this obscure perception of an absolute, hidden as well as revealed by means of divine or demonic mediations, sought even if not attained, and employing cultic forms which are structured culturally and repeated because they are imperatively imposed. In spite of its variations, it strikes me that a similar structure can be found in late Roman religion (see St. Augustine in the opening chapters of his *City of God*); among the Aztecs (see Tzvetan Todorov, *La Conquête de l'Amérique. La question de l'autre* [Paris, 1982], especially the chapter entitled "Moctezuma et les signes," 60–193), in the high plateaus of Vietnam (see Jacques Dournes, *Dieu aime les païens. Une mission de l'Église sur les plateaux du Viet-nam* [Paris: Aubier, 1963]), and among the Bambaras of Niger (see the wonderful film of Souleymane Cissé, "Yeelen," released in 1986).

because awareness of the analogy of language leads to great prudence in its affirmations and to constant self-criticism. For this very reason truth does not hesitate to make assertions with even greater determination than one would encounter in a thought world dominated by a dialectic of extremes. Such an intellectual orientation has consequences in the political life of a society as well as in its religious activity. A structure which rests on these two domains, each with its own laws and an articulation between them which does not involve the oppression of one over the other or the negation of one at the expense of the other, should be possible.

Limited Inculturation of the Church: The Acceptance of Hierarchy and Partial "Disenchantment" of the World

It would appear that the encounter of the Christian gospel and Hellenistic civilization was a positive one and contributed to making the patristic period a methodological model of mutual enrichment, to the extent that it has probably never been replicated. Christian thought and practice were nourished by Plato and Aristotle. Conversely, Christianity gave to this cultural substratum elements which transformed it and led it to an equilibrium it had not attained up to that time.

From the point of view of form first of all, Christianity includes the character of witness, is founded on the Word of God, and elicits faith: I believe. In itself such a contribution implies the refusal of a monopolistic rationality, and thereby introduces a sense of humility and incompleteness into the system of truth, elements which do not belong to the same family as the hard and lucid transparence of truth *(alētheia)* according to Plato. Truth in the Platonic sense issues from the obscure light of an illumination coming from the One or, in the opposite direction, truth proceeds from the resolute affirmation of a Reason that rests fearlessly on Being.

From the point of view of content, Christianity gave to the anxious civilization of the Hellenistic world a consistency and a reality unheard of up to then. It could name the One-beyond-everything, in identifying it with God, the Father of our savior Jesus Christ. It pointed to the goal of the ways of prayer and the cult. In this way it reduced the disquieting explosion of mediations, since it preached one sole Mediator between God and humanity, Jesus Christ, and one form of initiation and of the cult. Moreover, it purified the notion and the practice of other mediations, whether positive and beneficent (angels and saints), or negative and ultimately impotent (demons and the damned), and furnished a regulative principle to the multifarious forms of popular religion. In other words, the mystical search underlying the "Parmenidean culture" for its part submitted to a meaning that could be lived out, while at the same time this culture opened up for Christianity the possibility of emphasizing the spiritual realities in the gospel of Jesus Christ.

By introducing a certain sense of reality into the vision of the world and history, thanks to its foundational concepts of creation, covenant, and completion, on the philosophical and cultural levels, the Christian contribution tended to emphasize accents other than those of mysticism and hierarchy. Because of its spiritual realism, it situated the truth of *mystery* not only in what is beyond, but in eschatology and ultimately in time. It emphasized what *is* and thereby tended to promote a metaphysical theory of participation and an epistemology of analogy. All reality possesses a certain interior unity and a really objective consistency. The notions of unity and being, with their different degrees of intensity according to the level of reality at which one found oneself, were well suited to it. In this way, nothing needed to be condemned and nothing was absolutized. Here one is close to the Aristotelian idea of the equivalence of the One and Being.[3] God in God's self is the One and Being, and all reality, at its own level, manifests these two aspects. On the other hand, however, the need to speak carefully about the unique mediatorship of Jesus Christ demands a closer analysis, using a refined conceptuality when speaking about the divine and the various levels of existence or of the essence of the human, the soul, its faculties, etc. Real philosophical progress emerges in this way. As a result, Christianity involves the principle of a certain "disenchantment of the world." At the same time that it submits the world to divine creation and to created freedom, it declares the revealed character of its faith and the sacramentality of its institutions, while it also recognizes the social and political structures of society and allows them to emerge gradually in their proper sphere.

The Preference for Plato

The space opened up by the fundamental affirmations of the Christian Creed helped the Church to encounter and to advance the mystical and political perspectives of Plato, as well as the more scientific and ontological approach of Aristotle. Still, in Christianity, as in the thought world of paganism, Aristotle was regarded as providing a counterbalance to certain deleterious aspects of the dominant worldview of the One-beyond-everything. This can be explained by the fact that the world of late antiquity, which was that of the Fathers who drew on it unconsciously, was spiritu-

---

3. I would like to recall a text by George Florovsky which I cited many years ago in my *Structures et méthode dans la "Somme théologique" de saint Thomas d'Aquin* (Paris, 1960) 295, note 3: "In the philosophical interpretation of his eschatological hope, Christian theology from the very beginnings clings to Aristotle." The passage can be found in his "Eschatology in the Patristic Age: An Introduction" in *Studia Patristica*, vol. 2, eds. Kurt Aland and F. C. Cross (Berlin: Akademie, 1957) 235–50, at 246.

ally imbued with an anxious search that might be characterized as mystical, while it adopted the political organization of the empire. It highlights a type of thought dominated more by the theme of the One and its mediations than by the more down-to-earth world envisioned by Aristotle. This is what Jean Daniélou tried to express when he maintained that when the Fathers engaged in their preferred field of investigation, viz., mystical theology, they were "Platonists," but when they had to fashion precise dogmatic formulas in response to the controversies of the day, they were "Aristotelians." It is also possible that the continued delay of the parousia played a role in the Church's process of self-interpretation. Since Christ had not returned here to earth, he had to be sought in heaven. Increasingly, Christians attempted to define the spiritual stages which permitted union with God, without losing sight of the need to await the Lord, though this parousial horizon became rather remote. In other words, a relative "detemporalizing" interpretation emerged, and the intellectual and institutional structuration of Christianity assumed the unitary forms which were part of the contemporary culture.

In the long haul, such a "preference for Plato" had serious effects which go a long way in explaining the fate of Western civilization. However, I need to be more precise about one particular aspect, viz., the spiritual dynamism and the view of the world that were at stake. I will indicate the orientations which flow from what concerns the institutional forms.

Spiritual Dynamism and the View of the World

Among the elements constituting the spiritual dynamism of the time, we might include the following: an insistence on the quest for the Beyond considered as union with God; a spelling out of the spiritual sense of Scripture understood in an anagogical sense, i.e., the union with God above and beyond all things; emphasis upon the liturgical symbols as reflections and the first fruits of the contemplation of the ultimate; insistence on a spiritual authority capable of communicating the fruits of contemplation and of intimating the precise formulas for expressing the faith; development of an epistemology of illumination by which the inexpressible truth regarding the One is manifested to humans. But there are also somewhat disturbing elements which need to be added to the above-mentioned positive ones: the various malevolent forces which inhabit the lower spheres of the heavens in Hellenism and the significant presence of demons in the Gospels.

The image of the world that flows from this dynamism is dominated by a polarity between Christ the Victor, or the "Pantocrator," and Evil, or the "Prince of this World." Evil has two forms. The first one is static and sees the world as the battleground where the constant conflict between the "Prince of this World" and the "Pantocrator" rages, and which is reflected in the spiritual battle of each Christian. The second one is dynamic and corresponds to the conception of the world as a battleground: the way of *conversion,* i.e., the constant passing from one sphere to the other. A third attitude needs to be added to this double grounding attitude, and involves the failures of men and women in their spiritual combat, viz., *penance* both as an act of reparation for past faults and injuries incurred, and prevention of future faults.

Institutional Images and Leading Ideas

The overview I have given helps us understand the importance of the forms of authority that were in place in a world shot through with the mystical search for the One, with the war between good and evil, and with religiously tinged institutional hierarchies. The conception of the world divided in two is the background, in the final analysis, for explaining the institutions of the world of Christian antiquity. It is incumbent on each in his own way, the prince and the priest, to help humans pass from one world to the other and to assure that those who have been converted remain in the realm of Christ, even to the point of using force.

Both figures, the prince and the priest, are dominated by two leading ideas of the period: truth and unity. Truth is the proper characteristic of Christian revelation, and it is revelation which manifests the inexpressible One-beyond-everything which the Hellenist thirsted for. Truth is the value par excellence to illustrate and to defend against all error, even though this involves the danger of overshadowing the role of witness and of the freedom of faith, which are also essential traits of Christianity. Unity is not only the mark par excellence of the divine but also of the unique mediation of Jesus Christ. It should also characterize the Church and in particular its institutional mediations. Thus, the early councils are expected to demonstrate unanimity. But the question also arises with respect to persons who can effectively elicit unanimity in the truth. We have the experience of the painful efforts at defining matters and at installing a supreme religious authority to act as the expression of the ultimate mediation of God the One and the unique mediatorship of Christ: the emperor in the East, the pope in the West. To anticipate somewhat, we can say that, in the Eastern view, the fundamental politico-religious figure is the emperor and the council, later the emperor and the patriarch. But this could be maintained only so long as the emperor was strong, and so, e.g., the rise of Islam would strike a deadly blow against the vitality of the Church.[4] In the Western view, the vicissitudes of history, civil and religious, sometimes work to the advantage of the person

---

4. Later, the Church would reconstitute itself around the emperor of Russia and the patriarch of Moscow (until Peter the Great [1672–1725] suppressed the patriarchate, keeping supreme authority over the Church for himself).

of the emperor, and after him the absolute monarchies of a later period (usually in conflict situations), and sometimes, in the Church, the person of the Bishop of Rome, the "pope," the successor of Peter.

Modernity: Arrival of Space Created for the Human Exercise of Power

In a relatively large number of schools of thought scattered geographically and at different points in history, Christian antiquity managed, not without many a struggle, to attain a certain equilibrium in articulating the Christian realities of covenant, creation, and sin among themselves and relative to the contribution of Hellenistic culture in its double polar forms: Plato and Aristotle. We see this verified not only in strictly theological or ecclesiological matters, but also in philosophy and politics. We can name this ever fragile equilibrium "partial disenchantment."[5] "Disenchantment" to the extent that Christian revelation freed the reality of the divine and of the human and cosmic from the realm of fable and myth; "partial" because the return to the real does not bring about the disappearance of transcendence, spirituality, and mystery but places them in a new light. Such a partial disenchantment leads to a vision and to a practice in the world that can be called "hierarchical." The temptation is a recurring one: to break apart this equilibrium at the expense of a narrow mysticism of the One by concentrating exclusively on the following pair of ideas: sin and human weakness. How might we explain, then, that such a vision and practice in the world, regnant during the first thousand years of Christianity, would be contested and eventually supplanted by another one during the second millennium?

Let us formulate the hypothesis that, whatever we make of certain historical developments, contingent in themselves, there was a true development in the process of "disenchantment," based on a more or less lively awareness of the world as space for a creation, good in itself, handed over to humanity and animated by a dynamism of progress. We have seen how from the beginning the theme of creation formed an integral part of the deposit of Christian revelation and was opposed to the pagan themes of emanation. On the one hand, the realism of creation was underscored by the Christian truth of the incarnation: the unique authentic mediation between the world below and the abode of the One. In this sense we can speak of the effort at "demythicizing" the world from the beginnings of Christianity. Nonetheless, at the beginning, attention tended to be placed on creation as seen from the side of God—in the hierarchical perspective of the relation of a descending God vis-à-vis the world. Only slowly did the

---

5. I am borrowing the term evidently from Max Weber and Marcel Gauchet, *Le Désenchantement du monde. Une histoire politique de la religion* (Paris: Gallimard, 1985).

immanent consequences of the idea of creation emerge, viz., the coherence between reality and human values, and correlatively, the ability of human reason to assess these values, to deepen them, and to establish an appropriate practice and technique. The process was bound up with the influence of what I have called the realism of the Creed, but also with a series of historical circumstances which opened up men and women to the power they possessed.

They discovered a real autonomy of judgment and of action relative to material things and to their social relationships. They became conscious of their power to transform reality. At last, humanity and the world began to see themselves directly, apart from their condition of having fallen or being redeemed—a condition defined by the pitiless opposition between a triumphant Christ and the Prince of this world. Modernity began when the coordinates of sin and salvation, of Satan and Christ, were not the only ones taken into consideration in defining human existence, or when it was discovered by men and women that they had a certain autodetermination and a certain sense of control over others without reference to the grand drama of salvation. In other words, human realities such as sexuality, money, power, technology have gained the right to exist autonomously, in accordance with the laws of reality, which themselves are determined by human beings and by things in themselves, and all this in the very name of the value of creation. Human reason, which effected this discovery and the utility of these same values, acquired an importance unknown up to then. Behind this autonomous discovery stand the autonomy of science and of the reality of a history governed by freedom, the birth of those political forms called "democratic." They appear more satisfying to the degree that they presuppose in principle that reason is capable of indicating the path society should take, the forms of government it should establish, and the means of exercising control it should consider, viz., democracy and the separation of powers.

A Brief Chronology of Events

The first stage of the appearance and the development of modernity took place in the twelfth century, when the recently discovered conceptuality of Aristotle provided a language for speaking about reality. We might call this phase *anthropological,* in as much as it inquired concerning the immanent processes of knowledge and began to discover technology and urban life (while coexisting with a more rural and traditional civilization). In other words, men and women began to uncover the possibility of new relations with the world and among themselves. A second stage, which we can call *cosmological,* began in the sixteenth century when the idea of a solar system replaced the more classical view of the world with its ascending and descending mediations uniting heaven and earth. This new idea rocked the mentality of mediations and hierarchies to their foundations and opened the possibility of another way of composing reality. In this view, the epistemological element is decisive. On the positive side, it opened the way to the development of mathematics and the principles of reason. On the negative, it created difficulties for locating a place for revelation and the Scriptures in the emerging view, as well as the role of sensibility and symbols. If the first stage overturned the experience of space, the second, starting in the eighteenth century, profoundly involved the experience of time. It pointed to the areas of development and of *history,* of freedom and of *politics,* both on the cosmic and the human levels. In addition, instead of a perfect world at the beginning, but later vitiated, then redeemed while still awaiting its perfect restoration, modernity tried to substitute a world characterized by becoming, a humanity characterized by education, an all-encompassing dialectic, which meant the development of new methods of knowing, methods tied to the process of interpretation.

Conflict and Eventual Separation of the Two Worldviews

If I am correct in identifying these fundamental features of modernity and its evolution, questions nevertheless remain concerning how more exactly the modern worldview—born of the Christian worldview and developing within it, a worldview marked by hierarchy—emerged out of this world defined by an inescapable struggle between two sovereign realities, Evil and Christ, by the practice of penance, and, in the best of possible scenarios, by the way of mysticism: and all of this taking place within the very heart of the social and religious organizations where power comes down from on high, i.e., from the sacred.

Looking at history concretely, the discovery of a dimension of the world we might call "objective," whether beyond or at the very heart of the twofold, conflicted sovereignty of Evil and the Pantocrator, would seem to require an attitude of "emancipation." The autonomy that emerged frequently had to struggle for independence and assumed a posture of opposition, all the more so since the former institutions, founded on the waning worldview, not being able to comprehend the appearance of another conception of reality and a different set of practices, bitterly defended its legitimacy and only begrudgingly accepted the expressions of autonomy that were being deployed. In other words, it didn't become clear early on how the new understanding of the world also emphasized the idea of *creation* professed in the Christian Creed, a view which could be defended not only by viewing creation from the point of view of God the Creator, but also from the point of view of the creation as it already existed. The authorities did not know how to understand the autonomy of creation in its dependence on its Creator, could not evaluate the impact of revelation and covenant, of sin and redemption, on reality as it existed and on the development of created values. Such an effort at reordering has never been completed and continues to preoccupy us. But when modernity appeared, the need to do so was never perceived, either by the innovators or by the hierarchical authorities. Modernity needed to define certain lines of thought and to initiate certain actions which would have established a measured autonomy for humanity and world, all the while retaining the idea of a covenant and remaining realistic about the human risk of failure. Herein lies the historical tragedy at the birth of modernity: it was initiated and developed without ever really being thought through.

Because it was something new and difficult, modernity needed time to be accepted. It was a matter of articulating positively a statement about the essence and the existence of created values together with the determination of prohibitions that would permit these values to develop without endangering humanity, society, or nature and with clear indications of which injuries would impede its development. By "prohibitions" I mean to emphasize how the relation of human to human might lead to the limitation of the relationship between human and nature, and how the limitation of the relation of human to God might lead to a limitation in the human relation to nature and to other humans. It's a matter of what St. Paul meant when he said, "All belongs to you, but you are Christ's and Christ belongs to God" (1 Corinthians 3:22-23). Far from intending to restrict harmony between humanity, creation, and society, such "prohibitions" assure the fact that the ordering among these values and their interrelationships is a beneficial one. Ideally, modern persons should have perceived the organic need for a just use of the world, whereas in fact they plunged headlong into an attitude of exploitation. For their part, the hierarchical authorities became imprisoned in positions of rejection and condemnation.[6] If society does not find the correct prohibitions for channeling its efforts, these prohibitions develop in a way that is excessive, by extending their powers without limitation and by an uncontrolled accumulation of possessions. The latter engenders a disequilibrium in human relations, some having more, others having less of society's goods. As for the human relation with God, it is dulled to the point of disappearing eventually. Science has no need for God, and history is content to remain confined to the world.

6. *Prohibition* expresses the necessary limits in order to have a balanced development of autonomies. The negative aspect is merely the opposite of the positive content of a beneficent law of development. A *condemnation* applies to opinions and attitudes judged erroneous. But even if prohibitions turn out well in one set of circumstances, they do not limit *eo ipso* the positive contributions in a new situation; they risk mixing in the good with the bad. Sometimes, too, they turn out badly because they make their judgments on inadequate criteria. See below, "On the Law," p. 80.

In politics, a modernity that tends to be exclusive, that fosters a total rationalism, and that is cut off from other influences, implies a vicious circle: it pretends to be able to define its own norms. This self-definition can even be considered the very sign of liberalism. In particular, it isn't clear what place it gives to the sense of the religious. For modernity, the sacred does not have its own social location (with its laws and priests), since by definition it transcends the purely rational (at least to the extent that we are not speaking about the Enlightenment ideal of religion within the limits of reason), and it lacks any social location within an articulated politics, since this would involve some foreknowledge of religion's proper place. If it exists at all, the religious sensibility is restricted to the realm of the "private," i.e., to that sphere which has nothing in common with an individual's reason. Whatever one thinks about this last point, our "modernity" has its origins in an exclusive emphasis on one pole, the strictly rational. In the end, one is forced to ask whether such an insistence on reason alone is itself reasonable. Conversely, the ecclesiastical authorities, who acted out of a worldview that understood the world in an immediately religious and hierarchicized way, should have been able to recognize an aborning autonomy and guided it up to a point by emptying themselves in service of encouraging the human. On the contrary, they appear to have been more concerned with reasserting themselves and thereby contributed to nourishing a certain revolt in the human quest for "modernity," with the consequent signs of growing disorder.

Declarations of the Approach of the "End"

Historically, we can declare that the grafting of modernity on to the religious world defined by the inevitable struggle between Good and Evil has not succeeded. The worldview based on sin and grace simply did not know what to make of a worldview based on nature and power, and so tried to ignore it or even reject it. For its part, modernity developed its own autonomy in an independence increasingly marked by an ideology of rationality and progress, ignorant of its inherent disequilibrium.[7] The modernity which issued from this mixture had a correct insight into the nature of autonomy but developed a perverse sense of the autonomy of values, both of

---

7. This failure is due less to the intellectual incapacity of locating one of these two conceptions in relation to the other than with concrete historical struggles for power. In the worldview of the spiritual combat, humanity is subordinated to and assisted by the hierarchical authorities who have ultimate responsibility for the process of conversion already underway. Given a more rational and liberal conception of the world, the authorities need to redefine their role, whereas an emancipated humanity needs to recognize the limits of its newfound power. In the Church and in society at large (and indeed in religious life), the operative social forms have adapted poorly to the new situation.

nature and of humanity. Today we can easily ascertain the bitter fruits of this perversion (without necessarily being able to analyze their causes with great exactitude), and we are tempted to call into question the correctness of the perception from which it originated. Thus, we speak of "postmodernity"—bitterly lucid, disenchanted and terrified at the same time, indecisive and unsure of itself—a phenomenon that now in its secular form meets up again with the other world of guilt and grace, and in its turn, given the experience of failure that abounds, is tempted to emphasize the fact of guilt over that of grace. In both cases, a climate of "apocalyptic" finds a home.

I submit that this is undoubtedly why in recent years certain expressions have found a place in the language of the modern culture which describe our time as reaching its *end*. I will give just two of the most important ones: "the end of modernity"[8] and "the close of Western civilization."[9] If the first envisions a form of society, the second extends more broadly to include an entire vision, a history, and a system of practices in the world. And if we speak today of an "end," as these expressions would have us, what is really being pointed out is their "failure," even though they have implemented the very resources by which they are defined. Hierarchy and modernity have not only failed to produce what humanity has always waited for—what the ancients called happiness and the Church names "justice, peace and the protection of creation"—but they are themselves in a state of exhaustion. There is little more to expect from them.

The End of Modernity

In the case of "the end of modernity," the issues relate especially to the state of culture and of society, which I have already described, and which date from the late years of the Middle Ages, from the Renaissance or from the beginning of modern time. This culture is based on the individual, who grasps himself or herself as a subject and is governed only by the principle of reason, sufficient of itself to nurture the conviction of an irreversible order of progress. The critics of modernity are the philosophers and the sociologists who probe it and attest to the fact of its failure, both as regards the happiness

---

8. See Gianni Vattimo, *The End of Modernity: Nihilism and Hermeneutics in Postmodern Culture* (Baltimore, Md.: Johns Hopkins University Press, 1991). Heidegger's criticism of Hegelian rationalism, transformed into a negative judgment on the whole of the history of philosophy, has proven decisive for postmodernism. Along with many others, I have examined this in *God, Time, and Being,* trans. Leonard Maluf (Petersham, Mass.: St. Bede's Publications, 1992) 47–57. See also G. Sasso, *Tramonto di un mito* (2nd ed.; Bologna, 1988) 321–59 (= "Vergessenheit des Seins [intorno a Heidegger]").

9. The reference is to Jacques Derrida, *Of Grammatology,* trans. Gayatri Chakravorty Spivak (Baltimore, Md.: Johns Hopkins University Press, 1974) 18–26. See my *God, Time, and Being,* 57–68.

of the individual as well as its significance for society. Some of the indicators of the failure include the fact that war continues to be the backdrop of international existence; that sexuality continues to be subject to the immediacy of desire and leads to enslavement, literally and figuratively; the obsessive pursuit of money which determines economic structures; the loss of points of reference in one's personal and social life, in esthetics and politics, etc.

At many levels, attempts are not lacking which oppose this degeneration, but they come across as palliatives, indeed as indispensable emergency measures which if only fully implemented would put modernity back on its feet. It is modernity's principles which are lacking and not some cosmetic manifestations of decline. In light of the very real havoc in nature and in society wreaked by a modernity out of control and supported either by the Enlightenment or a simplistic ideology of progress, many of today's intellectuals are quick to reject modernity, declare it finished, pronounce it dead. They announce the arrival of a "postmodernism" which is itself markedly ideological and which tends to discredit any effort of reason and any affirmation of freedom in favor of silence, sentiment, and the rebirth of a sense of the sacred more or less the object of reflection. Then, too, all development on the planet is discredited. Finally, one notes a certain despair in the ceaseless search for different issues, or in the face of the absence of any realism in these projects, a despair that reveals a suicidal tendency.

The Close of Western Civilization

In truth, the end of modernity coincides in time with another, vaster "end," that of the whole of Western civilization. Modernity is only destined to pass away because its ineluctable end has already been programmed by past options and remote circumstances. I feel the need to expatiate on this topic of the "close of Western civilization," because it defines the essentially cultural options which explain this diagnosis of an "end."

When Martin Heidegger retraces the tragic path taken by Western philosophy, he considers Plato the initiator of an irreversible tendency of decline. The exact meaning of truth begins to take a wrong turn with him, while his answer to the question of being is also a false one. Plato is the father not only of the dominant philosophical tendency in the Greco-Latin world and up to our day,[10] but he is also the father of humanism and the practice of politics. It follows that the whole of Western civilization has been wounded by a double injury inflicted by Plato—to truth and to being. The dissolution of Plato's universe today is the tragic final act in a history of false interpretations. Even if Heidegger's interpretation is overly one-sided

10. In the Introduction to the proceedings of the Colloque de Royaumont, *Le Néo-platonisme* (Paris, 1971) 1, Pierre Hadot quoted Alfred North Whitehead's remark that "Western philosophy is nothing more than a series of footnotes appended to Plato's text."

and unreasonably pessimistic apropos of our civilization, it is surely justified to probe deeper into what might be called "the Platonic question." As
we shall see, to do so brings us to the very heart of yet another question—
"the question of the Church."

This is not the occasion to develop the philosophical and cultural aspects of "Western civilization" under the imprint of Plato.[11] Institutionally,
in both the political and the religious senses, we can say that we are approaching the "end of Western civilization" to the extent that we have exhausted
the possibilities of the political and cultural forms emerging out of the supremacy of the Mystical and the Political founded on the invisible One-beyond-everything. But so, too, have we exhausted the possibilities emerging
from the supremacy of an immanent rationality that is always capable of
grasping what is, of organizing, possessing, and dominating, i.e., of
modernity. The first form of dominance suppresses individuality and
human creativity, which are constantly menaced by interior divisions and
need to rely on some greater authority. The second covers over the person's
desire for the religious, exploits the planet, and creates relations of dependence
based on knowledge and wealth, rather than on spiritual contemplation.

An End Incapable of Fresh Initiatives?

The interpretation of the end I have presented is immensely tragic:
those who employ it have no idea of what lies ahead of this end. They are
the children of an abortive era and have no idea of what to do to gain a
sense of direction. In order to point to the inescapably paradoxical character of the situation of not being able to think without using the very means
furnished by their exhausted era, the philosophers and sociologists of the
End refuse to speak and when they write it is frequently marked by a tactic
of "erasing," crossing out certain words they employ, especially the word
"being," demonstrating thereby both the absence of any pertinence and the
inherent contradiction of being forced to use these words because no others are available. On the other hand, the announcement of this tragic End
is the simultaneous admission that they have no true understanding of
time, since the only time they can know is "abortive." Historical periods
come to their term without having produced anything: they are a sort of

---

11. See my *Histoire théologique de l'Église catholique. Itinéraire et formes de la théologie* (Paris: Cerf, 1994) for my inquiries into the cultural foundations of the present
book. I attempted to stress the importance for Western culture of the ideas of "the one"
and of "being," which lie at the very heart of all the forms of our culture, even the politico-
social. That is why I have described this culture with the expression "the Parmenidean
culture," alluding to Plato's dialogue *Parmenides,* in which he confronts these two paradoxes at length.

succession of instants that stand still, an evacuation of any possible meaning. Consequently, to speak about time is not to speak about a value but about a negative force which works destruction. In such situations, we are sent back to a previous situation, to a timeless origin, to a "once upon a time" that remains nameless and without any definable character, since one must refuse all mythology of an idyllic past.

We will have occasion to see that if presentations of the end of being and the end of time, which concentrate exclusively on the tragic element, err by excess, and if the different opinions taken together (and others too could be added) are open to discussion and to being nuanced, and if the approach of the year 2000 imparts a certain element of the mythic and the fantastic to the theme of the End, still we cannot deny that many persons today are unanimous in their opinion that what is at stake is not only a matter of a different optic on reality, but that in fact we have arrived at a decisive turning point of a long era. We can even maintain sincerely that none of what is transpiring before our very eyes argues indisputably for an indefinite prolongation of the painful situation in the world, still it is not illegitimate to acknowledge that this situation is deeply rooted in our civilization. We can avert this tragic excess only if we make the effort to sort out those elements of Western culture which have come to their end, and without rejecting the whole concentrate on stressing the authentically human elements in the culture. But we must also try to feel out what might constitute a new beginning and strive to foster its arrival, all the more so since the End of the World (whatever can this expression possibly mean?) is clearly not knocking on our door.

The End of Western Christianity?

Having arrived at this point, we must recall that during and after the Second Vatican Council, as we gradually became aware of the direction of these writings, Catholics too began to speak of an End. In this case, however, we spoke about "the end of the Constantinian Era." Many proclaimed the end of a highly hierarchical polity according to which norms for living together were devised and imposed from on high and where the real autonomy of individuals and groups representing intermediate levels of responsibility was severely restricted. It is significant that it was precisely many Catholics who proclaimed the end of such an era after Vatican II. Clearly, what they wanted to express was the end of a certain type of ecclesiastical government, and which we shall consider at greater length in the next chapter. In the politico-social world properly speaking, it appears that the Constantinian Era ceased to have any influence long before Vatican II. The revolutions of 1789 and 1848 and the efforts to establish world organizations after both World Wars of the first half of the twentieth century had already greatly modified the political mentality in the world. The Constantinian Era had already begun its decline in civil society with the advent of modernity. But the Church was determined to hold on to the institutions that had proven themselves in an earlier stage of Western civilization, and it resisted modern rationalism, except in a limited and timid form. In any event, for Christianity and in the West for Catholicism in particular, given its past influence in the societies of antiquity and the Middle Ages or given its polemical attitude toward modern societies, its reforms, counter-reforms, and its opposition became an integral part of what today is claimed as "at an end." The Church's antimodern attitude became so integrated into the very fiber of the culture that it came to be considered inseparable from it and indissolubly bound up with it. Should we then add yet a third item to our enumeration and speak of "the end of Western Christianity"? In the future, should we think of another form of Christianity, and if so, which one? Or should we consider something else entirely different from Christianity, and if so, what? Given the close and reciprocal dovetailing of Christianity and Western civilization, is it even a possibility for Christianity to "recoup its investment" when Western civilization itself is crumbling?

I believe that the questions I have just posed are justified and that for the believer they are frightening, even destabilizing. I am not sure that today theologians can risk saying anything valid for people in general and especially for their own Church, if they refuse to accept the fact that the world around them is tottering. This is all the more true for the members of the hierarchy. Unquestionably, the Church has the words of eternal life, but not every ecclesiastical form can make this claim. And if there is reason today for "imagining the Church," isn't this really because the forms in the Catholic Church, and perhaps in all the other churches, are too dependent on precisely what is moribund in Western civilization, the very civilization that in earlier times they helped create? Only if we do not avert our attention from the fact that the upheaval overwhelming Western civilization is also overwhelming the Church will we be able to imagine other forms that will permit the Church both to survive the crisis and to contribute to the much needed birth of another world. But if we give in to the reassuring thought that the current crisis is of no import for the Church but only for the world, we will rob ourselves of the opportunity of doing what must absolutely be done for the world and for the Church.

Judgments

Having said all this, I need to add some nuances to the judgment passed of "the end of the era" as it applies to actual relations between the world and the Church, since there are elements in this very relationship that open up a space for hope and even action.

The World of Culture

I have stressed the various points of opposition in the "Parmenidean culture": either it has little or no connection with our human rational and temporal condition, or it is submerged in it. I have indicated also how these two opposing forms correspond in time to different cultural, social and political stages: an "imperial" (hierarchical) world and a "bourgeois" (modern and democratic) world. To be more precise, one should also indicate how both forms to some extent corrected one another. Historically, neither form was ever purely "hierarchical" or purely "democratic."[12] When such corrections have been made, they have generally favored an inclusive attitude over an exclusive one. In the same way, in the course of making judgments about our future in the light of these various "closes" or "ends," we will have to incorporate those very values which Western civilization discovered, even if they have come to grief in the way we have tried to realize them. With a bit more tact than the prophets of the "End" bring to their claims, we will have to admit that Western civilization has not been entirely negative. Mysticism, thought, power, reason, and technology are not in themselves condemned to catastrophe. Perhaps we can detect more than a little arrogance in the attempt to write only while simultaneously "striking out" such grand notions, and in the claim that in the final analysis our ancestors were totally mistaken and that we—or maybe our children—stand a better chance of discovering the key that will unlock reality by starting over from scratch. What we really need to do is face up to the difficult judgments we have to make, judgments that are tied up with the possibility of imagining the future, in all humility and audacity, and doing so from within a tradition that is a melange of thought and action. Staying with the categories of the Hellenistic thought-world, one can say that side by side with Plato (considered to be the root of all our problems) stand such figures as Aristotle, Epicurus, and Zeno. We must also evaluate critically Aristotle's identification of the One and of Being, and the consequences of his understanding for thought and more generally for humanism. In this way we can render a better account of the role played by such an identification, so that from within the civilization of antiquity itself we might be able to correct the excesses of the "Parmenidean culture."

12. The "Debate between the elders and modern man" is a device employed by civilizations of various epochs to achieve a certain real, albeit precarious, equilibrium in society. See the chapters entitled "Antichi, moderni, postmoderni" and "'Idola' della modernità" in P. Rossi, *Paragone degli ingegni moderni e postmoderni* (Bologna, 1989).

Christianity

On the other hand, when one is tempted to pass judgment on the whole of Western civilization, it is important not to leave out Christianity and its vicissitudes, since it forms a whole with the history and the culture under consideration. Earlier, I tried to define the proper contribution the Christian faith made to Western culture, by examining the essential values expressed briefly and fundamentally in the ancient Apostles' Creed and the way these essential values contributed to correcting and enriching the patrimony bequeathed to the West by the Greeks. We should not minimize the value of the example set by the encounter of Christianity with the culture worked out during the first centuries of the Church. In this concrete encounter, we have a good example of a methodological paradigm.

None of this is a denial of the fact that when created, earthly realities, both cosmological and anthropological, began to attract the attention of the cultural world of Christians, and when the real danger of a rationalism, more and more enterprising and possessive began to appear, the Church, either in its organizational structures or in its horizon of theological propositions, had no viable alternative to offer. It should have been possible to develop a conceptuality of being arising out of the Church's understanding of creation and of the logic of analogy. Such ideas after all formed an essential part of the deposit of revelation in its belief in the parousia of Christ. The Catholic Church chose to be "antimodern" rather than "modern, but in a different sense." This failure has cost the Church dearly, but it has also been disastrous for civilization. Instead of offering each other possibilities of correcting one-sided positions and of mutually corroborating each other in the search for a just way for humanity to survive in a world increasingly abandoned by hierarchical thought, the Church and the world grew farther apart, each perilously weakened by the divorce. The Church lost its roots in humanity and could not find the right cultural habits which would have helped it avoid giving the impression of being only a "supernaturally perfect society." And the world was denied a sense of ultimate meaning which would have led it to a correct perception of being and a lively knowledge of time. The Christian faith held the possibility of opening up the world to the meaning of time by marking out the limits of rationalism and the need for certain creaturely restraints.

Conclusion

By approaching the Second Vatican Council in the way we have, it can be claimed that the Church saw the need for reform in the face of the tragic impasse of our time, at least to the extent that it affected the Church itself. That would be the ultimate meaning of the council. At least once the Church seems to have consciously discerned such a need before the other human societies took stock of their situation, and which exploded in the various movements of May 1968.

Placing the opening of the council in October 1962 parallel to the events of May 1968 might appear surprising, nevertheless, aren't they like the fabled tortoise and hare?[13] The council needed three years of preparation, followed by four years of debate, and even to this day it has perhaps implemented only a third or even less of the council's resolutions. Whatever is to be made of the lapse of so many years, a profound reform was adopted in principle and even part of the reform was undertaken in a courageous way. (One need only point to the reform of the liturgy!) This reform directly addresses the contemporary discourse of an "End." The political demonstrations of May 1968 bolted from the starting line like La Fontaine's hare, impulsively and violently sensing the absence of human meaning and the emptiness of life, whether manifested in the holding on to power at all costs by society's "hierarchies," or in the fruits of a modernity robbed of its project.

However, what resulted was that modernity remained fixed in an attitude of opposition. Thus, it could only oppose the anarchy of technology, of power, of progress with another anarchy, that of a sense of exaltation in the immediate moment, of suppressing all power, of simplistic ecological measures. It revealed a keenness for merging perspectives. Thus, the simplicity of the imperative, "Make love, not war" showed that it lacked any reflection on the different forms of love, as if love could succeed without the element of dying to oneself. In reality, the pretended purity of love and the pitilessness of war are just the two tragic faces of the same frightening misunderstanding. And when the analyses finally appeared on the scene, it was clear just how dreadfully ideological and frightfully deceptive they were. The youth of May 1968 were incapable of getting beyond their rhetoric, and their "seizing the word" produced no concrete results. And who could hold anything against their efforts?[14] But that said, October 1962 and May 1968 show the same awareness of the sense of impasse that urgently needed to be surmounted. Even the slow pace of postconciliar reform can serve to inspire hope. Though the full reality of the reform remains hidden, at least in

13. For those unfamiliar with the allusion, see La Fontaine's famous fable entitled "The Hare and the Tortoise." The point is that the one which is by nature the faster and the more agile of the two, wastes its time in distractions, while the more deliberate tortoise "makes haste slowly" and arrives at the goal first.

14. A moving witness and a clear analysis of what happened in May 1968 can be found in Guy Coq, *Que m'est-il donc arrivé? Un trajet vers la foi* (Paris: Seuil, 1993). This journey to the faith implies the Church, and the author treats this theme admirably on pp. 109f.

the end the need for it was squarely faced, and perhaps in the long term its impact on civil society will also be felt.

Some will object that it was not at all Pope John XXIII's intention to deal with the tragedy of the "close of Western civilization" and the "end of modernity." He certainly had no intention of bringing the "Constantinian Era" to an end. Instead, it does seem that he wanted to dust off an aging institution by challenging it to a modest *aggiornamento,* but also to work toward the unity of the churches (and one could argue that from this standpoint we have the germ of a much more extensive reform than the Pope himself was aware of). To comprehend the importance of the council as a decisive moment in world history, we cannot restrict ourselves to a lifeless historical-critical exegesis of the words of the Pope or even of the council's texts. For all the need to exegete in an historical-critical way the "literal meaning," i.e., the "intention of the author," (popes, the bishops, or the conciliar commissions) in order to arrive at the "first level of meaning," this effort, imperative though it may be, is not sufficient. Even if we choose the case of the conciliar documents, a text from the Dogmatic Constitution on the Church will take on a broader, more nuanced, more ambiguous meaning when it is brought into play with the ensemble of conciliar documents, i.e., when it is interpreted in the light of "the analogy of the faith."

A council does not assume importance because it is involved in the internal vicissitudes of its own intratextual history. It assumes greater significance when it is considered in relation to the human predicament out of which it was born, which profoundly influenced it, and which it too has modified. This is why I maintain that the event of the council, taken as a whole, grows in importance when it is brought into contact with the events of May 1968, and vice versa. Given the simultaneity and the violence of the search, May 1968 radicalizes the tragic character of the epoch and the urgency of "making a turn." It invites Christians to ask themselves: "What was ultimately at stake at Vatican II, and doesn't this far surpass our thoughts?" Conversely, might not the seriousness of Vatican II's reflections on the times and even the slow pace of its procedures during the council and in the postconciliar phase, cause the men and women of our day to pause to reflect on the gravity and the difficulty of the task of building something that can surmount the threat of an "end" to the world of value and meaning as we know it, and even offer them some modest method of reflection?

The challenge for Christians in the future will be to know how the Church can continue the course opened by Vatican II and its limited reforms. Taking nuanced account of the triple goal we have noted, i.e., the crisis of Western culture, the close of the Constantinian Era, and the end of modernity, how will the Church for its part contribute to clearing the way for a new beginning? Because the Church does not want to be carried off in the disaster of the "Parmenidean culture," but wants instead to set out on, and help the world find, new paths, the Church finds itself facing the fascinating task of imagining itself and constructing itself in a way very different from the forms of the past, helpful at the time but spent today and conserved by the Church for too long. The intent of my book, then, is quite simply to contribute to the task of finding a new vision of the Church, one that will emerge out of the courage to imagine its future.

Chapter 2

The Gregorian Form of the Church

We cannot undertake the task of "imagining the Church" without taking a closer look at the dominant form adopted by the Church in what we call Western Christianity (and without forgetting that this form was exported throughout the non-Western world in the course of the "discovery" and the "conquest" of these cultures). By defining this form emblematically as "Gregorian," we are clearly alluding to a form which bears the name of Pope Gregory VII (1073–85), the pope who was primarily responsible for implementing it. This form can be considered operative already before him, however, both because it is tied to an earlier political theology that it takes up and contributes to, and because it was never abandoned, at least as regards its essential structures, even though it was subjected to certain subsequent modifications. Beyond the Gregorian reform of the High Middle Ages and its consolidation up to the thirteenth century, its structures are found at the very heart of the Catholic reform at the end of the sixteenth century. They were reaffirmed by recent popes, and can be read even in the encyclical *Mystici corporis* (1943) of Pius XII, but in which, too, we can detect the tentative lines of a new form beginning to emerge.

This model highlights three supporting elements, or three axes that hold up the entire multiform reality of the Church. The first, and unquestionably the most important, since it informs the selection and implementation of the other two options, is the keen awareness of what might be called the *primacy of the truth* as it relates to salvation. Next, there must also be an institution for the proclamation and the defense of the truth. The *primacy of the pope* is central from this perspective and will continue to grow in importance with the passing of time, eventually weakening the other institutions which also serve truth and the salvation of men and women. And third, there must be a *holy and continent priesthood* which is charged with the pastoral care of the faithful. All three elements are derived from the same theological orientation and each is its expression in the realms of truth, power, and the sacred. Thus, together they constitute a *system*, with the result that it becomes impossible to maintain the Gregorian form if any one of these axes is seriously weakened.

But before we undertake a study of each systemic element, it might be helpful to note briefly that for the medieval understanding of God the ideas of *unity, immutability, and omnipotence* are determinative. Unity is the very foundation of theology to the extent that it is dominated by the idea of the One-beyond-everything. Immutability is characteristic of the very being of God who is opposed to the innate instability of creation (according to the phrase of the prophet most dear to St. Augustine: "I am the Lord and I do not change" [Mal 3:6]). Among the other divine attributes, omnipotence receives special attention because it is the basis of the power exercised by the hierarchical mediations in the order of salvation: God the Creator and initiator of all reality is alone almighty, but communicates this power to those whose authority is derived from various mediations, those coming from Christ's will as Founder of the Church, and those derived from the mediation of angels and priests. These themes are the indispensable background ideas for understanding this theology and as the foundation of all truth and authority. In what follows, they need to be kept in mind.

The Defense and Elucidation of Truth

We have briefly characterized the exaltation and the defense of truth as the primary element in the Gregorian form of the Church. This fact explains why, since the very origins of the Church, the bond between the true confession of the faith and eternal salvation has been so close. We need to remain aware of this connection before we take up the issue of heresy, i.e., the sin against truth, and before we determine some of the characteristics of the "Inquisition," the institution established to combat heresy and to maintain the Church in truth.

Truth and Salvation

There are three levels on which the value of truth is expanded and given expression: doctrinal, linguistic, and ecclesiological.

The Doctrinal Aspect

In the first place, only a person who is found in the truth is saved. This "Johannine" conviction is of theologal[1] significance because Jesus Christ is

1. The author uses this uncommon technical term rather than the more general "theological." In the theology of the virtues, faith, hope, and love are often called "the-

not only a witness to the truth, but is himself the Truth and the Life. His mission results in the knowledge of the true God: "To know you and him whom you have sent, Jesus Christ." On the other hand, this conviction is supported by those means of expression that formed the mentality, common to the Hellenistic world and shared by the Fathers of the Church and the doctors of the Middle Ages, viz., the double primacy of truth (*alētheia*) and knowledge (*gnōsis*) on the scale of human values. Truth is first because it reflects, on different levels, the essential attributes of God. Like God, it is one and immutable, opposed to all error and to the uncertainty of opinion (*doxa*).

The encounter between the Christian idea of the revelation of the Truth and the cultural conviction of the primacy of truth (whose true abode is "on high") results in the epistemological doctrine of *illumination:* all genuinely intelligible and spiritual knowledge descends on men and women by means of a light that both blinds and informs. From Augustine and Pseudo-Dionysius up to Bonaventure, Latin authors tried to elaborate philosophically the nature of this illumination. How does it come into the soul and how is the soul prepared to receive and appropriate it? Whatever different answers theologians gave to these questions, this conviction regarding illumination remained firm, and yet could not resolve new conflicts arising from the emergence of the autonomy of reason.

The Linguistic Aspect

The theological conviction apropos of the primacy of "knowledge" and of "truth," along with the illumination theory of knowledge, are the basis of the linguistic nature of truth, viz., that the formulations of the faith, e.g., the Scriptures, creeds, and other texts proposed by the Church, are an authentic expression of the Truth. There is a quasi-identity of revealed truth and the formulas expressing the truth, at the least in the negative sense that any other formulation of the same object is excluded if it does not contain the substance of the signification given in the authorized formulation. The latter becomes the point of reference in a twofold sense: doctrinally it is the norm of all teaching, and juridically it is the criterion for judging orthodoxy.[2] The mentality of knowledge by illumination also

---

ologal" with the intent to express the immediacy of these virtues with the divine life. These three are "theologal" because they are our graced participation in the life of God as it comes to expression in these three perfections of our fundamental human dimensions. We are defined by faith, hope, and love and are not simply called to the occasional exercise of these graced acts. By using the term "theologal" in this context, the author points to the bond between truth and God's own life. In philosophical language, we can say that revealed truth and God as Truth are convertible [translator].

2. This twofold acceptation, doctrinal and juridical, is contained in the expression "authorized formulation": the word "authorized" signifies (1) "what has authority"

plays an important role in this regard. According to Pseudo-Dionysius, the bishop receives illumination from on high in order to communicate the truth, with the result that his proper gift guarantees, as it were, the truth of the formulations. The faithful must simply accept the illumination coming from the bishop's teaching and hold these texts as an expression of saving truth. (As we shall see later on, more and more medieval theologians will apply these ideas to the pope and his role in enunciating and defending the truth.)

The Ecclesiological Aspect

A third nuance remains in this theory, the ecclesiological. The Truth, which in the Holy Spirit joins faith and the truths which formulate it, constitutes the Church as "foundation and pillar of the Truth" (1 Tim 4:15). Negatively, this means that those who do not confess the truth in the terms enunciated by the Church are separated from unity with it and find themselves rejected because they have not fulfilled an essential condition for salvation, viz., membership in the Church.[3] The confession of revealed truth in the terms which the Church uses to proclaim them is the final norm for access to eternal happiness. This ensemble of convictions regarding the central character of the Truth and its authorized expressions explains the passion of the Fathers of the Church in their polemics against heretical views. It also explains their anxiety in finding formulas which could be the object of unanimous consent among the bishops and thereby make available to the Christian people texts that function as normative expressions of the truth. In the course of time, the search for unanimity developed to the point that it became a demand for uniformity. This development reached its summit in the twelfth century, i.e., paradoxically just when the first signs of modernity began to appear and pose the question of the possibility of a pluralism of views.[4]

---

because of its "author" just as much as because of its content, and (2) "what is permitted," which includes a connotation that other formulations are excluded.

3. I reference here the words which conclude the recent definitions of the Immaculate Conception and the Assumption of the Virgin Mary: those who do not accept them "have made shipwreck of the faith and fallen from the unity of the Church." See H. Denzinger- A. Schönmetzer, *Enchiridion symbolorum definitionum et declarationum de rebus fidei et morum* (33rd ed.; Rome: Herder, 1965), nos. 2804 and 3904. E. T. in J. Neuner-J. Dupuis, eds. *The Christian Faith in the Doctrinal Documents of the Catholic Church* (rev. ed.; Staten Island, New York: Alba House, 1982), no. 709, p. 204.

4. "In all domains and at every level, western Christendom in the twelfth century was haunted by the veritable obsession for a *reductio ad unum*. In theology and ecclesiology, the fundamental preoccupation of most of the clergy was to reduce everything to unity, so that diversity became synonymous with something evil and pretty soon with something deviant. This option, which appears inhuman to us, did not lack a certain grandeur and the attempt to create on earth a perfect Christian society under the leader-

"Evidence" of the Truth

As the Gregorian reform was taking root in the High Middle Ages, it was taken for granted that the Church knew the truth and had established the necessary formulations, especially in its creeds and in its hierarchical structure. A person knew what was needed to be saved, and those who were baptized into the faith of the Church were judged to know the truth and were held to profess it. Any hesitation, any criticism was not justified, and if any did appear, they were culpable. Apostasy was the worst sin, a fact that was clear from the era of persecution in the early Church; heresy was next on the scale of grave matter.

The Episcopal Function of Teaching

To better situate this attitude, perhaps we should pause to reflect on certain facts that emerged out of the patristic period. At that time, three poles can be distinguished in the bishop's task of teaching. First of all, it was exercised in the bishop's *preaching of the faith, in the context of the liturgy, by employing the method of commenting on the Scriptures.* The homiletical and mystagogical task of the Fathers of the Church is at the center of their theology, or better, *is* their theology. Announcing the faith by engaging the spiritual sense of Scripture was addressed to the mind and the heart of the faithful in order to transform the liturgical assembly into a Christian church and to make each Christian into "one who knows God." Secondly, and parallel to the first, the encounter with the culture led to *employing a certain vocabulary, establishing theological structures, and composing doctrinal syntheses.* These efforts also aimed at the mind and heart of Christians, but with a more pronounced intellectual impact, more speculative and more practical. Bishops were often involved in this effort, but any Christian could do this by reflecting on the faith from the perspective of his or her gifts and under the influence of the Spirit. The third task of the episcopal ministry was the *correction of grave errors* emerging from the theological and doctrinal effort just mentioned. The bishop had to exclude certain formulas while proposing others. At this level, adhering to the faith implied a character of "obligation," i.e., some expressions could be used while others were definitely excluded, and this defining and coercive task was not practiced without considerable difficulty. Finally, the task was often a collective effort,

---

ship of a single leader, the pope, made for a project that was both utopian and fascinating at the same time. But the obverse of the medal was not only that a sense of intolerance continued to grow—for, at no period of their history did medieval society turn tolerance into a value, even if it was practiced occasionally—but that what today we call the right to be different, was rejected without any possibility of appeal." André Vauchez in J.-M. Mayeur, C. and L. Pietri, A. Vauchez, and M. Venard, eds., *Histoire du christianisme des origines à nos jours* (Paris: Desclée, 1993) 5:822.

the fruit of local or general councils. Scriptural and liturgical preaching, doctrinal initiatives, and the correction of errors—in that order of importance—were the ways in which bishops exercised their prophetic ministry.

The Correction of Error

In the High Middle Ages, the first two episcopal functions were somewhat neglected. The monasteries undertook the search for the spiritual meaning of the Scriptures and the theological fund of the Fathers seems to have become part of the general theoretical understanding of Christians, so much so that there was no need to change it. It was enough that its content be repeated in the local parishes. This fact explains why the Gregorian reform did not demand much in the way of the intellectual formation of priests. All that was needed was that they knew the rudiments of Christian morality in order to teach and exhort the faithful. But the third function remained lively at this time—that of correction of error—and it was exercised with so much zeal that the element of truth in the mentality of the Greco-Latin culture was seen as constitutive of salvation. But also, in a Christianity that was increasingly centered on the pope, concern for Christian unity seemed to demand a doctrinal unicity that was seamless. As the accent on the orthodoxy of the faith grew, the note of *obligatoriness* increased at the expense of a *spiritual listening* and the *understanding of the faith*. All this helps to explain why an institution was needed that would safeguard this sense of orthodoxy, now regarded as the foundation of eternal salvation and the unity of the Church here below. Given certain variations bound up with different cultural situations, from the Inquisition of Innocent III (1198–1216) to the Congregation for the Doctrine of the Faith of Paul VI (1963–78), the Church continues to cope with the same concern: how can it equip itself to guard revealed Truth, to maintain catholic unity, and combat errors fatal to the salvation of men and women?

The Sin of Heresy and Its Condemnation

Presupposing these two premises—the bond between truth and salvation on the one hand and the "evidence" of this truth in the Church on the other—there is no wonder that if someone were to question a received formula of the faith or an established ecclesiastical structure, it would be an inadmissible sin, i.e., an offense against God and a scandal for the Christian people, because it would be an attack on their theological faith and the coherence of the institutional Church.

We need to pause here to examine the model used in the Middle Ages to qualify something as heresy. It was considered a crime of *lèse majesté*, i.e., just as certain crimes against the prince were an affront to his majesty, so heresy was a grave affront to God's honor.[5] The underlying figure is that of the kingdom of God, of the royal transcendence of Christ the Pantocrator. The background idea explains how the prince, in his rather modest situation vis-à-vis the celestial hierarchies but in his supreme position as regards terrestrial hierarchies, functions as the expression of God's royalty and divine Truth—always in dependence on Christ, of course. This expressive function is the basis for his "majesty." Any crime against the prince is an affront to this majesty and is punishable by grave sanctions. So, too, if God is Supreme Truth beyond all knowledge, and if the Word is the very expression of this Truth, accessible to our world by the incarnation and glorified in death by his resurrection, then heresy is a blow against the Truth of the Word and a breach of the honor due him—a veritable crime of divine *lèse majesté*. It is a matter of an enormous offense which must be prosecuted and sanctioned in the same way one would proceed against the crime of royal *lèse majesté*. This assimilation of the earthly and the heavenly orders explains the seriousness of the procedure and the gravity of the punishment. Heretics must be prosecuted for two reasons: first, to lead them back to the truth, and second, to disarm them from further harming others. The Church's professions of the faith become juridical norms almost for judging whether someone belongs to the Church or not.[6] Such reasoning explains the importance of excommunication and the justification of its frequent use in Christendom.

We need to remember that society in the Middle Ages and in modern times was reputed to be entirely Christian. The Church not only had its visible structures, it also possessed juridical powers, since it could initiate actions that would not permit the heretic to remain in the same human and social condition. Furthermore, if one turned to the state, here the sin of heresy was considered a civil violation, even a crime, so that in addition to one's being persecuted in the Church one was also subject to corporal punishment and coercive measures by the civil authorities. It was inconceivable that a condemnation for heresy by the Church was not met in the state by the punishment of a heretic being banned from society, and this included being stripped of one's civil rights, the confiscation of one's property, imprisonment, etc. Conversely, the threat of civil sanctions that would

5. See the decretal of Innocent III, *Vergentis in senium* in *Decretales Gregorius IX*, V, 7, 10 (*Corpus juris canonici,* Emil Friedberg, vol. II [Graz: Akademische Druck- und Verlagsanstalt, 1959] 782).

6. Given the ambiguity between what characterizes something doctrinally or juridically, the juridical element begins to dominate. The High Middle Ages has no other cultural horizon for envisaging other ways of culturally conditioning the faith. Doctrine exists once and for all, and all that is needed is to become permeated by it. Otherwise, it is understood as a juridical norm.

make continued human existence extremely precarious for the heretic and his or her family was quite effective as a dissuasive measure. It is also evident that if the civil authorities refused to follow suit with the religious authorities in persecuting heretics, they would become complicit in the heresy and be open to sanction, especially excommunication. If we were to take these premises to their logical conclusion, a prince who was unwilling to support the action of the Church against heresy would himself cease to have authority over his subjects, because he refused to take the measures needed for keeping them in the sole and unique salvific truth. A heretical prince ceases to be a prince.[7] The religious authorities can undertake punitive and coercive measures if a prince refuses to employ them and if the Church has the means to do so. The political aspect becomes apparent in the Church's effort to maintain and safeguard the truth. We might ask whether it is possible to pursue a defense of the truth when the political means are no longer available, as is the case in modern societies, when the state no longer intervenes in properly religious questions. If this defense of truth is impossible, what other means hold out any hope of success?

The fundamental elements affirmed and defended, especially as we will see by the Roman pontiff, in the Gregorian form of the Church included the primacy of divine truth in order to be saved, a sufficient knowledge of this truth imparted by a rudimentary catechesis and the constant teaching of the priests, and the role of the truth confessed for the preservation of the unity and the liberty of the Church.

The Constant Elements of the "Inquisition"

From the approach we have taken, we can say that the Church fights a constant battle to defend itself against heresy on two fronts: the "intellectual" and the "spiritual." On the one hand, every new cultural contribution, whether because of a new set of concepts and terms, or because of new methodological demands, threatens the equilibrium established by a rudimentary catechesis and risks leading the faithful into error and compromising the unity of the Church. This explains a certain cognitive reservation in principle that assumes an attitude of vigilance, the detailed examination of documents inspired by new perspectives, and even

---

7. This explains the decision by Pius V (1559–65) to lift from the subjects of Elizabeth I of England, a heretical queen, their oath of obedience and their political allegiance to the queen. It also explains why Henry IV of France needed to be reconciled for the heresy of being a Protestant with Clement VIII (1592–1605), in order to be sure of the loyalty of his subjects, the vast majority of whom were Catholics. The background ideas for the bond between the true confession of the faith and its coherence with the political reality, can be found in Augustine, *The City of God,* Book 19, chs. 21–25. See *Corpus christianorum,* vol. 48 (Turnhout: Brepols, 1955) 687–96.

polemics—an ensemble resulting in condemnations and excommunications, with all the ecclesial and civil consequences these involve.

From Peter Abelard (1079–1142) and the School of Chartres up to the modernism at the beginning of the twentieth century, and everything in between, e.g., the introduction of Aristotle to Christendom in the thirteenth century, the appearance of scientific methods in the sixteenth, the historical approach to the Scriptures by Richard Simon (1638–1712) in the seventeenth, the Chinese rites controversy, and the morality of loaning at interest in the eighteenth, the same tactics always emerge. Vigilance and warnings are always employed in the short term, since it is true that new disciplines threaten the existing doctrinal equilibrium and because one does not find a new theological structure overnight that integrates these new ideas without imperiling revealed Truth. Perhaps most important of all though, the new ideas coming from "somewhere else" question the epistemology of illumination which for centuries had been employed in the interpretation of revealed Truth by introducing a certain competence proper to reason. The hierarchy feels disarmed before such strange and even foreign propositions, both because of their content and their methodology, and it does not have the means, at least not immediately, of integrating these new ideas into the apostolic proclamation of the faith.

If the "intellectual" front corresponds to the second outline of the responsibility of the bishops for the faith, i.e., the one that deals with the dangerous encounter between cultures, the "spiritual" front corresponds to the bishops' first task, viz., the exposition of the Scriptures and mystagogical commentary on them. There are always Christians who yearn for something more than the rudimentary catechesis and the morality insisted on by the competent ecclesiastical authorities; they yearn to return to the sources of their faith, especially the Scriptures, and they long for something spiritually profound and for mystical experience. Groups dedicated to this search arise spontaneously. In respect to the meaning of their symbolic language, their points of departure, and the esotericism of such groups, the authorities fear that they will fail in the effort to grasp salvific truth. The same is true of their practices, where the fear that the spiritual search will soon turn into something carnal is quite real, or where there are groups which exclude participation by priests because their spirituality is impoverished and their learning mediocre. In such instances, these groups risk inflicting considerable harm on the sacramental life of the Church and its hierarchical structure. It is not hard to understand why, from the Humiliati and the Cathars up to the Alumbrados and the Reformers, the Church has called for prudence in reading the Scriptures and in accepting mystical pretensions, and why inversely it has insisted on the continued importance of hierarchical mediation. On the other hand, it has tried to engage these spiritual movements by channeling their enthusiasm and by a process of sacerdotalizing their leaders, so that those judged susceptible of effecting balanced reform in the Church are helped in their efforts.

The Primacy of the Pope

Such an overview of the centrality of truth for salvation helps us understand why the function of regulating the truth of the faith and the struggles against heresy passes more and more to a single person: the Roman pontiff. This way of reflection opens up for us the second element in the Gregorian form of the Church: a precise theology of the primacy of the pope, the successor of the apostle Peter who received from Christ the mission to strengthen his brothers. In fact, as we will see, the theology of the primacy of the pope goes far beyond the question properly speaking of truth, even though it continues to be a central one. It is rooted in the broad cultural context we have already noted and which we must now take up in greater detail.

The primacy of Peter, established by Jesus Christ and transmitted to the bishop of the community where the Prince of the Apostles suffered martyrdom, is an article of the Catholic faith. The successor of Peter at the head of this community effectively receives the prerogatives of its founder.[8] But Scripture does not determine rigorously the lines of this primacy. Instead, it was concrete circumstances that determined how and when the papacy came to be responsible for the preservation of the faith and the unity of the Church. Vice versa, such a "practice of the primacy" contributed to establishing an institutional tradition, i.e., what we have called the "Gregorian form" of the Church. It has a long history, of course, but one I cannot avoid treating it by recalling its principal elements and their theological interpretation.

The Background: The Roman Empire and Its Religious Interpretation

To understand the Gregorian interpretation of Petrine primacy,[9] we need to study its origins and inspiration well before the High Middle Ages, and not only as far back as the patristic period, but even before Christianity. We need to examine the politico-social form that dominated the

8. See the many works that appeared in the previous generation in response to the book by Oscar Cullmann, *Peter: Disciple–Apostle–Martyr. A Historical and Theological Study,* trans. Floyd V. Filson (2nd ed.; Pa: Westminster, 1962). More recently, see J.-M.R. Tillard, *The Bishop of Rome,* trans. John de Satgé (Wilmington, Del.: Michael Glazier, 1983); Gérard Claudel, *La Confession de Pierre. Trajectoire d'une péricope évangélique* (Paris: J. Gabalda, 1988); Christian Grappe, *D'un Temple à l'autre. Pierre et l'Église primitive de Jérusalem* (Paris: Presses Universitaires de France, 1992), together with the review by Gérard Claudel, *Cristianesimo nella storia* 14 (1993) 402–6.

9. See M. Maccarrone, "I fondamenti 'petrini' del primato romano in Gregorio VII," *Studia gregoriana* 13 (1989) 55–96.

Mediterranean world from Augustus (27 B.C.E.–14 C.E.) through the fifteenth century—the empire. Christianity spread its message throughout the empire and, without sacrificing its originality, developed its own organization in the imperial world, a world shot through with a specific political theology which the Church both borrowed and transformed.

To understand the form of the empire, we need to reflect on several successive factors. First, there is the birth of a political institution that emerged out of the rivalry among the great military leaders of Rome in the first century before Christ. In the Mediterranean world, more and more subject to Rome's hegemony, this process tended to revive the memory of the historical and the mythic person of Alexander the Great (356–323 B.C.E.). Consequently, even though the origins of the imperial form cannot be separated entirely from the republican ideology, the vast empire must have appeared more and more like a unique political reality, increasingly organized in large territorial administrative units and no longer by cities and countries having their own local character, and in which individuals became the backbone of the empire.[10] Secondly, as the Roman imperial idea and reality encountered the theologies of power in the East, which held that the king was divine, the Roman imperial interpretation took on a certain divine character that the Roman emperors adopted as they extended the empire throughout the East. The juridico-political order and the reverence due the emperor became tinged with religious connotations, sometimes evidenced in the public cult—precisely the aspect of the imperial order that the Christians steadfastly refused to participate in.[11] And thirdly, we must take note of the political impact of the philosophical notion of emanation and return, a characteristic of middle and late Platonism. According to this idea, hypostases proceed one from the other. In this system of ideas, the prince is situated at the boundary *(metaxu)* of the invisible and visible orders; he communicates what he receives from the invisible to the visible, which is organized starting with him and based on the law which has its source in him. We understand better the mystical element in this political theology. Finally, it would be necessary to examine the extent to which the emperor's assuming the role of the Sovereign Pontiff in the pagan cult ended in turning him into the privileged cultic mediator between the gods and men and women.

10. See Jean-Jacques Chevallier, *Histoire des idées politiques* (Paris: Payot, 1979) 1:115–44.

11. Recognizing the "divinity" of the emperor did not mean for the pagans that the emperor was a "god" *tout court,* but that he had a special place in the empire's highly articulated and organic system of divinities, and hence had a right to a corresponding cult. The refusal of the emperor's divinity was thus tantamount to refusing the cult to all the other divinities of the empire, the world of gods subordinated to the One-beyond-everything.

As the empire became Christian, but not without first submitting to certain corrections, it assumed this political theology which tended to make the empire the more comprehensive structure for Christian society, and to make the emperor into a preeminent mediator between Christ the Pantocrator and the people in his charge. Naturally, there were the properly religious authorities, and Constantine's successors did not retain the title of Sovereign Pontiff which they had inherited from their pagan ancestors. The dogmatic controversies of the fourth and fifth centuries contributed to the bishops taking their distance from the doctrinal preferences of the emperors. For his part, whenever the occasion presented itself or demanded it, the Bishop of Rome emphasized his particular authority. In this way, tensions soon arose between the emperor and the bishops, between the bishops of the empire and the Bishop of Rome, and between the emperor and the Bishop of Rome. Nevertheless, it seems that for most the structures of the empire furnished a providential framework for the Church to grow and an ultimate defense of its unity. A sort of give and take between the imperial and the religious authorities regarding political theory showed the privileged nature of the situation. From the very beginnings of the Church, the elaboration of ecclesiastical power in general, and the authority of the pope in particular, always took place with reference to the practice and theory of civil authority.[12] Only with the help of the empire's cultural, juridical, and philosophical resources, viz., its political theology, was it possible to interpret and to establish the Church's institutional tradition. Thus, it is more accurate to say that authority in the Church is not so much modeled on specific human institutions as sharing in the same perspective. The converse, too, is sometimes true: in certain circumstances the Church's institutions can serve to inspire the formation of identical structures in the state.[13]

The West

The Role of the Bishop of Rome

The gradual crumbling and eventual disappearance of the empire in the West and the distance which prevented Byzantium from safeguarding

---

12. This happened rather quickly in the Church, if the picture painted by Pierre Nautin is to be believed. See idem, "L'Évolution des ministères au IIe et au IIIe siècle," *Revue de droit canonique* 23 (1973) 47–58.

13. See J. Verger, "Le Transfert de modèles d'organisation de l'Église à l'État à la fin du Moyen Âge," in Jean-Philippe Genet and Bernard Vincent, eds., *État et Église dans la genèse de l'État moderne* (Madrid: Casa de Velazquez, 1986) 31–40. For the East, see Hélène Ahrweiler, *L'Idéologie politique de l'Empire byzantin* (Paris: Presses Universitaires de France, 1975).

its western territories, led the Bishop of Rome to assume greater importance, even in the realm of politics, not because the popes at that time craved power, but because they sought to defend and organize their faithful in the face of the twofold menace of invasion by the "barbarians" and the Arian heresy. They tried to preserve in the troubled West the heritage of the Pax Romana, which had now devolved to the Christians, since the popes were often the only ones to assure it. One thinks of such personalities as Leo the Great (440–61) and Gregory the Great (590–604), whose political authority was no less important than the ecclesial authority or their exceptional holiness. If later they handed over responsibility to the former "barbarians," e.g., Charlemagne, to create a new Western empire, the Church of Rome remained the source of inspiration and the Bishop of Rome never failed to claim his unique religious authority.

The Central Question: The Salvation of Souls

At this point, the specifically Christian factor appears, viz., when it is a question of the state of a politico-religious society like the empire, and more particularly in the West which was preoccupied with the question of salvation, which it understood as the eternal salvation of souls. Now it saw its responsibility in terms of advancing this as much as possible, all the more so since it took the words of the gospel literally, "Many are called, but few are chosen" (Matt 22:14). Access to salvation is first of all bound to the absolute necessity of the sacrament of baptism. (The conviction of the absolute necessity of being baptized in order to be saved had a powerful impact on its missionary activity, every time it faced an unevangelized territory.) But even after the door had been opened by baptism, salvation remained something difficult. First of all, it was tied to the inscrutable mystery of predestination, for if the Catholic Church periodically opposed a doctrine of strict predestination[14] (which always generates either despair or its opposite, libertinism), it also retained a strong sense of predestination from its Augustinian upbringing, viz., something indecipherable about the gravity of human existence and the gratuity of grace entrusted to human freedom which is itself incapable of salvation. Jansenism in its various stripes is a constant temptation in the Church: though always rejected in its teaching, it appears again and again in its concrete life.

But salvation is hard to achieve because in Adam men and women are sinners, wounded by a powerful concupiscence that leads them astray and leaves them ignorant of God, the commandments, and God's plan, but which also induces them to acts of cupidity, violence, and lust. If one looks at

---

14. At the Council of Valencia (DS 628) in the ninth century; at the Council of Trent (DS 1567) in the sixteenth century; and later against various forms of Jansenism.

humanity in the concrete, it is hard to nurture a sense of hope for the vast majority of men and women. In such circumstances, the task of the Church authorities is an urgent one: to keep available for sinners the essential means of salvation, viz., a rudimentary catechesis repeated over and over again and the sacraments to help sinners escape their condition, baptism, of course, but especially the practice of penance. Even more advanced Christians need access to the Church's doctrinal guidance and to affective bonds that will permit them to advance on the way of salvation. The sense of urgency nurtured by the anxiety over the magnitude of the difficulty of salvation goes a long way in explaining the importance of the role of papal primacy as having ultimate responsibility for announcing and defending the faith and for administering the means of salvation, but also in explaining the responsibility of priests in their turn for this grave need of men and women.

The Medieval Problematic: Pope and Emperor

We come at last to the proximate cause of the Gregorian form under examination: the interpretation of the primacy of Peter is dependent on the medieval problem of the *regnum–sacerdotium*. We note that this binome was first understood and lived in the context of the dominant ideology in the Mediterranean world since Augustus, that of the *imperium,* and that later it was nuanced and qualified by the contributions of Germanic law.[15] This means that the authority of the pope is defined in a mental framework which can be called "imperial." To the extent that their sovereignty is effective, the pope's and the emperor's are both limited in their exercise. The pope is responsible for administering the patrimony of St. Peter, while the emperor has responsibility for the states that redound to him, not from his imperial dignity but by reason of birth and the settling of his family in the territories concerned. Far exceeding this minimal but nonetheless essential territorial claim, the pope as emperor lays claim to a universal authority, one capable of imparting a global direction to the empire, now inseparable from Christendom. Both sovereigns also accede to their dignity by means of an election which a liturgy of coronation publicly broadcasts to the churches and to the nations of the empire. The significant analogies between the two functions explains why the authority of the pope is expressed increasingly in legal terms, as "jurisdiction." His mission, received directly from God (the election is only a manifestation of God's choice) consists in declaring the law (the pope makes the law or legislates, and not only explains it) and in seeing to it that it is observed.

15. See P. Toubert, "État et Église au XIe siècle: la signification du moment grégorien pour la genèse de l'État moderne," in Genet and Vincent, eds., *État et Église dans la genèse de l'État moderne,* 9–22.

There is a theoretically fundamental difference between pope and emperor though, if we consider the raison d'être of their respective authority. The classical doctrine holds that just as the emperor is responsible for the temporal commonweal of the peoples of the empire, the pope's responsibility is for their eternal salvation. In practice, however, the difference is not so glaring, since one could not imagine a Christian prince who would not consider it his responsibility to assure the possibility that his subjects will be able to accomplish their religious duties, and one could not imagine that the pope would not have at his disposal the means of at least regulating the politics of the empire in order to avoid obstacles to the kingdom of God.[16] The emperor, and every prince under him, would want to be involved in the election of bishops, just as the pope, after agreeing to crown the emperor or not, would search for ways to intervene in matters of war and peace.

These premises explain why the relations between pope and emperor are pregnant with conflict, due to the fact that both individuals have reasons to assert their superiority over the other. The emperor can consider the pope and the bishops as imperial functionaries in charge of religious matters; the pope can consider the emperor and the princes as secular agents of Christendom. When circumstances favored the hegemony of the *regnum,* it imposed its will on the *sacerdotium,* but it also had the duty of assuring the traditional "liberties of the Church." On the other hand, whenever the Church was persecuted by the princes, the *sacerdotium* insisted on the liberty of the Church and made this liberty its first structural principle, even in political matters of Christendom. Thus, little by little, the primacy of the pope in the Church, i.e., vis-à-vis the bishops and the local churches, moved in the direction of laying claim to a primacy over the world, and in this way led to the idea that the pope is not only the moderator of the Church's life but that, in a certain sense, he is the *source* even of the secular institutions which have no meaning and real life apart from his authority.

This point of view received strong support from a theological source we have mentioned only in passing up to now, the Christian speculation on the theory of hierarchies conducted by a bishop in the sixth century who studied late Platonism under the last pagan teachers in Athens. He was probably of Syrian origin and his patron was Denis the Areopagite. In an attempt to enlist the thought of late Platonism in the last great school of Athens, this thinker undertook the audacious enterprise of interpreting the structures and the sacraments of the Church in light of Neoplatonism. The author of the work *Ecclesiastical Hierarchy* saw in the person of the

---

16. He justifies his interventions by employing a specific formula, *ratione peccati*—"by reason of sin"—the reasons for which emerge in the relations among princes or in the measures they take.

bishop the mediator between the angelic hierarchies, which had their source in God the Principle-beyond-principle, and the faithful of the Church. In a way, we can say that Pseudo-Dionysius applied to the Christian order what had already been accomplished in the religious dimension of politics in Hellenistic thought.[17] In addition to the other elements of political theology mentioned above, our recourse to the thought of Pseudo-Dionysius helps us understand the ecclesiological theory for the primacy of the pope, an interpretation that is inspired by late Platonism.[18] Regarding the pope, studies on the ecclesiological thought of St. Bonaventure (1221–74)[19] in particular have shown the dependence of the papal theology at the end of the thirteenth century on the thought of Pseudo-Dionysius. The bull *Unam Sanctam* of Boniface VIII (1302) marks a culmination of this interpretation, in as much as it subjects both the ecclesiastical and the political orders to a hierarchical interpretation of the encompassing hegemony of the pope.[20]

The Development of the Form in Modern Times

Even if today we can make the judgment that the attempt to assassinate the pope at Anagni (1302) symbolically marks the end of the papal

17. Pseudo-Dionysius does not represent any form of political theology; he never speaks of or quotes the emperor or any secular prince. In its ecclesiology, the *Ecclesiastical Hierarchy*, in as much as it is a mystagogical commentary on the sacramental life of a specific church, never treats the question of the plurality of bishops, and hence does not consider the possibility of a principle of unity, ecclesiastical or civil. Thus, for example, the emperor of the East is situated higher on the ladder of hierarchies and so has a certain mediatorial activity vis-à-vis the bishops. I believe that western ecclesiology located this unifying principle in the person of the pope.

18. The landmarks which trace the development from the writings of Pseudo-Dionysius to medieval pontifical theology are to be sought in the translations of the writings of Pseudo-Dionysius, and in particular by John Scot Eriugena in the ninth century. He is at the origin of the identification of Pseudo-Dionysius with the bishop of Paris of the same name. The influence of these translations explains why Pseudo-Dionysius became one of the founding Fathers of the Church for Western theology. See H. Dondaine, *Le Corpus dionysien à l'université de Paris au XIIIe siècle* (Rome, 1953). In the English literature, the translator recommends Paul Rorem, *Pseudo-Dionysius: A Commentary on the Texts and an Introduction to Their Significance* (New York and Oxford: Oxford University Press, 1993).

19. See Yves Congar, "Aspects ecclésiologiques de la querelle entre mendiants et séculiers dans la seconde moitié du XIIIe siècle et le début du XIVe," *Archives d'histoire doctrinale et littéraire du Moyen Âge* 28 (1961) 35–151; Joseph Ratzinger, "Der Einfluss des Bettelordensstreites auf die Entwicklung der Lehre vom päpstlichen Universalprimat, unter besonderer Berücksichtigung des heiligen Bonaventura," in Johann Auer and Hermann Volk, eds., *Theologie in Geschichte und Gegenwart* [Festschrift für Michael Schmaus](Munich: Karl Zink, 1957) 697–724.

20. See Emil Friedberg, *Corpus juris canonici*, vol. II, 1245–46.

claim to total hegemony, the papacy did not recognize this fact so quickly. It would take several more centuries, up to the French Revolution, before another status of the primacy of Peter, one less bound to direct and even indirect political aspirations, would emerge. This is not the place to survey the history of how the papacy moderated its Gregorian form. I only want to suggest that this study can be done along two lines: one is the progressive disappearance of pontifical authority over the political order, and conversely, a growing influence of this authority in ecclesial life itself.

The Humiliation of the Papacy

We could trace the political humiliation of the papacy from the disastrous period of the Avignon papacy and its manifest failure in the Great Western Schism, through the period of humanism, when the popes exercised great influence as sovereigns of the Papal States in an Italy in full growth and vibrant reconstruction. At this time, whatever the eventual pretensions of the popes in Christendom, their occasionally helpful interventions (e.g., in the Affair of Padroãdo) were aimed especially at avoiding a rupture in relations with the courts and the constitution of the national churches, such as when the Concordat of Bologna was signed with France (1516), annulling the Pragmatic Sanction of Bourges (1438). The papacy in the late Middle Ages and the Renaissance comes across as rather "provincial" and concerned with humanism, until the sack of Rome in 1527 provoked stupefaction and moved the papacy to convoke the Council of Trent (1545–63). After the council, at least in political matters, the papacy was obliged to fight to receive and spend funds to conduct negotiations to withstand ever-growing nationalist tendencies such as Gallicanism and Josephenism (and the various forms of Jansenism allied to them either by sympathy or simple expediency in the eighteenth century) in the parts of Europe that had not gone over to the Reform. It even had to sacrifice the Society of Jesus and, under persecution, helplessly stand by during the nationalization of the French Church, at the start of the French Revolution and beyond.

This development is negative only if we compare it to the growth of papal primacy in the Middle Ages, since we can also view it as a liberation, painful and incomprehensible to those who lived through it, of the institutional structure adapted under circumstances when the imperial ideology was the only one available to the Western world, but an ideology that remained foreign to the evolution of political structures and ideas operative since the fourteenth century. To view this development in a positive light, however, we have to rethink afresh the question of Church and state, no longer in terms of pope and emperor, or even pope and civil powers, but in terms of Church and state. But what is the Church? What is the state? We have to wait for Leo XIII (1878–1903) for the reflection on the problem to take this new path.

The Glorification of the Papacy

Even if the popes, against their will, had to abandon an imperial political interpretation of their office, they never succeeded in arriving at a nuanced understanding of their primacy in the Church itself, since it remained just as strong as in the time of Gregory VII. The Gregorian form and its expression in the hierarchical terms of Pseudo-Dionysius found a new form of expression in the popes' insistence on the rights of the Church. Whatever miseries might have been the fate of the Avignon papacy and the disastrous results of the Great Western Schism, the papacy never accepted the conciliarist structure which the Council of Constance (1414–18) arrived at, and whose inherent weakness the Council of Basel (1431–37) amply demonstrated. The popes never accepted the reforming resolutions of the Fifth Lateran Council (1512–17), and if they convoked an ecumenical council to deal with the tragedy of the Protestant Reform, they guided its proceedings so closely that, whatever the vicissitudes, the concerns of the Roman See were never far from view. The "conciliar question" remained an issue in the Church, and even if one could still read it in between the lines, in the form of the issue of the "divine right of bishops to their residence," and even if the issue was not given a definite answer at the council, it was regulated by the popes to their satisfaction by their application of the council. In Rome, the papacy established a pontifical Curia to regulate the life of the churches as closely as possible, while beyond Rome it urged a vigorous program of Catholic Reform wherever possible. One could say that the popes changed their direction from a defensive posture of opposing conciliarism after the post-Avignon period of the papacy, to an offensive strategy of regulating the life of the Church after the Council of Trent.

It took the French Revolution to point to the inevitable, not only in regard to the political forces but also concerning the primacy of the pope. Though Napoleon Bonaparte had to acknowledge the papacy in order to restore religious peace to France, he saw it as an element of civil tranquility. It provided him with an extraordinary means of expressing himself, when Pius VII (1800–23) demanded in an unheard of way that all French bishops, legitimate or constitutional, submit their resignation. If there ever was a way for the pope to manifest his primacy, that would be the means of doing so. The nineteenth century, therefore, can be considered the century in which the Church understood itself as a "perfect society," possessing all the structures necessary to constitute a sociopolitical body, but with the added fact that it also understood itself as based on a divine institution where the primacy of the pope enjoyed considerable extension and where it penetrated the understanding of the faithful. This happened through the adoption of the Roman Liturgy, the founding of numerous missionary congregations under the aegis of the Holy See, the personality of the popes themselves, especially Pius IX (1846–78), all of which led to the dogmatic constitution *Pastor aeternus* of the First Vatican Council (1869–70), with its double proclamation of a universal primacy of jurisdiction of the Roman pontiff and the infallibility of his doctrinal definitions. Even the loss of the Papal States, with its directly local political responsibility, could be interpreted as encouraging an understanding of the pope's universal mission now freed of political entanglements. Finally, the Code of Canon Law of 1917, valid for the whole Church, served to translate the papal primacy into the daily life of the Church. Even the technological progress made in transporting materials, in printing and distributing books, and in rapid communications were put in service of an almost immediate presence of the Holy See in the life of the local churches.

Conclusion

In this description of the pontifical form of the Gregorian theology of the Church, I have wanted to illustrate that the fact of the revelation of the primacy of Peter over the other apostles and of his mission of unity for all the apostolic churches was interpreted by means of a specific vision of a political theology, one that insisted on the One God, the principle and end of all mediations, but in particular that power over men and women is exercised in a hierarchical way, proceeding from God or the hypostases closest to God. This vision was the basis of the imperial ideology, from Augustus up to the *Golden Bull* of Emperor Henry VII (1213). In the context of Christianity, the papacy sought to interpret itself within the framework of this ideology, common property for over a century. After a time of relative success, culminating in the pontifical Christianity of the thirteenth century, it became increasingly aware of the more directly ecclesial character of its mission and progressively, though not exclusively, refocused itself on the universal Church. But the means of interpretation remained the same theology of imperial politics, only now it found expression in the papacy as a direct relation of the pontiff, chosen and invested with power by God. For the Church this meant a highly centralized structure in which everything issued from the center and returned to it.[21]

21. It is possible to illustrate this intra-ecclesial consolidation of papal primacy by simply enumerating the stages of the progressive centralization of law in the Church from the Gregorian reform to our own day: the lessening of participation by the bishops in the elaboration of the common law of the Church; Rome's progressive limiting of the diffusion of common law; the control by Rome of the local synodal activity of the bishops; the growth in the Apostolic See's involvement in legislation; the restriction

The Priest

The Holiness of the Priest

The third pole of the Gregorian form of the Church is the *priest*. Given the constant urgency of salvation and its connection with truth, the priest is the one who is divinely invested with the power needed to wrest men and women from ever-present sin and whose knowledge of the mystery of salvation makes it possible for him to teach the truth.[22] Because of his direct contact with the Christian people, whom he baptizes, catechizes, and reconciles, proof of the holiness and integrity of his life in harmony with his ministry emerge as the primary objectives of the Catholic Reform whenever it is undertaken. This importance explains Gregory VII's struggle to overcome "simony" by advancing evangelical poverty and "nicholaism" by favoring clerical continence.[23] In an ecclesiastical system for the administration of goods organized around the principle of the "benefice," i.e., the system by which the priest is supported on the basis of the revenues which accrue to the church to which he is assigned, there was always the temptation to seek out the most lucrative benefices, indeed even to accumulate them by receiving their revenues without really fulfilling the pastoral ministry. The latter was entrusted to another priest, who was paid less and was undoubtedly less qualified. The constant clamor for reform always included such examples of priestly indifference for the ministry.

---

by Rome of the right to guard the faith; Rome's right to restrict the normal and ordinary authority of the bishops (including the exclusive right reserved to Rome to nominate bishops of the Latin Rite); the increasingly heavy control by Rome over the local churches and religious institutes. See Michel Dortel-Claudot, *Églises locales, Église universelle. Comment se gouverne le peuple de Dieu* (Lyons: Chalet, 1973) (= Chapter 5: "Rome et l'Église universelle du XIIe au début du XXe siècle"). —It seems very important, when reflecting on this process of centralization of the Church's law, to understand how it is tied up with a certain theology of power, viz., if power comes directly from God to the pope alone, it is his responsibility to take all the necessary measures to assure the fact that God's authority will be respected, and eventually this means the diminution of the competences of others enjoying partial authority, in order the better to assure the general line to be followed by the body.

22. On the history of the priesthood, see Gustave Martelet, *Deux mille ans d'Église en question*, 3 vols. (Paris: Cerf, 1984–90), in which the author strives to develop a hermeneutic of this itinerary of the priesthood for the Church and for the faith. Readers of English might want to consult the work by Kenan B. Osborne, *The Priesthood: A History of the Ordained Ministry in the Roman Catholic Church* (New York: Paulist, 1988) [translator].

23. "Simony" is derived from the account of Simon Magus in Acts of the Apostles 8:18-23 and "Nicholaism" takes its name from Revelation 2:6 and 14 [translator].

As for the connection between continence and the priesthood, it was held to be a theological necessity. According to the commonly held sexual morality of the times, even in marriage the sexual act retained a certain sinfulness, since it was considered that concupiscence was to some extent identified with original sin or, after baptism, with what remained from it as wounds. The fact that the priest celebrated the sacrifice of Christ's death seemed to be diametrically opposed to the state of marriage in which it would be unavoidable to perform something illicit. This demand for the priest's holiness, and its double pillars of continence and poverty, explains the popularity of groups of priests *(collegia)* who lived in common and celebrated the choral recitation of the divine office. The life of a "canon" seemed normal for the support of the priest's holiness. On the other hand, if monks in the High Middle Ages and later mendicants were vowed to God in poverty and chastity, then it followed that their ordination equipped them for the celebration of Mass "for the living and the dead," for setting an example of Christian living for the secular clergy, as well as for certain ministries.[24] Little by little, these monks and religious, who were systematically ordained priests, became a special cadre available to the Apostolic See.[25]

After the Council of Trent, new nuances appeared. The reform of the clergy was always seen as necessary, but the council stressed even more forcefully, in opposition to the Protestant understanding, the connection between sacramental mediation and salvation. The Tridentine reform was greatly abetted by local initiatives, energetically supported by Rome, in matters of formation and regarding the holiness of priests. The religious orders for their part, too, reformed themselves, while other congregations were born to implement the reforms of Trent. In passing, it could be said that the strong spiritual tone of the reform among the secular clergy, up to this time unheard of in this degree of intensity, highlighted their distinctiveness vis-à-vis the form of religious life and that of the canons regular. In the perspectives opened up by the French School in the seventeenth century, priests were not expected to be religious. If they gathered in common, it was in societies that did not take vows. The reason for this refusal of the religious life can be attributed to the conviction that the priest did not need the vows: in itself and because of the holiness proper to the sacrament of

24. See the article "Sacerdozio" in Guerrino Pelliccia and Giancarlo Rocca, eds., *Dizionario degli Istituti di Perfezione,* vol. 8 (Rome: Edizioni Paoline, 1988), especially the study by Jacques Dubois entitled "Il sacerdozio nel monachesimo dall'alto Medioevo a oggi," 77–90.

25. Though I have spoken about priests, in reality the Gregorian reform properly speaking was aimed especially at the bishops and included the reassertion of holiness of life and the pastoral ministry. Nonetheless, there was a particular significance in the insistence on the canons relative to continence among the lower clergy as well.

order, the priest is situated in a spiritual dimension which, on the one hand, calls for the style of life lived by religious but employing different means, and on the other, is endowed with its own resources needed to achieve its end. Priestly celibacy is an example of what was considered essential in the Gregorian perspective, since it was thought to be a higher, or more profound, or more essential expression than the religious vow of chastity. On the level of the priestly ministry, celibate priests, because they are always available, would have a predilection for spiritual direction, in order to lead other Christians, sensitive to their inspiration, further or higher in the spiritual life.

The Pope and Priests

It would be interesting to study to what extent the ideas of Pseudo-Dionysius influenced the teaching of the priesthood in the Middle Ages, and in particular in regard to an understanding of the priest as the holy and consecrated mediator of the sacramental life of Christians, but also as ordained specifically for the celebration of the Eucharist.[26] If this is so, we can say that the thought of Pseudo-Dionysius regarding the bishop can be divided along two lines. First, it permits a conception of the pope as the "source of all fullness" *(plenitudo fontalis)* for the life of the Church, given his unique mediatorial position, viz., his position as mediator between God and humanity. Second, it would lead to viewing the priest, contemplative and mystical celebrant of the sacraments, and most especially of the Eucharist. There is a clear distinction between the *power of jurisdiction,* one and universal, spiritual and intermediate between God and humanity, with the pope as its source, and the *power of order,* capable of being multiplied with a view to forgiving sins and for the sanctification of men and women, whose source is the sacrament of order proper to priests.[27] Such a distinction would be properly theological, founded on the idea of a descending hierarchy that is ordered in terms of all the necessary spiritual gifts and grounded in the Unity of God. Paradoxically, such a theological vision has nothing to say regarding the bishop, since it is concerned exclusively with the pope and priests, even though the former was the sole focus for Pseudo-Dionysius. In the Western Church, the bishop, whose administrative and pastoral importance is real, emerges as an intermediate expression between the pope on the one hand and the priests and faithful on the other.

26. See Paul Cochois, "Bérulle, hiérarque dionysien," *Revue d'ascétique et de mystique* 37 (1961) 314–53; idem, "Bérulle et le Pseudo-Denys," *Revue de l'histoire des religions* 159 (1961) 173–204; Michel Dupuy, *Bérulle et le Sacerdoce: Étude historique et doctrinale. Textes inédits* (Paris: Lethielleux, 1969).

27. According to this theology, its source is not the bishop, who does not have a sacramental authority greater than that of the priest himself, since both can celebrate the fundamental sacrament, the Eucharist.

The Traditional Image of the Priest: Sacramental Character and Ministry

All that has been said helps us understand what, until the very recent past, was the common image of the priest. In this context, two elements were emphasized: the "character" of the sacrament of order and the call to ministry that knows no bounds. Sacramental character was conceived as a sacred instrumental power, immanent to the person of the priest and indelible, that rendered him capable of positing certain acts otherwise forbidden to other Christians. He could confect the transubstantiation of the eucharistic species, and thereby render the sacrifice of the Cross, the source of redemption, sacramentally present by reason of the sacramental character. This character came to be regarded increasingly in the priest himself and available to him in his task of applying the fruits of salvation to specific individuals rather than in terms of a particular community entrusted to his responsibility. The same is true of penance, where the power of remitting the sins of individual penitents was exercised without any connection between the penitent and a community with its liturgies of forgiveness. And so, the theology and the spirituality of the priesthood rested largely on a theory almost of the hypostasizing of the character as a sacramental power. According to the understanding of the time, there was a transferal of attention away from the permanence of the priest's possessing an "instrumental power" to the "being of the priest," which made the priest into a Christian who existed on another ontological level than that defined by baptism and confirmation. The result of such ideas regarding priestly character was to insist on the necessity of celibacy as an essential characteristic of this new ontological level of priestly existence.

Corresponding to the exclusive competence of the priest in sacramental matters—with its stress on his "immense dignity"—went a corresponding exclusiveness regarding his competence in pastoral affairs, at least in modern times. Until very recently, the life of the Church redounded fundamentally and almost exclusively to the priest, whose vocation was viewed as the highest. The scope of his ministry included catechesis, preaching, theology, Catholic instruction, youth work, visiting the sick, missions at home and abroad, finances, sacramental catechesis, administering the sacraments, etc. In the absence of any distinctions, all of this was seen as the province of the priest. Nor should we fail to note the paradox in all this: despite the almost total limitation of all this vast field of ministry to the priest, what still defined him was his celebrating the Eucharist. If being a priest meant essentially celebrating the Eucharist and pardoning sins, why was it necessary to turn him into the privileged agent in the mission of the Church to the point that the apostolate of the laity was considered a collaboration with the priest?

At this point, we must distinguish the theoretical point of view from the practical. In the Church's official theology, what we call the "priestly task" *(munus sacerdotalis)* does not flow directly from the sacrament of order but from the "jurisdiction" given to the priest by the bishop, who can give it definitively to others, as has happened in history. But in practice the priest, who by the sacrament of order has a specific relationship to the sacraments and to the Church, is also *celibate,* drawing his livelihood from an ecclesiastical office rather than from what society would understand to be an occupation, and so, by reason of his celibate condition, it is he who is always available for the pastoral needs of the parish and who becomes the pastoral focal point. From this point of view, it is clear that there can never be enough priests to meet all the tasks, especially if priests are chosen and formed, as has been the case since the Catholic Reform, so that the salvation of souls and the pastoral work of the Church are at the center of their spirituality. This fact also explains why, almost all male religious since the Middle Ages have been ordained priests, even if they did not have this intention when the order was founded, and which, among others, we can see clearly in the case of the Franciscan Order. The numerous congregations that have arisen since Trent reveal the character of "clerical active congregations," as if "action" implied "clerical status."

The Priesthood and the Sacred

This survey of the period from Gregory VII to the present indicates strikingly the ever-growing importance of the place occupied by the priest in the life and thought of the Catholic Church: larger, nobler, more demanding. One way of evoking this understanding is to use the term *the sacred,* even though it suffers from a certain vagueness. The priest, consecrated by priestly ordination—itself essentially a sacred rite ordered to the celebration of the Eucharist—is endowed with the sacred character of holy orders—itself understood as a power over the sacred, i.e., the sacraments. The priest, consecrated to be configured to Christ the Priest, is considered in himself to be a sacred person: he is allowed to touch sacred things, both the elements of the sacraments as well as the sacred vessels that are given to him at his ordination;[28] his hands were consecrated at ordination by a special anointing; his body is consecrated by his celibacy; and he is the one who properly offers the official prayer of the Church, the Divine Office.[29]Given his condition of holiness and separateness, the priest is truly

28. Up to the Constitution of Pius XII *Sacramentum ordinis* (November 30, 1947), this was considered an essential element of the sacrament's valid celebration. See *Acta Apostolicae Sedis* 40 (1948) 6 [5–7].

29. In the middle of the nineteenth century, a Czech bishop, A. de Roskovany, published thirteen volumes of documentation significantly entitled *Coelibatus et Breviar-*

the one on whose shoulders the whole matter of salvation rests: the full proclamation of the gospel and the complete education and sanctification of the faithful. An indication of the importance of the priest himself and in the sensibility of the Christian people is the high number of communities of women religious founded, especially last century, to pray for the holiness of priests. Many women lived and suffered, sacrificed in a variety of ways, as it were to obtain from God the holiness and zeal of priests.

If we measure the growth of the authority of the pope and what can be called the devotion to the pope, on the one hand, and the ever-growing importance of the person of the priest, on the other, it becomes clear how the faithful fit into a solid and holy structure that truly helps them achieve salvation, provided they do not separate themselves from it. The authority of the parish priest is directed immediately at the "sheep" entrusted to him and demands the requisite priestly dispositions. But the salvation of the faithful presupposes a general organization of the Church that permits everyone to remain true to the faith and is conducted in peaceful conditions. This organization rests on the primacy of the pope.

Conclusion

A Text of Pius XII

To conclude this study of the "Gregorian form of the Church," I propose to cite a text of Pius XII which succinctly but clearly traces the outline of this form, implemented and practiced throughout the centuries:

> By virtue of God's Will, the faithful are divided into two classes: the clergy and the laity. By virtue of the same Will is established the twofold sacred hierarchy, namely, of orders and jurisdiction. Besides—as has also been divinely established—the power of orders (through which the ecclesiastical hierarchy is composed of Bishops, priests, and ministers) comes from receiving the Sacrament of Holy Orders. But the power of jurisdiction, which is conferred upon the Supreme Pontiff directly by divine right flows to the Bishops by the same right, but only through the Successor of St. Peter.[30]

---

ium. Due gravissima clericorum officia, a monumentis omnium saeculorum demonstrata (Pest, 1861; Nitra, 1888).

30. *"Qua profecto divina voluntate christifideles in duos ordines distribuuntur, clericorum laicorumque; eademque voluntate duplex constituitur sacra postestas ordinis nempe et iurisdictionis. Ac praeterea—quod divinitus pariter statutum est—ad postestatem ordinis, qua Ecclesiastica Hierarchia ex Episcopis constat, presbyteris et administris, acceditur per acceptum sacri ordinis sacramentum; iurisdictionis autem potestas, quae Supremo Pontifici iure ipso divino directe confertur, Episcopis ex eodem provenit iure, at nonnisi per Petri Successorem."* Ad Sinarum gentem (October 7, 1954) in *Acta Apostolicae Sedis* 47 (1955) 9 [5–14]; E. T. *The Pope Speaks* 1 (1954) 400 [397–403]. A similarly inspired

This text is very clear: it begins with the distinction between clergy and laity, but says nothing more about the latter, who do not even figure in the synthesis. As for the clergy, they are defined by power. But the power is twofold, distinct both with respect to its object (which is not precisely given in the text) and regarding its origin. The power of order has a sacramental origin, viz., it is conferred by a sacred action attributed to Christ himself. Though the reason for the distinction of orders is not given, the implication is that what "makes the difference" is the sacerdotal quality of the priest, which renders its recipient competent *(habilis)* to celebrate the fundamental sacraments of the Eucharist and penance. The power of jurisdiction is of juridical origin (the "divine right" mentioned) and is conferred directly by God in the case of the pope, while in the case of bishops by the mediation of the pope. One could say that what unites both powers is the "will of Christ," the principle and the giver of both, and which establishes in the world a specific form of representation: the Roman pontiff is the "Vicar of Christ" and the Priest is "Another Christ." In this form of the double powers, the bishop emerges as the "orphan" in the triple hierarchy of orders: he has no sacramental power that is truly proper to him (since the Eucharist is already a "priestly" power) and as regards jurisdiction, the situation is not any clearer, since though he receives his authority "from God" it is always "through the pope." As far as the laity is concerned, they are not even players in the game of power described. Their role, if there even is one, remains entirely implicit: Christ's will regarding them is not specified, nor is the place of the sacraments they have received.

Toward an Evaluation

It could be argued that the Gregorian form of the Church, in all the forms it has known over the centuries, has played a positive role, *but only as long as the world was dominated by the idea of hierarchy and was understood as a movement of proceeding from God and returning to God.* At the time of Gregory VII, the reform took the shape that he gave it. It was a service not only to the Church but to society as well, even though this means not taking a position on one or another episode from his life or from the popes who followed him. The tragedy we note today is that this form sought to perpetuate itself even though the structures of medieval society, and of the empire in particular, crumbled around it and a new—"modern"—view of the world took shape. A keen prophetic sense of what was happening would probably have been needed to see the change. The monarchs who

text can be found in Pius XII's "Address to the Second World Congress for the Lay Apostolate" (October 5, 1957) in *AAS* 49 (1957) 924–25 [922–39]; E. T. "The Lay Apostolate," *The Pope Speaks* 4 (1957) 119–34.

launched the modern view, nevertheless retained an imperial attitude for a long time. After a brief experiment involving the municipalities, royal absolutism and later an enlightened despotism took over, but without really changing the unitary form of power. Whatever the reason, the Church was not really open to modernity in terms of its higher values, viz., the responsibility of each subject to take control of his or her life, both personally and collectively.

Even now, after the fact, the Church can still make restitution for the "sum total of expenses" for what should have been done since the end of the thirteenth century and start to draw an outline of an ecclesial reform which is not only moral (or "spiritual") in the polemical sense of the word, i.e., in an anti-institutional sense, but that would be creative and organic with society. What might such a reform look like? It could progressively reactivate the conciliar practice and the responsibility of the bishops; renounce a mysticism of illumination in favor of listening to reason and helping men and women decide for themselves which means are best for the harmonious and not the anarchic development of reason; lessen the impact of truth as *alētheia*[31] and set free a less ambitious vision of the scope of knowledge by insisting concurrently on the value of love. It is a matter of changing the hermeneutical grid by which the faith and the Church are interpreted, of undertaking the process of *aggiornamento* which would make it possible for the Church to be more present to men and women and free them from their infatuation with an exaggerated autonomy. In reality, this was never done, so that an increasingly anarchic modernity set itself in opposition to a Church that more and more resembled a fortress.

It is this double failure which is envisioned today when people speak of the "end of the Constantinian era" for the Church and the "end of modernity" for the world. The question, then, is: How can we resume the effort of restoring and building something from its roots up that would at the same time have an effect on the world and the Church? There is no questioning the fact that the Church can no longer act directly on the world. But if the Church can so effect its own reform, by finding a form that would no longer be "Gregorian" and yet would not cease to be Christian and Catholic, it could help the world too find its way. This approach would be more preferable than for the Church to remain in the same condition and continue to dictate solutions to the world's problems.

Let us face the paradox involved in this double crisis. On the one hand, it is a question of finding the right attitude vis-à-vis a sick modernity, and which the Church also finds itself in to some extent. The task is not for the Church to be converted to a world which it had allowed to develop its own

---

31. See the discussion above of truth as *alētheia*, pp. 14–17 [translator].

understanding of reason and power in a unilateral way, and now gives every sign of dying of its excesses, but also not to continue to close itself off from the world by being content to dictate what humanity must do if it is to be just and if it is to find a way to salvation.

Somehow, in its own structures, the Church must find a way of articulating exactly what is human and what belongs to the Christian community in its expectation of an announced End, but without the Church trying to fully disclose the times or trying to supplant their human, immanent capacity to understand the world and act on it.

On the other hand, it is a matter of restoring to the understanding and the practice of the Church the primacy of Sacrament and of the Holy Spirit, and consequently of lessening the degree of centralization and an oppressive insistence on what risks hiding the more important elements of the faith and of Christian life, and not of denying the necessity of juridical elements in the Church. I am talking about the active presence of the mission of the Word in the sacramental symbols and of the mission of the Spirit in the hierarchical and charismatic gifts from which the Church lives. It is a matter of rethinking in a new way the whole ensemble of life, mission, and law of the Church, and this is decisive, *in order to pass from such a renewed understanding to corresponding action.* These two elements, Sacrament and Spirit, are simply too absent in the ecclesiology of the Gregorian form. Such a restoration will imply and provoke both an education for freedom in the Church, a model of education for freedom of any and all who desire it. It will also permit the renewal of the status of truth in the Church, and suggest some coordinates to contemporary philosophy which are lacking it. In this way, perhaps the Church can modestly contribute to philosophy's regaining a sense of direction in its quest and meaning in its universal investigation of all the elements it ceaselessly gathers without being able to mobilize them to bring about human happiness.

Part II

Vatican II: Toward a
New Form of the Church

I have tried to define the historical and theological background for a new reform of the Church, more fundamental and more extensive than any that have taken place in the long history of Western Christianity. The idea of such a reform is the product of Vatican II: without it and what it has prepared us for, as well as the often painful conflicts over its interpretation, the very idea of imagining a new form of the Church would not be possible. I believe that, starting with these very orientations, we can safely engage in the effort of beginning the journey toward an authentic "utopia."[1]

If I were asked to indicate where more precisely the call to reform by Vatican II can be found, I would not point immediately to the properly ecclesiological questions or practices dealt with by the council. Something more important and more fundamental undergirds the work of the council and in the final analysis explains the notorious difficulties of its development, its uncertainties, and even the polemics which have characterized the postconciliar period. The issue is precisely that of an *important evolution in the question of truth itself,* i.e., what I referred to above as the first axis of the Gregorian form of the Church. What is important is to try to define the status of truth in Christianity, not so much by criticizing the

1. I borrow this term, in the positive sense of a creative imagining, from a remark by Paul VI in his encyclical, dated May 14, 1971, *Octogesima adveniens,* no. 37: "We are witnessing the rebirth of what it is agreed to call 'utopias.' These claim to resolve the political problem of modern societies better than the ideologies. It would be dangerous to disregard this. The appeal to a utopia is often a convenient excuse for those who wish to escape from concrete tasks in order to take refuge in an imaginary world. To live in a hypothetical future is a facile alibi for rejecting immediate responsibilities. But it must clearly be recognized that this kind of criticism of existing society often provokes a forward-looking imagination both to perceive in the present the disregarded possibility hidden within it, and to direct itself towards a fresh future; it thus sustains social dynamism by the confidence that it gives to the inventive powers of the human mind and heart; and, if it refuses no overture, it can also meet the Christian appeal." See Joseph Gremillion, *The Gospel of Peace and Justice: Catholic Social Teaching since Pope John* (Maryknoll, N.Y.: Orbis, 1976) 502.

various positive or polemical opinions which have emerged in the course of time, but by attempting a new explanation of what is dominant in the status of the Christian faith as highlighted by Vatican II: the essentially eschatological character of truth, its symbolic and narrative elements, and the primacy of the Scriptures as the final basis of the faith. This will be my first task.

Next, if I am correct in maintaining the dominance of the theme of truth and its interpretation, and which in the past dictated the institutional practices of the Western Church, especially its heavy accentuation of the persons of the pope and the priest, then it seems to follow that certain changes in the understanding of truth will necessarily provoke other changes on the level of the Church's institutional life. In other words, we have to examine carefully the larger issue, something that does greater justice to all the movements of the Spirit in the Church and in the world of men and women, in order to be of service to the coming of the reign of God. In this perspective of reform of the whole and not just isolated elements, the two figures of the pope and the priest, viewed almost monopolistically up until very recently, will find their just and indispensable place in the Church. In the remaining chapters, in an effort not to ignore the second and third axes of the Gregorian form, I will attempt to study how the Church is a "structured communion."

Chapter 3

The Status of Truth

The reform introduced by Vatican II is first of all a reform of *language.* Today, after more than thirty years of lectures, commentaries, and interpretations, the language of the conciliar texts seems a bit jaded, threadbare, and ready to be consigned to the repertory of theological stereotypes. On the other hand, the language of the council is anything but univocal and coherent; on the contrary it is characterized by a mélange of styles that betray a mixture of theologies themselves more or less compatible. If examined more closely, it becomes apparent that words began to be used differently at the council than in the recent or even the more distant past in the Western Church. An early indication of this concern can be found in the council's beginning with the liturgy, i.e., with that space in the life of the Church which is expressed in the language of images, gesture, and song, and which structures the Church in terms of the persons who speak this type of language and who are different yet ordered to each other. Without doubt, the council began its deliberations with the liturgy, with the explicit intention of emphasizing a religious language that was both wider and less precise than the customary theological language. For all that, once the choice was made, the discussion centered on the nature and the value of religious language.

It is not my intention to claim that the more logical and metaphysical language used in the precise formulas of the faith, which are to be confessed under threat of disastrous consequences for the faith, simply disappears, but that the latter is included in the heart of a language that is more global, or perhaps one could say more human, where narrative, poetry, and rhetoric prevail.[1] Now, if it is true that a certain form of listening and

---

1. I will have occasion to define more precisely in this chapter that it is entirely possible that the reinsertion of logic and metaphysics into a vaster epistemological whole, really works in favor of their regaining the truth proper to them. When logic and

responding corresponds to a specific type of language, then an indication of a change of style equally implies a change in the way the message is received and responded to. We will need to examine briefly this change of style, which will lead us to see yet another transformation, that between the relation of reason and faith. This more global language, be it witness-language or response-language, invites us to a renewed attention to the human sciences, more than to the influence of the exact (or "hard") sciences, particularly cosmology and then metaphysics. To conclude, we will see how we are led to rediscover and to implement in a new way the sequence that governs the levels of presenting the apostolic witness: Scripture and mystagogy, and then theological reflection, first in its cultural context, and then as a defense of the faith against error.[2]

Even concerning the question of theology's defense of the truth, a certain adaptation has taken place, but which is not easy to spell out in an epistemological theory. Today it is a matter of "dialogue" with other Christian confessions and with non-Christian religions, but the rules of such dialogue are not easy to determine. It cannot be a matter of polemics or of controversy, but of a genuine exchange of words, i.e., one that avoids any attempt to ignore all differences in a reductionistic way. I will attempt to offer some brief reflections on this subject also.

Style

The Forms of Discourse

Lumen gentium *1 and 2*

Let us begin with a very precise example: the first two chapters of the Dogmatic Constitution on the Church. In an attempt to introduce the mystery of the Church, and consequently to address absolutely fundamental matters, as well as indicate a general direction for the thought of the whole work of the council, the text employs language that is trinitarian, based on images, and comprehensive in scope.

First of all, the Church exists, and could not exist in any other way, than in its being rooted in the Trinity and in its configuration to Christ (LG 2–4). The council here has made a fundamental epistemological option: stress is put on the operation of each divine Person, in their coordination among themselves, for establishing and advancing the life of the

---

metaphysics are treated in total independence of the sensible and the symbolical orders, they run the risk of developing in total autonomy, and hence in a rationalistic way—a development that is actually baneful to their authenticity.

2. See above, p. 41.

Church. In its analysis of the Church's origins, the council could have begun by speaking about "God," i.e., by privileging the unitary character of the revelation of God rather than that of the communion of persons. The mere fact that the Father, the Son, and the Holy Spirit are highlighted is already a sign that the Church is a communion and something dynamic. Had the council highlighted the monolithic unity of the Church by employing the image of the unity of the one God,[3] it would have made allusion immediately to the ecclesiastical representatives of this unique God vis-à-vis the crowd of believers in all their multiplicity.

Secondly, and this observation is connected with the option of the trinitarian perspective for speaking about God, the language appropriated for speaking about the mystery is scriptural. The images used here are primary, not the concepts: sheepfold, field, house, family, temple, spouse (LG 6), the body of Christ (LG 7), and the People of God (LG 9–17). Even if some of these words are used in a more-than-metaphorical sense, they still retain the form of images, and this means that they suggest a reality which more sophisticated formulas are less capable of expressing, and furthermore that they retain a normative value over against such technical formulas. We simply cannot think about the Church without recourse to the world of images, emotions, experiences, and affections, and which suggest symbolic fields: pasturing, farming, architecture, sexuality, and ritual. Scripture points us in their direction and invites us to wander about through them. The liturgy takes them up and invests them with vibrant actuality. For their part, too, psychology and sociology can be of assistance to us in helping unmask the implications they hold for analogically expressing the Infinite. Theology rests on the fact that it can never exhaust their meaning or take their place, but that it must constantly have recourse to them.

Finally, this trinitarian and biblical language is always directed to the whole Church, "the assembly of those who look toward Jesus Christ, the principle of unity and of peace" (LG 9). Whatever distinctions we make, functional or otherwise, they must be understood within a vision that is global or, as some today prefer to say, "holistic." If there is a diversity of "hierarchical and charismatic gifts" (LG 4), they are given to the *whole,* in and

---

3. On the level of epistemology, this preference by the council does not prejudge the theological question of what precisely is to be attributed to the various divine Persons regarding their specific influences on the Church's constitution. Nor does it attempt to deny or call into question Christian monotheism. The theological issues being what they are, the trinitarian preference here for speaking about God is all the more significant, since the theology of the Church was considered in terms of its being conditioned by the unity of God, the foundation of the unicity of the Church, the unicity of the apostolic ministry, the unicity of the papacy, etc.

for the *whole,* which is the true subject of God's action and of the mission that flows from this action.[4]

Story, Image, Concept

What has just been said of the Dogmatic Constitution on the Church can also be said of the Dogmatic Constitution on Divine Revelation and the Decree on the Missionary Activity of the Church. All three documents start from an "economic" understanding of the Trinity, which immediately calls to mind the primacy of the narrative style. We *narrate* what the Father, the Son and the Spirit, in their distinctiveness as persons and in the unity of their essence, have done to reveal themselves to the world, to call forth the Church, and to spread the knowledge of the gospel. The full weight of this conciliar perception demands an effort on our part to evaluate it properly. The trinitarian understanding itself calls for a narrative structure, or beginning the other way round, the narrative structure is the necessary linguistic way to be initiated into the trinitarian mystery.[5] In saying this, a rough sketch of what truth means in Christianity is detected. When credence is given to a story, it presupposes and induces a person's engagement in the story's point; in this case, "knowledge" is inseparable from "interest." We can also say that "truth" is first of all a matter of "meaning": the story recounted concerning divine revelation and the birth and development of the Church is only able to be accepted to the extent that the hearer perceives meaning and significance for his or her existence, but also meaning and significance for humanity and the entire universe.

Likewise, the council did not recoil from using *images* in speaking about the Church, and even favored them. In other words, it appealed to our imagination as constitutive or creative, capable of forming as it were a "literal" image of reality with all its objects, their form, their colors, their brightness and shadows, their interplay, their fullness and void, their sounds and the music accompanying them. And not only all of this, but their affective and emotional range also, i.e., the full range of the passions involved: to what extent do they arouse pleasure or pain, joy or sorrow, enthusiasm or depression? And what about their intellectual suggestiveness, since an image is capable of giving rise to a happiness coming from the clarity of

---

4. Later on, we will see that for me the word "whole" does not mean the universal Church, but the "Church in its entirety," where the body of Christ exists in qualitative plenitude.

5. Though I have said that narrative is the "necessary" way, I do not hold that it is "sufficient." I have tried to show elsewhere that the stress today on the "economic Trinity" does not make talk of the "immanent Trinity" useless or tautological, just as talk of "time" does not nullify or diminish the impact of "being." See my *God, Time and Being,* trans. Leonard Maluf (Petersham, Mass.: St. Bede's Publications, 1992) 257–324.

the concept, the joy of knowing something? Out of all this arises the choice between images or an ensemble of images: metaphors are born, i.e., the unconscious transpositions, scarcely controlled or voluntary, of one image or ensemble of images among others, with the result that wide berth is given to our passions or to the knowledge that springs out of them. Here, the play of poetry is infinite.

If the council employs images, it is undoubtedly because it finds them in the Bible and judges it opportune to call them to mind. Nevertheless, in doing so it appeals to our imagination as constitutive and makes this capacity the final judge of the understanding of ecclesiology. We cannot avoid observing that "to know" something in theology has the connotation of what "knowledge" means in the Bible. We "know" the mysteries of God's dealings with us very much like a man "knows" a woman, or better, the way a wife "knows" her husband. Such images are not meant to be surpassed; on the contrary, they create the framework within which the concept makes sense.[6]

To summarize, we can say that the style of the council is first of all that of narrative and poetry. I say "first of all" because other styles, too, can be found in the documents of the council, styles that are more conceptual and that correspond to other perceptions and ways of expressing reality but which are also necessary for formulating the faith. Still, the question of *precedence* among these styles is important. A clear development can be noted when we compare the conciliar style with that connected with the Gregorian form of the Church: whereas the latter is dominated by the category of unity, that of the council stresses communion and the Trinity, as far as the mystery of God is concerned. With its element of time, story imparts a different tone to the mystical, which no longer functions in so apophatic and atemporal a way as in the earlier discourse. The object of our senses is neither condemned nor shunned, but welcomed because it has been transformed, and the "spiritual senses" of Scripture are important because of their value for initiating the faithful. From another perspective, the change of the former heavy accent on unity means a change of approach in human and ecclesial politics, and, as we will see in greater detail later on, invites us to reconsider the role of mediations in this area of human existence.

But the change also has implications for the question of Being: our more speculative expressions can now be purified of the temptation of theological rationalism. On the one hand, they have been incorporated into a framework of thought that surpasses pure intellectualism and so receive a different orientation from their new placement. On the other hand, now they only speak from the perspective of the analogy of being and the analogy

6. Later on, I will underscore that the primacy of metaphor is not an exclusive one and that theological language also demands the use of analogy.

of faith: they retain a certain subtlety, a sense of mystery that refuses to have anything to do with possessiveness. Though fragile they are necessary, since they open the way for our language to have real consistency, both ontologically and/or ecclesiologically. In concluding this section, let us recall that what sets the tone to the ensemble of discourse of faith is not the ontological structure, but the historically dynamic structure, not the hardness of the concept,[7] but the suggestiveness of the image.[8]

The Meaning (Direction) of Discourse

Story, Time, and Truth

Story and poetry—Christian discourse has a character all its own. It is entirely open to the future and transformative of the present. It neither ignores suffering and death, nor is it a story of a paradise lost or an irreversible tragedy, but a narrative that connects us to the past only to the extent that remembering the latter is necessary to understand the future that still awaits us and which imparts definitive meaning—the parousia of Christ and communion with God. From one end of Scripture to the other, the story is told of what the divine persons, who are committed to their creatures and with whom they have sealed a covenant, have done to fulfill their plan. All this is realized in the course of a dramatic struggle of divine and human freedom, and within the context of a promise of an End that is no illusion. The outcome of this struggle is never in doubt, but time is unaware of it. The whole of Christian thought is under the sign of time and expectation: we do not know when the covenant will bring creation and the testing of freedom to their definitive completion. Every affirmation, every intimation is made in vigilance and obscurity.

---

7. The hardness of the concept can be deceptive, if we lose sight of the profoundly analogical character of words used to express revealed truth. See the resolute yet moving remarks of Karl Rahner, *Expériences d'un théologien catholique,* trans. Raymond Mengus (Paris: Cariscript, 1985) 15–20.

8. A typical example of articulation in historical language and in ontological language can be found in the Dogmatic Constitution on Divine Revelation: "It pleased God, in his goodness and wisdom, to reveal himself and to make known the mystery of his will, which was that people can draw near to the Father, through Christ, the Word made flesh, in the holy Spirit, and thus become sharers in the divine nature" (DV 2). The vocabulary is entirely scriptural, and still it begins its account with its origin in the Trinity and viewing the fulfillment of human history in terms of communion (i.e., a historical and symbolic style), and only then does it speak of participation in the divine nature (i.e., an ontological style). The council's presentation of matters in historical language first is entirely characteristic of the first two chapters of the constitution, whereas that is not the case for the texts of Trent and Vatican I. See my "La Constitution *Dei Verbum* et ses précédents conciliaires," *Nouvelle revue théologique* 110 (1988) 58–73.

In reality, we must admit that Christianity has often done a poor job of avoiding the aspect of human nostalgia for a "once upon a time" somewhere between time and eternity. This characteristic of the founding myths to locate the meaning of history in its beginnings is found all too often in their being repeated and transposed by Christians, even though the same cannot be said for the biblical narrative. Then, too, there is the problem of evil, also taken up by Christians in their retelling the myths and exorcised only with great difficulty. This deviation goes hand in hand with an excessive insistence on the dimension of unity, and can apply to the understanding of God or to the image of the road humanity must travel. In the Christian story, time is a preparation, even an anticipation of an End "which eye has not seen and ear has not heard, but which God has prepared for those whom he loves" (1 Cor 2:9). Without the negative component there would be no story, since the object of the account is to reprise and comprehend the moments of rupture in the effort to understand it, and yet the negative needs to be interpreted with the utmost care as a step on the painful and barely comprehensible history that finds its completion in communion. The Christian narrative demands a delicate discernment of the genuine structures of time: between the moments in time, the ruptures in the exchange of words, sins which are refusals, suffering which brings redemption and reorientation, the economies of gift. The role of the theology of history is to truly appreciate time in all the diversity of its moments as what is at stake in the narrative. Whatever else it is, story is an "invitation to a journey" which is both adventure and discovery, not some circular orbit in which everything is in principle given over to oblivion, where the point of departure is already the point of return. In this sense, the more speculative elements of Christian propositions can be considered more modestly as the "compass" for the journey and not the point of the trip itself.

The Engagement Truth Demands

Clinging to the language of revelation takes the form that corresponds to the style of this language; it is essentially "faith." Faith is the way of knowing proper to every story. One tells a story so that, with the help of language, the events recounted can be laid out before the listener. In this way, the listener can evaluate its probability and decide if he or she will become engaged with the narrator and the persons concerned in the direction indicated by the story. In other words, story is the language proper to testimony, and testimony demands a faith that is a knowing and an engagement.

I would like to illustrate this by commenting on a position maintained by some opponents of the council, who do not feel bound to obedience because it was a pastoral council and did not teach anything infallibly or impose any obligations. I could contest this proposal by remarking that the council did in fact issue statements that call for "obedience" to the extent that they speak solemnly about the faith of the Church on certain points, notably the sacramentality of the office of bishop. But such a riposte would not quite touch on the point of their objection. And so, I venture to say that it is precisely because the texts of the council are not presented in a juridical form demanding the believer's conformity or in the form of propositions to be accepted under pain of anathema that these texts are worthy of faith and demand our adherence and reception. Everything that the council said, even in juridical and theological matters, is in the order of a restatement that bears the stamp of originality and yet has been elaborated in line with the narrative and poetic forms proper to it. The council remained faithful to the witness confided to the Church from its beginnings. An intellectual adherence or a juridico-ethical obedience must be viewed in a broader context of knowing that also calls for engagement and implies the totality of the person, both as an individual and in the community which offers the testimony.[9]

The reception of the council surpasses merely consenting to the formal correctness of a formula or a norm. However, paradoxically, just as professing the Creed is broader and more global in scope, so too is it more critical. The effort of discernment by both the individual and the particular community is inseparable from authentic knowledge and real engagement. The language of story and the language of poetry call for a qualified, nuanced, response because epistemologically they are not derived from the category of the demonstrative but from the probable.[10] One might say that

9. One could ask whether the exclusive insistence on adhering to propositions in their conceptual and theological form, or on submission to canonical norms, is a remnant of the age of "Christendom." If the whole world is Christian, if its Christianity is incarnated in ecclesiastical and civil institutions, in short, if the visible structure is strong, one risks taking it for granted, forgetting that its foundation, at once solid and fragile, is the testimony which the Spirit gives to the gospel. If one considers the foundation self-referential, forgetting the need to welcome the Mystery again and again, one will depend on formulas and norms as though they had their existence, their truth, and their force of obligation in themselves, and as though they did not depend on a testimony composed of historical and metahistorical elements and the type of faith they elicit, viz., faith and engagement inseparably linked to one another. I will have more to say on the question of authority and obedience in chapter 7.

10. When I speak of what is "probable," I am referring to what the Greeks called *doxa,* and what the scholastics called *"scientia quia"* as opposed to *"scientia quid"* or even *"scientia per causas."* More precisely, it is a matter of a something held as "true" and involving specific comportment. However, the intellect which understands such a truth, after careful examination, is not totally at rest, since a margin of inaccessibility remains: another *doxa* is possible regarding the same object. At this level of knowing, the mind decides to cease the discussion and to hold a given proposition as true, for

these languages call for a restatement that is faithful and original, one that permits the individual or community that has accepted the witness now to bear it itself, but in the words of tradition as well as in their own words, the words they have used to assimilate and interiorize that very tradition. If one begins with this kind of reflection, then one will arrive safely at a correct understanding of dogma and norms: they are languages which, in the framework of a specific culture, have refined the interiorization of the testimony to the faith and made possible a more just response.[11]

Finally, everything I have proposed regarding the evolution of the "style" of truth is meant to give more concrete significance to what is called the *sensus fidelium,* as well as to the primary way the ecclesiastical magisterium is exercised, viz., biblical and mystagogical preaching.[12] If it is no longer a matter of guaranteeing an exact formulation of the words used to proclaim the gospel and that one can believe in absolutely, but rather of evoking and introducing the mystery of Christ with a view to a person's engagement, then it follows that the truly fundamental levels of communication are

---

reasons that have a sufficient basis. The notion of "probability" is concerned exclusively with the issue of the "object" of truth, and is completely distinct from the notion of "certitude." The latter designates an attitude of the "subject" and points to the state of the mind's repose, of its security based on the definiteness of the position it has taken. Someone can be completely certain about a probable truth, if that truth is such that one can reasonably and affectively make it one's own and so rest content in it. Conversely, someone can remain uncertain about something that is evident or has been demonstrated. Thus, even the proofs for the existence of God have demonstrative force, and even if someone was eventually convinced by their demonstration, that person, as a "subject," could still remain uncertain. The passage from affirming something intellectually to a subject's global certitude is always a hard one. See the old but still quite remarkable book by Yves Simon, *Critique de la connaissance morale* (Paris, 1939).

It follows from these precisions that all truths of the Christian faith, even those which defy demonstration, are "probable" truths on the level of their epistemological coherence. As such, they can be affirmed, thanks to the study of the faith and the gift of the Spirit. Finally, they are certain as far as the "subject" is concerned, because the Christian's intellect rests on the witness of God's act of revelation and on the indeceivable interior instinct of faith.

11. It is not my intention to claim that these specific languages have validity only so long as the culture continues. In so far as every culture is human culture its languages speak partially to everyone and the ways the apostolic witness has been received, considered diachronically and synchronically, are not completely heterogeneous. But the precise point is that a critical judgment is necessary to appreciate the exact meaning of these cultural languages as actually received, i.e., in time and space that are truly different. In part, they still can serve to advance the interiorization of the process of reception, but at the very least they will become elements in a different way of receiving the faith.

12. We have already addressed the different functions of the magisterium. See above, p. 41.

those by which individuals and communities testify to Jesus Christ in the Spirit. The goal is the same for explanations of texts and rites that nourish the faith and make engagement by persons possible. Some form of regulation will always be necessary, but tributary to the rhythms and methods that are needed to "imagine" in a fresh way, and not to obfuscate, the primary role and meaning of story, symbol, Creed, and expectation.

Reason and Faith: A New Status

To favor the narrative and poetic expressions of testimony and its reception, as the council clearly did, and do so without denying the roles of dogma and law, calls for conversion of men and women in all the complexity of their nature. It goes deeper than just their ability to know something to be true and to act justly. History, poetry, and rhetoric are not exact disciplines, susceptible to precise formulation and demonstrative argumentation. Epistemologically, they pertain more to probability than to direct or logically reasoned evidence.

Until very recently, the faith was more characterized by the elements of logic and metaphysics in its formulations and this fact tended to nurture an intellectualist understanding of the person as a kind of "gnostic,"[13] potentially or actively engaged in knowing something, or at least on the way to full knowledge. A renewed interest in philosophical anthropology has opened the way to other dimensions, less intellectually satisfying but more humanly significant, such as rhetoric and poetry. Vice versa, liberated from such intellectualist inhibitions, Christians are free to appreciate the human sciences which open them to the mystery of their personal conduct, of collective reactions, of developments (but not necessarily always progress) that time initiates, and of their necessary hermeneutic.

The Human Sciences

Generally speaking, we might say that this new form of knowing opens two essential dimensions of human existence, sensibility and relation. Nor is it possible for this new form of knowing to understand the person if it remains trapped in an impasse which refuses to accept the mysterious connections between our senses and our mind. Instead, by studying the various possibilities of convergence and how different elements affect one another (temperament, differences in character, etc.), it rediscovers the complexity of human passions, especially fear. On the other hand, it investigates the full range of relations: its structures, its interplay, and its pathologies. Exam-

---

13. I am not using the term in its pejorative sense, but have chosen it to highlight the primacy of knowledge in the hierarchy of human values, so characteristic of the Hellenistic mentality discussed earlier. See above, pp. 14–17.

ples include language—verbal and nonverbal, chitchat and mute silence, transparence and dissimulation, etc.—and sexuality—tempestuousness and coldness, identification and otherness, etc. It makes clear once and for all the difficulty of articulating for oneself what is the "same" and what is "other," and in which attempt is found the key to understanding concrete human existence. Nor is this study purely theoretical: it is a "hunt," a "cunning"; it "tracks down" our comportment, our weaknesses, our erring; it lets go of our ceaseless clash with the unconscious. On the level of group activity, too, the human sciences deepen their common interests. This occurs first of all in what concerns life's daily activities: eating, drinking, sleeping—in a given geographical place and climate; working, production, earning a salary; communicating in the whole range of languages; play, i.e., our attempt to symbolize in profane and sacred ways the most fundamental relations that evoke ultimate hidden meaning and that are not foreign to the great issues of war and peace. All this implies an evaluation of ideas, the languages of myth, and ideologies that express a group's culture and progressively define a tradition. And finally, they uncover and analyze the reality of hierarchies: Why are we not all equal? What is power and where does it come from? What are the norms justifying the right use of authority?

This complex of inquiries and interests can be called a *return of wisdom*. In the sapiential books of Scripture, there are sublime passages which describe wisdom in the transcendence of its hidden relation with God. But these passages frame a series or collections of proverbs drawn from human life, with the result that it is not possible literarily or theologically to separate the sublime from the earthly. The human sciences today, together with other resources and other methodologies, function like a new invitation to wisdom and open up an art of interpretation. On the question under study here, viz., the truth of faith and the language of faith, it is most important that we accept the principle of creating space for the development of the human in these different disciplines—psychology and human social life, the senses, symbols, and relationality—and not try to absorb them directly into the supernatural or the ecclesial domain, i.e., without trying to interpret them right off in terms of grace and sin. On the other hand, in the interpretation of the faith, we must take them into account, or in other words, we need to develop a new form of the *intellectus fidei,* one less "intellectualist," more "human." We must avoid a form of intellectual monophysitism without falling into a Nestorianism of the superhuman. We can fruitfully project the light of faith, of symbols, and of rites on all these areas of human life. This would certainly help us better understand them as phenomena and better understand humanity which lives from them, but also, where called for, to work for their healing. Nor should we forget that this effort would help us to understand the impact of grace and of sin in all these phenomena. Finally, this complex point of departure is perhaps what the Pastoral Constitution on the Church in the Modern World wanted to indicate and outline in the cultural context of the 1960s and 1970s.

On Law

We could make the same claims for the notion and the reality of law. The word "law" can be aimed at the *contents* of moral action and indicate *what* is to be done, prescribed either by reflective reason or by divine revelation. It refers to structures of creatures, as God created them, and to their dynamisms. Epistemologically, in general they demand our attention and investigation, and in particular cases our discernment of what is to be done specifically; they proceed from the process of moral knowledge I spoke of earlier in connection with probability and certitude. But (and this is true especially in the case of the human sciences, which shed light on revelation and covenant in another way) the word "law" indicates what I must submit myself to *in order to encounter another.* We cannot really encounter another unless we eliminate personal relationships that are not perhaps wrong in themselves but that prevent the formation of a "we" and unless we perform the requisite actions. As others have remarked, a law in the sense of an "interdiction" is what permits us to "speak among ourselves":[14] to talk, to encounter. The law which "the other" represents and created laws are not opposed to each other in principle but, on the contrary, support each other. Primacy, however, belongs to the law which is "the other," since created law owes its form to it. The double commandment of Jesus (cf. Mark 12:29-31) is a perfect expression of my point, and, if one must err, let it be on the side of preserving the quality of the relations between persons rather than on the fact of safeguarding the full content of the law, even though in the ideal order the quality of interpersonal relations presupposes the authenticity of a law's content, and vice versa.[15]

14. See Michel de Certeau, "La Rupture instauratrice," *La Faiblesse de croire* (Paris: Seuil, 1987) 208–27. —The author is playing on the Latin words *dicere inter* which are the basis of the French *dire entre,* and which explain etymologically the word for a prohibition or an *inter-diction* [translator].

15. Anyone who refers to the difficult concept of a "natural law" (though the idea is not without some foundation), needs to take into account the fact that in ethics there is really a *twofold* natural law: that which is dictated by the objective demands of a given way of acting, and that which the defined relations themselves command in terms of the conduct. The human condition of sinfulness explains why these two aspects of natural law sometimes conflict with one another. The whole issue of moral discernment can be summed up in how a person reestablishes, for better or for worse, the balance between the objective and the relational dimensions (and not forgetting what has already been said above about the notion of "probability").

The Exact Sciences: On Physics and Metaphysics

What has just been said about the need to take into account the human dimensions of the senses and relationality, but also what this implies regarding the rules of establishing truth, is just as valid in another, though seemingly opposed, sector, viz., the exact sciences. Even if the methods are considerably different, here too we rediscover the questions posed by the ancients. After having considered the mutual relations between humanity and the world, the symbols that they give rise to and their immense fecundity, humanity has still another desire, the desire to *know* properly speaking, an appetite to know something in itself, or what has been called "basic research" and which results in the discovery of truth in all its purity.

There is no point in contesting or minimizing this desire to know, since it is also characteristic of the status of Christian truth. But it might be helpful to notice the difference we must face in this field when we act out of a broader mentality that includes testimony, story, and symbol rather than one that stresses the perspective of the knowing subject's limitless self-affirmation—a subject who is sole master of his or her rationality. It is pointless to contest the emergence of rigorous reason, inspired by mathematics, and the perfectly real aspects of the cosmos it discovers, even if it is hard to determine the coherence between these facts and the symbols we spoke about. If I am not mistaken, the philosophy of science moves in two directions. Paradoxically, the first attempts to insert the rigorously mathematical (the domain par excellence of human reason), and whose truth is confirmed by its ability to produce results, into the domain of the "probable" associated with humanity and the cosmos. This is a theoretical problem concerning the nature of knowledge,[16] but it is also an ethical problem. To the degree that the "rigorous" finds itself thrown in with the "probable" (whose extent is much larger), the former's ability to produce results because of its mathematical clarity is not the only criterion of research and application. There are others. This area of research is very delicate, since obstacles to the rigor of science should not be created for moral reasons that might prove to be poorly framed or that are bound to a certain stage in science's development. Furthermore, if the knowing subject is no longer sole master of the terrain, it is a priori essential to define which human, political, and even religious criteria are needed to sketch out a deontology of knowledge. Finally, in a concrete situation, a strategy of research must

---

16. I am referring to the current research on the status of scientific objectivity (called "soft"), on the principle of uncertainty, etc. See B. d'Espagnat, *Une incertaine réalité. Le monde quantique. La connaissance et la durée* (Paris, 1985); idem, *Penser la science, ou les Enjeux du savoir* (Paris, 1990); E. Klein, *Conversations avec le sphinx. Les paradoxes physiques* (Paris, 1991).

also be defined, since we never start from square one, neither in the attempt to investigate what is real nor in the field of "knowledge of good and evil." The attempt is to some extent a matter of "hit and miss."

The direction taken by the philosophy of science seeks to situate in a larger context the problem we can simply call "physical" in a very general way. I am here thinking of the renewed interest today in the question, Can we have science and God? Frankly, this way of posing the question runs the risk of being very misleading. After two thousand years of Christianity, believers and nonbelievers alike think they have some understanding of what the word "God" means, but how true is it? In reality, the point of the question is not God but the absolute or partial autonomy of the physical order. This last problematic calls to mind the urgency of the concern in antiquity for the "metaphysical" question, i.e., something necessary for the physical order itself and beyond it (regardless of the latter's methods which are evidently very different today than earlier). Like many others, I have been struck by Stephen W. Hawking's treatment in his famous book *A Brief History of Time*,[17] where according to him, if we could find a "formula of the universe," one that reconciled relativity with quantum theory, all men and women, and not just scientists, would know *the mind of God*,[18] and in this sense we could say that they would become "like the gods." But even in this case, the question "Why?" would remain unanswered. Assuming that we can reach the end of the series of questions regarding the essences of things (how are they affected by space and time? by nature and history? how are these questions interrelated? etc., etc.), we would not be able to suppress the sense of wonder we would experience in knowing that all this is really true. And yet even at this point we would still not have posed, but only opened, the question of God, so that a new light would shine on these beings whose secrets we know exhaustively, except for their very last secret: what are they?[19] At this very point, having posed the ultimate question, we

17. *A Brief History of Time: From the Big Bang to Black Holes* (New York: Bantam, 1988).

18. But just what does this expression mean: the mind of God? the divine intelligence? the intention of God?

19. Hawking's approach is extremely enlightening, because it casts new light on old issues. Ultimately, the question comes down to the meaning of "to be." If we give it the meaning of an absolutely rational articulation of all essences, in themselves and in their relations, we remain fixed in the outlook of modernity which defines reality in function of the reputedly infinite capacity of the human mind. This is the point of Hegel's axiom: "All of reality is knowable." But it is also perhaps Plato's insight, in the second hypothesis of the *Parmenides*, when he maintains that being, unlike the One, is what can be predicated of all things. There can be no doubt that the understanding of being as the exclusive token of identity espoused by Leibnitz and Hegel is just what Heidegger opposed throughout his life. And finally this is the way neo-Thomism under-

gain some insight into what was at stake for the ancients and medieval thinkers concerning the *creation* of the world, as opposed to its emanation, and concerning the relations between creation and time. I don't think we can be more radically fundamental in our questioning reality than the medievals when they clashed with each other over the question of the beginning of the world and the exact relation between time, being, and God.[20] Be that as it may, it is interesting to see how today as in the past the desire to know and the results of the exact sciences both contain the metaphysical question, just as centuries of reflection on the biblical theme of creation brought it to such a refined state.

The Status of Christian Knowing

A Return to the Primacy of Scripture

In all that I have said thus far, one can detect the outline of a new balance between reason and faith. Epistemologically, current studies show no sign of rationalism in the strict sense. Taking its inspiration from mathematics and modernity, such an understanding of rationalism had a decisive influence on the way reason and faith were understood in the Church. But we have also seen that an act of affirming one's faith is not only a matter of the intellect. More precisely, the epistemological dimension for a conceptualization of the faith takes place at the heart of a complex ensemble that includes recognition and personal engagement. The encounter between a reason that knows itself to be rooted in the "senses" and a more "global" understanding of faith is something very delicate, more human and, perhaps too, more divine, even though none of this is a rejection of the strictly theoretical and speculative elements at its very heart, viz., a transcendent convergence of dimensions. In other words, the conditions for understanding thought now in place demand a reworking by Christians of the conditions that obtained when they understood reason solely in terms of logic and metaphysics, i.e., when they formerly occupied the front of the stage. A delicate equilibrium must be sought. If the human and exact sciences can stir up another way of thinking and believing, faith itself, so human

---

stands being, marked as it is by the principle of sufficient reason. But in its depths being is much more than that; it is a matter of all reality and the whole of reality, but considered in light of the immanent and mysterious principle of its sudden emerging. This way of thinking about being is extremely subtle and delicate, and includes and develops ideas of creation and participation. Epistemologically, it assumes both the reality of sensible perception, the basis of all knowing, and the analogical quality of the idea of being, when it is understood in this way.

20. See F. J. Jimenez Rios, *Dios e la Historia del tempo* (Rome: Gregorian University Press, 1992).

and divine at once, might be of some help in shedding light on the human sense of expectation and human powerlessness when left to ourselves.

Such theoretical observations lead to underscoring the fact that we are in a position today, as in antiquity, to rediscover theological expressions that are primarily a commentary on Scripture, or we might say are our dialogue with Scripture. If contemporary human thought is rediscovering a certain primacy of the literary dimension, it ought to be open to the affinity between it and the literary character of the books of the Bible. A new method of exegesis can now emerge, one that is not simply a return to the old forms but their creative revival.[21]

Theologies

The investigations conducted in the human sciences, as well as in the exact sciences and metaphysics, point to something characteristic both of the present moment and the beginnings of the Christian tradition: the human search conducted in a faith that is open to the witness of the Spirit. The language of revelation is mediated by one's culture. Such an effort focuses on the distinctiveness of the *sensus fidelium* of the whole Church. We no longer find ourselves in an exclusionist epistemology of illumination. Moreover, Christians are in daily contact with the men and women who work in the various domains of life, and so are in the position of acknowledging not only their competence in principle but also a certain moral capacity on their part to judge the moral necessity of their research, even if it is conducted apart from any religious option. This presupposes an effort at dialogue, the progressive defining of fields of activity and methodologies, the acceptance of differences between researchers and thinkers, everything that might help, little by little, to find the way to truth. And, of course, this means a certain experimentation and the possibility of making mistakes. Time will be needed to find one's way around a question, and so, one must be ready to admit that a fresh posing of the question can help one see the narrowness, regionalism, and even the "provincialism" of one's perspective regarding what one once believed to be absolutely true, everywhere and always. Finally, if redemption is still unfolding, one needs to learn how to participate in God's patience. Since evil cannot be avoided absolutely, one has to try to limit it, and that means not excluding myself from the effort. Truth involves a strategy, and it always arises out of the probable, not out of what can be demonstrated.

---

21. I tried to give a brief sketch of the possible general lines of such a method at the end of my book *Histoire théologique de l'Église catholique. Itinéraire et formes de la théologie* (Paris: Cerf, 1994) 453–56.

On the other hand, Christian faith is quite capable of shedding light on many human realities whose principles and operations the culture seeks to investigate. If the Church presents itself as a community that renders testimony to Jesus Christ and makes the resources of its tradition available, it can open its riches in service to humanity. What it can teach about the covenant between God and humanity, and between men and women themselves, but also what it can teach about *sin* as a breaking of the covenant and hence introducing a principle that perverts *redemption* as the ever-new possibility of life, can be extremely helpful to society in this regard. Such coordinates, welcomed as partial if not complete hypotheses, can have a real impact on the culture. Since Christianity belongs to the cultural tradition of a large majority of humanity, it is not impossible for it to recover some of its influence—perhaps a more secularized influence in one or another domain—and thereby be of service to humanity by advancing what, even though known by other names and belonging to other social systems, still pertains to a patrimony which the Church wants to put at the disposition of all.

Finally, the concept of tradition assumes all the force that the Dogmatic Constitution on Divine Revelation accorded it, when it spoke of its "progress" and its "growth" (DV 8). As the domains of knowledge gradually grow out of the different levels of study by Christians, it just might mean that the worldview might change. What is needed is "to arrange things differently,"[22] with the result that their meaning and significance for the appreciation of the whole regarding humanity, the world, and God changes, but not their immanent truth.

Dialogue

The steps taken by Vatican II on the question of truth would have been almost unimaginable in other eras. Suffice it to say that it accepted the existence of other languages and practices that were incomplete approximations of the truth, or different and even false expressions of it, and that it adopted a policy of dialogue with these languages in order to establish or rediscover points of convergence between the Catholic Church and the churches and confessions that spoke these languages. At the same time, it made efforts to acknowledge the real dignity of other religions and other systems of worship. What is to be made of all this?

22. "It should not be claimed that I have not said anything new: the arrangement of the matter is new. When one plays tennis, both players play with the same ball, but one hits it better." This text of Blaise Pascal is cited and commented on by G. Genette, "Enseignement et rhétorique," *Annales, économies, sociétés, civilisations* (1963) 292–305.

The Primacy of Witness

Behind this new attitude of tolerance and dialogue was a more lively awareness that Christian truth concerned revelation and came about because of the encounter between the Church's testimony and the faith of the person responding to it. The only thing the Church can do is render its witness, in word and in the very life of Christian communities, to the Word of life (cf. 1 John 1:1) who is manifested in it, and to ask the Spirit to give faith to those who hear their word. In other words, adherence to Christian truth happens only when it is free of any coercion. The text of the Declaration on Religious Liberty on the way Jesus fulfilled his apostolic mission (cf. DH 11) became the charter for this conviction about the primacy of witness. But mention should also be made to the classical teaching on the act of faith according to which everything takes place between God and the innermost recesses of the person. Faith's content is recognized only because of an "interior instinct of truth" which, thanks to the inspiration of the Spirit, responds to the "authority of God revealing." If the Word of God which is heard in the Church is to effect a change in a person's life, it can be accepted only because this interior instinct of faith opens the person to see that this word actually proceeds from God.

God Alone Saves in Jesus Christ

It follows that the Church is led to admit its own ignorance on how God saves, even if it knows that salvation comes always from Jesus Christ. More than in the past, it is challenged to take seriously the passage from St. Paul where he shows that all are saved through obedience to the law written in their hearts and which is related to the gospel (cf. Rom 2:12-16), and to understand that God's mercy extends to our weakness, and even includes our errors. Can we attribute the rigidity of the ancient Fathers to their having too intellectual an understanding of truth and too unquestioning a commitment to the way of illumination for explaining how people arrive at the truth? From the very first moment that truth was proclaimed in the world (and for them, that meant the area around the Mediterranean) it shone so brightly that the failure to recognize it was already a fault, whereas erroneous interpretations were immediately explained by culpably bad faith. Our perspective today is much more nuanced, perhaps because after so many centuries the fact that so many nonbelievers and heretics have still not been converted, we are forced to reexamine our criteria of judging them. The work in this area is delicate because the missionary perspective opened by the Council of Trent remained in the same "exclusivist" line of thought of the ancient Fathers. The attempt was to import Catholicism in the form it has received not only from Trent but also from the unifying and centralizing currents that followed it. Under these conditions, as the question of the Chinese rites in the seventeenth and eighteenth centuries amply demonstrates,[23] it was difficult to acknowledge the impact of culture on the faith, mixed and ambiguous as culture always is.

The Church, Disciple of the Truth

But even more needs to be said. Ecumenical dialogue and dialogue with non-Christian religions are based on something else, something not insisted on very much but important nonetheless: the Church engages in dialogue because it senses that it has something to learn from others, even though it rarely admits this or openly says so to others. In dialogue it recognizes the legitimate but limited character of its own accents, e.g., concerning the sacraments, Scripture, law, the Spirit, etc., and senses the need to make room for other, possibly neglected accents in a global presentation of truth, accents which the other confessions in their own right tend to employ excessively and exclusively. Consequently, if the other confessions can find room for certain Catholic orientations, and if the Church can make room for what it has neglected, both should be able to settle on an agreement that is wider than their current discourse betrays. Such an agreement does not mean necessarily that the language must be uniform, but that what must be recognized is the validity of various languages permitting the originality of different communities and their sensibilities, of their liturgical practices, and possibly of their different moral positions, provided that all remain true to the light of the gospel.

The Church, One and Plural

But this ecumenical approach also means that the Church has to acknowledge this same need within itself: it needs to rediscover a sense of diversity at the very heart of orthodoxy. In the life of the non-Latin, Eastern Catholic Churches, there already exists a way of fully acknowledging a difference in rites, in theological orientations, in juridical provisions, and in social practices. This implies that if real diversity has been accepted, even on some necessarily very important points, what could it possibly mean to insist on a uniform discourse regarding the contents of the faith, if such were even possible. The "process of Latinizing" which has for so long characterized the Catholic Church vis-à-vis the Oriental churches (and which one would like to say sincerely has finally ended), is bound to the "Gregorian form of the Church," ill suited to welcome plurality in doctrinal and

---

23. On the Chinese rites controversy, Matteo Ricci, S.J., and the Congregation *de Propaganda Fide*, see Aylward Shorter, *Toward a Theology of Inculturation* (Maryknoll, New York: Orbis, 1988) 157–59 [Translator].

liturgical expressions of the faith. It was Gregory VII who wanted to suppress the Mozarabic liturgy and Pius IX (1846–78) who urged the universal acceptance of the Latin Liturgy throughout the Western world at the expense of those local expressions that still remained. Likewise, as useful as it might have been in other areas, the imposition of "Thomism" as the official doctrine of the Church, the insistence on "the" social doctrine of the Church as unitary, and other such efforts at uniformity, took their inspiration from a notion of unity that was not one of a convergence of perspectives but of the exclusion of differences. The Church can be truly ecumenical and open to religions *ad extra* only if it succeeds in determining fair norms in regard to its plurality *ad intra*.

The Eschatological Quality of the Tradition

But even more profoundly, we need to note the impact of Vatican II's teaching in the Dogmatic Constitution on Divine Revelation on tradition. Article 8 insists that our knowledge will not be perfect until the end of time, when the meaning of the Christian Mystery will have manifested all its admirable correspondence with the treasures of human wisdom, which will be purified and transfigured, and when Christianity too will have welcomed the wisdom and symbols of nonbelievers, the sciences, and all the domains of human knowledge, in order to learn from them and so deepen its knowledge of the faith. Thus, even for Catholics, the full potential of revelation has not yet been discovered. The way to self-discovery by the Church will be the patient listening to others.

Conclusion

Today, truth appears in the complexity of all its dimensions. During the past millennium, little by little we lost sight of certain essential dimensions for grasping and expressing reality. The primordial and permanent dimension of sense knowledge especially lost its impact and with it the infinite play of metaphors and of spiritual meanings in the act of knowing. The communional dimensions of knowing were not stressed, as though language was less symbolic, or less concerned with the process of communication among speakers than signifying, or more concerned with indicating content. Another, more general reason is that our human *desire for communion* gave way almost totally to the *desire to know*. The dimension of witness, important for a large part of our knowing, gradually came to be understood as a prior condition of our knowing rather than as belonging to the very structure of truth. The conceptual and metaphysical dimensions of knowing ceded the sense of being as mystery and participation, and the correlative meaning of the analogy of language, to a desiccated or purely pragmatic rationalism. Thus, one had no other option but to search for a spiritual breath of fresh air in the mysticism of the Totally Other, itself divested of anything sensible, having no language, and beyond intelligibility. The Church was not the only one liable for this kind of "decadence" regarding the Truth. On the contrary. Still, it is not clear why, from the Middle Ages to the present, the Church devoted so much attention to the issue of truth. From the High Middle Ages it became imprisoned in a doctrinal, liturgical, and ecclesiological understanding of the truth, and continued to maintain the corresponding strategies of illumination theory, gathering evidence, fighting heresy, conducting inquisitions, so preoccupied was it to defend a certain number of convictions. Without even noticing it, it often lagged behind in ways of interpreting the faith that were marked by a rigid and impoverished rationalism.

Today, the Church is following the lead of a more cultural understanding of truth, but it is also trying to inform the latter with a sense of realism endemic to Christian revelation. In this way it is slowly rediscovering the essential aspects I tried to outline above and by opening itself to new ideas is discovering the wealth of its own tradition. The fruit of this new epistemology can be found already in the documents of Vatican II. *But it is clear that the present awareness of the status of truth demands modes of testimony, preaching, theology, instruction, and when necessary of defending itself which have yet to be imagined.* There are areas where the renewal has already begun to be implemented. The whole catechetical movement, even if it is currently enjoying some breathing space, is a testament to this fact, as are theological research and instruction. But this movement in support of the new awareness and presentation of Christian truth demands yet another conviction of the Church as witness to this truth: the vision of exclusive unicity (only one God, only one Christ, only one pope, only one priesthood), the vision inspired by Neoplatonism (mystical, juridical, and political), which served as the grid for interpreting the revealed truths of the Church, its charisms and ministries, must finally give way to another criteriology, one that is broader and less monolithic. That is what the Second Vatican Council set about to accomplish. Our task now will be to turn our attention toward the Church as a "structured communion."

Chapter 4

The Church: A Structured Communion

We had occasion to emphasize the trinitarian, figurative, and more encompassing language used to present the Church in the Dogmatic Constitution on the Church, and taken up and refined at the beginning of the Dogmatic Constitution on Divine Revelation and the Decree on the Missionary Activity of the Church. At the beginning of this chapter, it will be our task to develop somewhat the effect of this very initial presentation of the Church, since the consequences for the life of the Church are significant. Let us be honest: we are sorely tempted to recoil from these consequences when we begin to catch a glimmer of what they mean *in practice* for the Church, i.e., in terms of the process of restructuring the Church's institutions that will be required.

In this chapter, I will consider in greater detail the two connected themes of the body of Christ and the People of God in their richness. But paradoxically this consideration will lead to drawing attention in certain passages of these documents of Vatican II to the real ecclesiological uncertainties, ambiguities, and inconsistencies they contain, and that we will have to attend to. I will try to sketch a theological perspective that will help eliminate these ambiguities and permit us to give full force to the essential intuitions presented at the beginning of the chapter.

Body and People

Expressing the Whole

Body

Three successive approaches can be distinguished in the text that discusses the Church as the body. Each depends on how it views Christ's relation to the Church. The first speaks of the *mysterious identity* between the dead and risen body of Christ, animated by the Spirit, and the Church; the same image of identity is employed to speak of Christ and the Church. Second, there is *a double relation of distinction and communication:* Christ is *head* of the body and as such is the principle from which the life of the Church flows, by means of the gift of the Spirit. Here, the image is one of physiological perfection which both surpasses and communicates itself. And third, Christ is the *spouse* of his Church. The image has sexual connotations, but a sexuality that has already been reflected on: the spousal gift of self, body, soul, and mind by which a woman becomes a wife. The community of believers is rendered fruitful by Christ's gift of himself in the Spirit.

In all three figurative uses, but perhaps most clearly in the first case, it is a matter of the crucified and risen body of Christ, in the plenitude of the Spirit. We are contemplating a body which has transcended the state of opposition between life and death (and which we know all too well from our experience) but still remains in what might be called the eschatological equivalent of this opposition. In other words, Christ's glorified body is a body that is always and totally accepted by God the Father and that is returned to him entirely as an eternal offering. It is a body that is fully son-like, living by the Spirit of generation and sonship. The visible Church, the community of believers, already *is* this body. It is only a visible community of believers in as much as it is the surface appearance of this hidden identity (mysterious, secret, in mystery) with the dead and risen body of Christ, and which is manifested in the specific acts of the Spirit who animates it. This bond, at once invisible and constitutive of the Church as the body of Christ, takes three forms.

The first shows forth the *initiatory, ritual, and festive character* of the Church as body. The Church becomes body and is manifested as body through the richness of symbolic acts which culminate in the celebration of the Eucharist (which in itself is not an ethical and product-oriented activity) that causes the believer to pass from a condition of finitude to one of resurrection. The Eucharist keeps the community in this identity with the Body of Christ by means of the festive meal whose symbolic signification is one of identity by exchange. We eat the body and drink the blood needed for life, which are gifts, *and* we do this together. Thus, there is a twofold, complementary exchange between Christ and the believer that makes the guests into the Body that represents the world beyond our present condition *and* what is most closely connected to our bodily condition.

The second points to the *organic solidarity* that exists among the members of the body and that makes their diversity a source of complementarity and convergence. This solidarity grounds in this world both the practices of communication and compassion which the Spirit inspires (and hence is the ethical dimension of the body) and an articulation of the diversity of functions and ministries which are of service to the body's symbolic and ethical practices.[1]

The third expresses the *real conformity* of the Church with Christ in its present condition. It reproduces in its present pilgrim state the path taken by Christ in the past, so that its life, too, is marked through and through by the same tragic reality that Christ experienced. Nevertheless, there is a difference which demands theological expression, viz., that although Christ's battle was one of a pure man, one who had assumed but did not share in our sins, the Church must constantly make the difficult choice between three types of struggle: the properly Christian type of obedience to the word of God; the type that is born of the opposition of those who live outside of Christ and whose refusal to enter runs the risk of persecuting him; and the type of that which is born in the heart of the Church, indeed in each of its members, between the given identity and the active identification to Christ and the refusal of this identity–identification.

People

After speaking about the "body," the council seems most eager to speak of a "people," because the Dogmatic Constitution on the Church dedicates the whole of chapter 2 to it. A careful examination of the introductory material in articles 9 and 10 reveals two essential points. First, there is the idea that salvation comes to humanity in its being joined again to the very heart of a community which, under the direction of Christ, is capable of recognizing the covenant proposed by God and of responding to it in dedicated service. The second point is that the Church is a historical reality, prepared in the Old Testament, gathered again by Jesus Christ, and on a journey toward the completion of all things in the parousia of Christ.

By stressing the twofold character of sociality and historicity, the Church, even in spite of its small size, has appeared and must be able to appear as a seed of hope and salvation for all humanity. Defined by the basic communional identity of its faith and sacraments, the People of God is immersed in culture, suffers and toils, is renewed and reformed constantly

---

1. Though I would prefer to use the word "hierarchies" to describe this articulation of diversity, because it expresses quite precisely the idea of "sacred principles" that traverse the social body and confer unity and effectiveness to it, I will not do so for two reasons. First, in common theological parlance, the word "hierarchy" has come to express the Neoplatonic idea of "ladder-like" subordination of what is lower vis-à-vis the higher and from which it receives its being and action. This can lead to a rigidity which is out of place in this context. Second, for some time now in ecclesiology it has been reserved for the subjects of the apostolic ministry, the bishops charged with assuring the correct transmission of the tradition received from Christ to the Church. But the "hierarchies" I am speaking about are much more extensive than these.

by the action of the Spirit. It is a priestly people, a prophetic people equipped with charisms by the Spirit, a catholic and universal people, qualities which in a preliminary way the text tries to define in reference to the other Christian churches and other religious groupings. The People of God offers a sketch, it initiates and prepares the journey of humanity toward the eschatological moment of a "pure offering."

By choosing to employ the Church as body and people, each provides certain corrections to the other. At the Extraordinary Synod of 1985, the importance of the theme of the People of God receded somewhat out of fear that its usage had become too "political" and too focused on "democracy" in the Church, and so it was proposed that "communion" be substituted for it. In fact, there is some danger of the "People of God" falling into the same genre of political ambiguity that the ecclesiology of the "perfect society" or of the "pontifical theocracy" succumbed to in the Middle Ages and in modern times. In the latter case, "democracy" replaces "theocracy," but with the same drawbacks. Nevertheless, even if we admit that "communion" does effectively suggest the quality of "sociality" proper to the Church of God, especially as a term that is juxtaposed to the "People of God," it is not entirely adequate since it does not appropriately underscore the liturgical reality stressed so often in the prayers of the Roman Missal with their regular invocation in such formulas as "Listen to your people, O Lord," nor does it give sufficient attention to the aspect of historicity, the concrete historical vicissitudes, and the process of inculturation, all of which are so forcefully presented in chapter 2. Left to itself, the term "communion" offers too "spiritual" an impression not to awaken certain suspicions on our part. It can remind us of the anti-institutional ecclesiologies of former times, ecclesiologies founded exclusively on holiness or on the Bible alone. But it can especially awaken the fear that, once we have defined the Church as communion, we feel quite free to develop a juridical structure that is even more restrictive and burdensome than the idea of communion will bear. That is why I maintain that the body of Christ and the People of God, used in tandem, attain a certain equilibrium. They permit us to have a preview of an ecclesiology as "structured communion," and whose general lines I want to spell out in my book.

A Communion of Communities

If we are going to do justice to the Church as body of the whole Christ and People of God, not merely in theory but also in practice, we have to consider it in the concrete communities where men and women gather. Effectively, the Church—body and People of God—is found where the gospel is announced, the sacraments are celebrated, and one's gifts are employed. If I keep insisting on the word "effectively," it is to support those vivid images used in article 6 of the Dogmatic Constitution on the Church, images which are lively and operative in the liturgy: the flock, family, house, temple, spouse are all realities of human dimensions. If each person is to take his or her place, there must first be some such determined place. If tiny groups are gathered on the basis of one or another gift, they must be able to find expression in the playing out of the same "might,"[2] there must be a common space which is not too big, lest the individual gets lost. If we fail to understand the images of the Church in human dimensions, they cannot have any practical meaning for us. They are quickly forgotten as so much rhetorical verbiage. And even if these images are open to universal significance, when it is a matter of speaking of the communion and communication among all the particular communities, even that transposition must rest on the reality of particular experiences. An immediately universal idea of the Church does not allow a *real* playing out of might and holiness. There would only be so many individuals and the supreme Power, or presupposing the existence of intermediate degrees, these would be like so many necessary platoons of more or less passive individuals, where power is passed down from a supreme authority. The question needs to be asked: In reality, how are symbolic languages essential to having might and to holiness?

When we speak of particularity we touch on the concreteness of the human: the family of God, the flock of Christ gathers men and women in a particular place, with their language, and their local cultural customs, starting in a determined geographical place, with a certain social structure, and a definite political form. The Church adopts this ensemble of elements, and by the might and holiness coming from the Spirit, offers its criticism, contests some elements, heals others, and so in the end promotes it. Here is the place where the tone and color of specific rituals,[3] a proper ethical accent, and an art of living remain always open to further refinement.

Undoubtedly, these grounding particularities are to find an articulation among themselves, and that will not be easy, especially when account is taken of these communities in communion not being contemporaneous

2. Here I am giving the word the sense of "dynamism" and "vitality," of what makes a body or a people express itself, manifest itself, and find itself in this expression. Earlier, we saw that this included a liturgical moment, an ethical moment, and a moment that can be called hierarchical or diaconal. I think we can locate this notion of "power" by taking certain sociological studies, such as those of Michel Maffesoli, *Le Temps des tribus* (Paris, 1988), and transposing them for theological reflection.

3. We need only think of the diversity of Eucharistic Prayers (anaphoras) in the different liturgical rites of the early Church. It would be highly important in this regard to study the juridical decisions of the various churches, from their beginnings to the present, to see the evolution of art and ethics, in order to verify how institutions of communion were worked out.

(we are speaking of old and new churches) and the different relations they have with the surrounding cultures, sometimes polemical, sometimes peaceful, sometimes uncertain. In these circumstances, the institution of the synod, local or universal, will prove indispensable, on condition that we re-define what a council is, who takes part in it, and how each community and each person will appropriate the decisions taken.[4]

Ambiguities and Uncertainties

As great as the evolution has been in the way the Church is envisaged, the text of the Dogmatic Constitution on the Church (but also other texts, which we will have occasion to look at), leave the reader unsatisfied. I would call it a "positive sense of not being satisfied," since it is an invitation to pursue with greater theological determination the basic orientation of the council. I would like to indicate three areas of a lack of satisfaction: the question of the holiness of the Church, of its "hierarchical constitution," and of the subject and persons responsible for mission.

The Holiness of the Church

If we consider the Church as the body of Christ, animated by the Spirit, it would appear that the first thing to be said about it is its holiness. If "Holy" is the name par excellence of God, and so does not signify anything except God, this name is God's first gift to the Church. It points to the level at which its life should develop, and suggests the mystical thread that runs through it, the interior desire that moves it, and is identical in the final analysis with a participation in the mutual life of the divine Persons, the ambiguity and the tension which is its permanent passion, so long as Christ is not "all in all" (Col 3:11) and so long as he is not yet fully realized in it.

It is astonishing that article 7 of the Dogmatic Constitution on the Church, which describes the body, does not mention this holiness explicitly. On the other hand, even though in speaking about the People of God, it does here and there speak of the "holy People of God," again no special article is dedicated specifically to the treatment of holiness as a gift of God appropriate to this people, to the point that it becomes an immanent characteristic of it. The constitution deferred speaking about holiness until chapter 5, and did so in the perspective of a call ("On the Universal Call to Sanctity in the Church"), which led it to describe the response to this appeal and so to put it in an ethical and active perspective rather than in a theological and receptive one. This problematic can be understood from an historical viewpoint.

---

4. This paragraph has tried to say in the context of our development here, what J.M.R. Tillard has expressed in his aptly entitled book *Church of Churches: The Ecclesiology of Communion,* trans. R. C. De Peaux (Collegeville: The Liturgical Press, 1992).

Before the council it was customary to distinguish two categories of Christians in the Church and their position regarding holiness. There are those who follow the "ordinary way" and can scarcely aim at sanctity, so encumbered are they by the worries stemming from marriage, family, and one's occupation. But there are others who are in the "state of the pursuit of perfection" for whom sanctity is their primary objective and for which they have sacrificed certain possible avenues in life, marriage certainly and involvement in the labor of this world.[5] After treating priests and laity, the council finally took up the life of religious only to find itself face to face with the classical doctrine of the two states in life which it wanted to change. Its will was to proclaim the call of all Christians to holiness or to the perfection of evangelical life, but what then would it teach about those members of the Church, known as "religious," who had dedicated themselves to a particular way of living the gospel? What was this way, and was it right to say it was a "higher" way? This background explains somewhat the difficulties chapters 6 and 7 of the constitution had to consider. Thus, the question of the holiness of the Church surfaced only when the council took up the question of religious life.

Today, with the passage of time and upon greater reflection, we are free to maintain that it would have been better for the council to speak about holiness either in the chapter on the People of God itself or immediately thereafter, in a chapter all its own devoted to the issue of holiness. Before it is a vocation, holiness is God's first gift to the Church, the proper note of a body animated by the Spirit, of a people that is the People *of God*. If it had spoken about holiness right off and before any other considerations, the council would have been faithful to the formulation of the Creed which speaks of the Church as "one, holy, catholic, and apostolic," and would have put holiness at the forefront in defining the Church. After recognizing its quality as gift, it would have been possible to define how Christ has distributed various states of life, complementary but sometimes in conflict with one another, so that Christians might receive and live out this holiness, whether collectively or personally. It could have highlighted the human dimension of this gift, of a particular vocation, and of the various states of life. It could have considered next the various distinctions of states of life, their tasks and ministries (even those included in chapters 3 and 6) and thereby considered them under the direction of holiness, i.e., under the aegis of the Name of God written on the Church and the Spirit of God who directs it toward the Father in Christ. Awareness of the primacy of holiness among the "notes" of the Church, could have led to a certain reversal of the

5. See René Carpentier, *Life in the City of God: An Introduction to the Religious Life*, trans. John Joyce (New York: Benziger, 1959) 11–15.

constitution's order of treatment. What I have to say now about the mission of the Church is an invitation to execute such a shift of themes.

The Mission of the Church: Subjects and Those Responsible

The question we have raised regarding the holiness of the Church finds an important echo in another issue, the mission of the Church. Do not these two words "holiness" and "mission" express the very work of the Spirit in the Church and through it? Just as holiness is a primordial gift to the whole Church, so too is the mission a global sending forth of the body and the people to announce the gospel. But in reading the text of Vatican II, it seems that this perspective is not the only one retained, so that once again we find ourselves face to face with an ambiguity: who are subjects of the Church's mission? Is it the whole Church which exercises this responsibility, thanks to the charisms of the Spirit (including, of course, the charism of the apostolic ministry), which are the product of discernment, recognition, and articulation among them? Or is it the bishops, successors of the apostles, who exercise this as a function of the authority communicated to them by the sacrament of order, received in the hierarchical communion of the Church, and when necessary with the collaboration of the Church? I consider the alternative not to be pertinent. It creates an opposition that the whole of my book rejects. The council's texts nonetheless—and we must be honest about the matter—create a tone that is somewhat ambiguous, and we need to listen to its dissonance.

Dogmatic Constitution on the Church 17 and 18

At the end of chapter 2, in discussing the missionary character of the People of God, the council based it on the sending forth of the apostles in John 20:21 and on the Great Missionary Command of Matthew 28:20. It states that this sending and this command was received by "the Church from the apostles to be accomplished to the ends of the earth," in reference to Acts 1:8. There follows a description of the mission which is applied to the whole Church and to each disciple, and noting at the end of the text that the proper office of the priest is to gather in the Eucharist the offering of all the nations already evangelized.

At the beginning of chapter 3, which explains the hierarchical constitution of the Church, article 18 appears to disrupt slightly the balance in the presentation. The council says that Christ established the Church by sending forth the apostles, as he had been sent forth by the Father[6] (see

---

6. *Jesum Christum Pastorem Aeternum sanctam edificasse Ecclesiam, missis Apostolis sicut ipse missus erat a Patre* ("Jesus Christ, the eternal pastor, established the holy church by sending the apostles as he himself had been sent by the Father"). The ablative ab-

John 20:21). In other words, the apostles have the role of an active subject, while the Church appears to be the fruit of their labor. Then the text moves on to the successors of the apostles whom Christ willed to be pastors of the Church "until the end of the times" (Matt 28:20). The logic of these formulas and their citations moves in the direction of maintaining that the "mission of building up the Church" belongs to the bishops. Moreover, it is not without significance that the vocabulary used concerns a building: it is a matter of "building up." Both the image and the use of a transitive verb imply an "object," and that this cannot be other than the Church. But the Church cannot be considered both the object of the "building up" and the active subject of mission at the same time. Thus, this second perspective disappears from consideration. And yet, in a very real sense, the Church itself builds up itself (according to article 4) thanks to the hierarchical gifts, which in this context can be interpreted as the ministry of the bishops, (even though the expression is much broader than that) and the charismatic gifts. Here, then, is our problem: Is it the whole Church or the bishops who exercise mission?

Dogmatic Constitution on Divine Revelation 7 and 8

In this section the perspective is that of the "transmission" of revelation, an expression which calls for missionary activity and fidelity to what has been handed on. The text proceeds something like this: we begin with the apostles in the strict sense of the term, i.e., those disciples Jesus personally chose, those who heard Jesus and preached what they received from their contact with Jesus. Next come the bishops, those who have inherited the apostolic magisterium and are responsible for the living preservation of the gospel *(ut evangelium integrum et vivum servaretur)*. The stress is more on fidelity *(integrum, servaretur)*, but life *(vivum)* is not excluded, and it can mean both the evangelical life that Christians lead and the apostolic vitality of the message. Very discreetly, mission is included in the text. In what follows, the stress on fidelity is increased when the exhortation of the apostles (again in the strict sense) to hold to the tradition of the faith and to fight for it is emphasized. However, when the text turns to the active mission *(transmittit),* the subject once again is the Church, i.e., the one "who hands on all that it is and that it believes," without any explicit distinction of functions (which does not negate the distinction, of course, since it is mentioned in other contexts).

And so, in article 7, we can discern a certain distinction and articulation in the transmission of revelation: the whole People of God (and this

---

solute in the Latin, *missis apostolis,* can only serve as a complement of the agent involved, i.e., it is Jesus who builds up the Church by the sending forth of the apostles.

includes persons in positions of authority and their specific tasks) seem to be viewed as the subject of mission, the bishops as those who actively guarantee fidelity to the message, whereas only the apostles in the strict sense actually constituted the tradition and the Church which incarnates and continues it.

Decree on the Missionary Activity in the Church 5 and 6

The Decree on the Missionary Activity in the Church was written at the end of the council and shows a more reasoned understanding of the problem. It says explicitly that "the apostles were both the seeds of the New Israel and the origin of the sacred hierarchy." In short, it recognizes an "apostolic succession" communicated to the whole Church and an "apostolic succession" communicated only to the bishops. In employing this distinction, which is not a separation, the council again uses the same scriptural passages (Matt 28:20 and John 20:21) to speak of the global mission of the Church. The text offers the following explanation: this office *(officium)* which is incumbent on the Church as a whole is exercised either in virtue of an express mandate of Christ transmitted from the apostles to the "order of bishops, whom the priests assist, together with the Successor of Peter," or in virtue of the "life which Christ communicates to his members." Further on, it speaks again about the Church as subject of mission, which is made present to all of humanity in so far as it "remains obedient to the commandment of Christ (making reference to the order of bishops) and is equipped with the grace and charity of the Spirit" (making reference to the "life communicated" by Christ). One might take exception to this division between an "order" that issues from a *commandment* of Christ and a "life" which is a gift of Christ animated by the *Spirit*.[7] The fact remains, however, that in this passage it is the Church which is always the active subject of mission, its "office."

It is all the more surprising that after these developments, no doubt theologically inadequate, but clear in the statement that the Church is the ultimate subject involved here, to see the shifts that take place at the beginning of article 6. It sums up the content of the previous paragraph with the expression *hoc munus* (which forms a pair of expressions together with the term *officium*), but the subject is no longer the same: "This responsibility,

---

7. This distinction between "order" and "life" reminds the author of the article by Yves Congar, "The Holy Spirit and the Apostolic College, Promoters of the Work of Christ," *The Mystery of the Church*, trans. A. V. Littledale (2nd ed.; London: Geoffrey Chapman, 1965) 105–45. Even then it left me confused, and I am not convinced that it covers the reality of the Church which is life and institution *at the same time*. For the same reaction, see Hans Urs von Balthasar, *L'Heure de l'Église: Entretien avec Angelo Scola* (Paris: Fayard, 1986) 74.

which the order of bishops, presided over by the Successor of Peter, must accomplish, thanks to the prayer and the cooperation of the whole Church, is one and identical"! Now the subject is the episcopal order, and one does not say any longer "together with" *(una cum)* the Successor of Peter, but one underscores his superior authority with the expression "who presides over" *(cui praeest)*, and there is no more mention of the specific assistance of the priests within the center of the hierarchy of order.[8] As for "the whole Church" (and here we must understand all those who do not belong to the order of bishops, the priests and laity therefore), it makes its contribution by its prayer and its cooperation: it still occupies a position of being a support, but it is no longer the primary subject.

The texts that I have just analyzed, and most especially the last one, manifest a double ambiguity relative to our question. First of all, who fundamentally is the subject of Christian action, the Church presided over by the bishops, assisted by their priests and united to the pope, or the order of bishops under the effective presidency of the pope *(cum Petro et sub Petro)*, and with the possible collaboration of the entire Church? Supposing that we choose the first alternative, is the distinction between the *commandment* of Christ giving rise to a hierarchy and the *life* of Christ communicated to the Church adequate any more? Nevertheless, before considering these questions, we must examine a third ambiguity left by the ecclesiology of Vatican II, which deals with the hierarchical constitution of the Church.

The Hierarchical Constitution of the Church

The title of chapter 3 of Vatican II's Dogmatic Constitution on the Church is somewhat discomfiting. The word "constitution" has a precise literary meaning when it refers to a certain form of the text produced and solemnly promulgated, such as those of recent councils.[9] In itself though, it is a political term which was widely used in the nineteenth and twentieth centuries, with the fall of authoritarian governments, to define the political foundation of a state, by using a foundational text adopted by a parliament. I admit that I am not familiar with the history of its use in ecclesiastical

---

8. We are back in the perspective of Pius XII in his encyclical *Ad Sinarum gentem* of 1954 and the address in Assisi in 1958, which we have already commented on. See above, pp. 61–62.

9. We speak of the "decrees" of the Council of Trent, of the "constitutions" of the First and Second Vatican Councils (though the latter also produced a number of "decrees," apparently enjoying lesser solemnity, as well as "declarations" in cases which treated matters not directly related to Christian practice), and of "bulls," as in the cases of the recent proclamations of Marian dogmas, *Ineffabilis Deus* (1854) and *Munificentissimus Deus* (1950). What are the nuances in these expressions, when it is a matter of the exercise of the extraordinary magisterium of the Church?

texts before the French Revolution or even since then. What is clear is that we begin to find political and administrative terms (e.g., *monarchia, institutum,* etc.) used to speak of the Church, and that in the range of the institutional vocabulary employed in the nineteenth century, the word "constitution" enjoys a special weight. However, I wonder whether the celebrated book of Dom Adrien Gréa, *L'Église et sa divine constitution*[10] was responsible for introducing this modern political term into our ecclesiological discourse. In the title of this book, the adjective "divine" underscores the fact that, if there is a "constitution" of the Church (or as we are wont to say more recently, a "fundamental law"), it comes from God and not from us. We do not vote on it; all we can do is receive it. Up to this point this poses no problems. But what we note is that the word "divine" used by Dom Gréa begins to be replaced by the word "hierarchical," which designates exclusively the structure of the apostolic ministry. If the Church is a totality, a body, a people, shouldn't all of its constitutive elements without exception be considered as "constitutional"? When Pseudo-Dionysius spoke of "hierarchies," he was not only thinking of persons but also of the sacraments and the Scriptures. And when Vatican II, in article 4 of the Dogmatic Constitution on the Church, spoke of "hierarchical gifts" in contradistinction to "charismatic gifts," aren't we supposed to understand the sacraments as belonging to the "hierarchy"? If baptism and confirmation make a Christian, doesn't that person belong to the constitution of the Church, thanks to a "hierarchical gift," even though he or she is not necessarily a member of the "hierarchy of apostolic ministry"? Furthermore, in the case of religious life, we can say that almost from the beginnings of the Church, celibacy, which can be considered the determinative element of religious life (and is clearly attested to in Jesus' words in Matthew 19:12) was understood as a "charismatic gift" that the Church needed if as a whole it was to be fulfilled.[11]

As for the diversity of charisms St. Paul enumerates for us in different lists, which permit the Church to live and to offer its witness, and which in a general way we can call "diaconal charisms," aren't they too essential to the constitution of the Church? On this very subject, when the council in

---

10. Originally published in 1885, it was reissued recently with a preface by Louis Bouyer (Tournai: Casterman, 1965) [translator].

11. If not, we must have recourse to the distinction between "structure" and "life" we examined above (see p. 100, note 7), and which we said was unsatisfactory. "The state of life which is constituted by the profession of the evangelical counsels, though it does not pertain to the hierarchical structure of the Church, clearly does belong to its life and holiness" (LG 44). Religious life also possesses firm structures, as we will have occasion to see in the next chapter. It would be highly simplistic to consider the hierarchy alone as formally defining the constitution of the Church.

chapter 3 tried to define the various tasks of the People of God, it used the categories of priesthood, of prophecy and mission, and even government; in other words, the very ones mentioned in the same chapter to define the specific offices of those who are pastors among the people. We are entitled to deduce from the identity of terms used that what constitutes the People of God is as "constitutional" as the "hierarchical" ministries. On the other hand, this interchangeability of terms creates certain problems in distinguishing concretely between the People of God as a whole and its ministers: who does what and in whose name? The general approach of Vatican II is not sufficiently thought out, and this failure can have grave consequences on the practical level. It risks creating competition among institutions that in reality should converge in mutual support or at the very least benefit from distinctions that permit us to better distinguish among them.

For all these reasons, I think it would have been of greater help had chapter 3 been entitled "The Hierarchical [or better: Ministerial] Aspect of the Constitution of the Church." This change is not insignificant, for if the foundational term "constitution" is immediately qualified by the term "hierarchical," it tends to signify that what is essential for the Church is found in this ministerial structure, while all the rest pertains to the *bene esse*, not the *esse* of the Church, something that is evidently false.[12] Vice versa, if one treats the apostolic ministry like one of the elements of the Church's constitution, the question can be asked anew regarding its exact place in the whole of the constitution and in the ecclesial dynamism that flows from it.[13]

Conclusion

Following this overview of all these ambiguities and uncertainties in the presentation of Vatican II on the Church, we might ask ourselves if they do not arise out of a certain lack of appreciation and failure to stress the gift par excellence which Jesus gave to his Church after the resurrection—the Holy Spirit. Thus, holiness is the gift par excellence of the Spirit and at the same time the ultimate vocation of the Church. And mission, too, is attributable to the Spirit, who at the same time inspires the whole body of the Church, the different missionary initiatives in regards to their goals as well as their institutional forms, regardless of their origin in the People of God,

12. Likewise, there is the real danger that such a hierarchical structure will not be considered formally in its "sacramental" understanding, i.e., the primary meaning of "hierarchical," and justified in this case because the sacrament of order is what is constitutive, but more from its immediately "constitutional" aspect, viz., its "power" before, outside of, and above the sacrament.

13. On the manifold of issues involved, see the judicious reflections of Libero Gerosa on the significance of the categories "institution" and "constitution" in the Church in *Carisma e Diritto nella Chiesa* (Milan, 1989) 108–25.

and the dynamic responsibility of the episcopal college presided over by the Bishop of Rome. Finally, the ministerial aspect of the constitution of the Church (even if its institution is from Christ) must be concretized over the passing of time by the movement of the Spirit who inspires the process of discernment and the necessary decisions to be taken, and who articulates the episcopal ministry among the other diaconal ministries in the Church. In order to understand better the vocation of the Church, its mission, its various institutions, with pride of place given to its sacramental life, I think we can profit from a reexamination of this manifold of issues in light of a theology of the Spirit in the Church. Here are a few indications by way of a possible outline.

On the Spirit and Institution in the Church

The preceding observations bring us to a deeper reflection on the fundamental ministry of holiness and mission in the Church, the ministry of the Holy Spirit. Whenever the Church tries to define itself, it rediscovers the One who is the "social bond," the author of its communion and its coherence, the One who permits it to contemplate itself in its totality as organic, holy, and missionary, the One who is at the origin of all its actions and was formerly called the soul of the Church. Our concern will be to consider if we can adopt a more highly articulated perspective on this ministry of the Holy Spirit, in order to implement in a better way the fundamental intuitions of chapters 1 and 2 of the Dogmatic Constitution on the Church. This reflection will help us cover the diverse levels of life in the Church without separating them: the fundamental and constant presence of the Spirit in the whole of the Church; the various types of gifts ("charisms") which concretize this presence; the levels of truth, of sacrament, and of institution which these gifts make possible and which in turn invest them with human depth.

The Might of the Spirit

In order to conduct such an investigation, I would like to start with the notion of *might*, to see if it is true that the Spirit appears first of all as "might," according to the Jerusalem Bible.[14] Such *might* is the source of the

14. See the long footnote on Acts 1:8, where it is noted that the word "might" *(puissance)* is used here with connotations that have their origin more in the word "strength" *(force)* than in "power" *(pouvoir)*, even if it remains true that "power" is one (but not the only) manifestation of the "might" of the Spirit. [The somewhat archaic word "might" which I am using to translate *puissance* better communicates the meaning of divine power. The English word "power" often connotes a right which comes externally to a person or a person's capacity to coerce others. The French *puissance* connotes more an

holiness and the dynamisms that run through the Church; the *might* of the Spirit is like a dynamic link that keeps the Church in holiness and unity and that comes to expression in its various gifts.

The Church's "social being" is permeated by the *might* to be transformed and to reform itself, not first of all by reason of criteria founded in reason (even if there were such criteria) but by reason of the very dynamism that constitutes it. This very *might* is at the same time immanent because it dwells in the Church, and transcendent because its source is and remains the Spirit of God. It initiates acts of witness, of mission and of challenge to humanity wherever the gospel is announced and established among peoples. In reality, it is the Spirit's *might* that manifests great diversity and is constantly being realized in mission. We need to attend to these multiple manifestations in order to discern the origin of the Church's "social being" and learn how to promote this movement by bold supervision and energetic implementation.

Might and Charisms

An Approach to Charisms

Perhaps this is the place to be more precise and say that the manifestations of the Spirit's influence are the *charisms* of the Church, on condition that we give the word its primitive meaning of "gifts of the Spirit," diverse yet originating from the same living root—the "might" of the Spirit.[15] For historical and theological reasons, the word "charism" has not yet found its proper place. Sometimes it is used in opposition to "ministry," where the latter is given a signification derived from the reception of the sacrament of order, and sometimes in opposition to "institution," where this term is used in a political and juridical sense. Both forms of opposition seem to be bound to the Gregorian form of the Church already discussed. Thus, charism is characterized by activities in the Church that do not arise from either the "power of order" or the "power of jurisdiction," but are found where there is no connection with a sacrament or where the Church's jurisdictional authority (and here we are talking essentially about the pope's)

internal quality which founds a person's capacity to influence others or change situations. Formerly, we referred often to "Almighty God," and that form of address accurately reflects the distinction Lafont is trying to make. See Gerhard Friedrich, *Exegetical Dictionary of the New Testament,* vol. 1, eds. Horst Balz and Gerhard Schneider (Grand Rapids, Mich.: Eerdmans, 1990), s.v. "*dynamis,* power, might," 355–58. A helpful article in English on this matter is John A. Coleman's "Authority, Power, Leadership: Sociological Understandings," *New Theology Review* 10 (3) (August 1997) 31–44. [Translator.]

15. For "charisms" we can almost substitute the word "hierarchies," which I proposed earlier should be expanded beyond its narrowly Neoplatonic and juridical meaning.

has not yet begun to exercise control. Since the Gregorian form does not leave much room for such free activity to find room to express itself, except in a very provisional way, "charism" necessarily has come to take on a marginal meaning, given the narrow gap it is permitted to occupy. It is found primarily in expressions that reveal a "spirit of opposition" and a "spirit of claiming rights," or it appears as a "spirit of devotion" in contexts that make few claims. As a "spirit of opposition" it emerges in history whenever the sacramental is opposed to the institutional, or the Bible is opposed to holiness.[16] As a "spirit of claiming rights" it emerges at moments when persons who have no access to orders or jurisdiction but desire to have a role in the Church lay claims to such (and not entirely without justification) but remain stuck in the framework of "powers" and functions to be performed. Moreover, because the Gregorian form smacks of an "imperial" Church, those opposed to it necessarily demand a "democratic" Church.

Charism, Institution, Power

In order to avoid thinking of charisms in this destructive way of inherent opposition to institutions, it is necessary to look deeper into the reality of the "influence of the Spirit." The latter is found both in sacramental liturgy as well as in the search for holiness, in missionary initiatives as well as in the institution of law and rights, in the confession of the faith as well as in catechetical and theological research. Every initiative of the Spirit, i.e., *charism,* gives rise to some *institution,* to some expression or organization in space and time, however tenuous, in the concrete life of the Church's communion.[17] Moreover, the institution of a charism implies a certain *power* which is proportional to the goal pursued.[18]

All of the above is a retrieval of St. Paul's teaching on charisms: as soon as the Spirit imparts a gift, we can speak of an institution that is more or less permanent or more or less passing. Even the sacraments come from the influence of the Spirit and reciprocally give access to the Spirit. In the Church, such a way of looking at things leads to constant vigilance and to a certain flexibility, even in areas that seem the most fixed. It accounts for a certain climate where lively attentiveness leads to a tempering of rigidity

16. On the question of "reform" and its historical forms, see my *Histoire théologique de l'Église catholique. Itinéraire et formes de la théologie* (Paris: Cerf, 1994) 138–42 and 223–25.

17. In the course of our study, we will examine the multiple relations between institution and sacrament.

18. I have examined this question apropos of religious life in "L'Esprit Saint et le Droit dans l'institution religieuse," *Le Supplément,* nos. 82 and 83 (1967) 473–501 and 594–639. See also Libero Gerosa, *Carisma e Diritto nella Chiesa* (Milan, 1989) 205–42, where he considers new movements in the Church.

and so helps maintain a spirit of cohesiveness and consistency. If there is Church in the sense of a body and a people, it is this "social being," transfused by holiness and *might,* and by the gifts that are both hierarchical (i.e., articulated and ordered among themselves and in the structure of the body) and charismatic (i.e., marked by the Spirit in their origin, form, and goal), that makes this holiness and *might* concrete.

I propose the following distinction between gifts, together with their institutions and powers and if necessary the sacraments connected with them: those arising from *states in life,* more or less directly connected with the holiness and the humanity of the Church; those arising from *diakonia,* i.e., from the ensemble of the Church's service to the gospel; and those arising from *presidency,* i.e., from governing the Church as a whole and from "moderating" the gifts found in it. With this last gift we have found our way back to the apostolic ministry.[19] Let me say from the start that such a reflection on charisms, one that proceeds from the Spirit and gives birth to institutions, would by its very nature eliminate the ambiguities noted above.

In the trinitarian vision of the Dogmatic Constitution on the Church, the Church as a whole is made holy by the Spirit's gift of the Body and Blood of Christ and by the diversified institutions according to the states in life that support this gift of holiness. The whole Church is the subject of mission, thanks to the ensemble of *diakoniai* ("services") stirred up by the Spirit in the body of Christ, under the impetus and presidency of those who have received the charism of apostolic ministry by sacramental consecration. Finally, everything that has its source in the gift of the Spirit—holiness, charism, sacrament—belongs to the Church's constitution, albeit for different but mutually reinforcing reasons.[20]

---

19. The following three chapters will deal with these three generic gifts to the Church and can also serve as divisions for a text on canon law that would deal with the Church as a structured communion. The introduction to such a text would speak of the Eucharist as both the source and the fulfillment of the charismatic life of the Church, while the conclusion would make allusion to what eludes the grasp of canon law but which accounts for the latter's very existence: the Church's attentive awaiting of the parousia of Christ.

20. In what follows, the reader will come across many ideas and proposals that are not at all original and that have been treated fully elsewhere, including a few documents originating from the Holy See. Likewise, many of my observations are already realities in the life of the Church. What is perhaps of interest in my presenting this reprise of the whole area is found in the principle inspiring all the individual elements: charisms are instituted by the Spirit. Far from intending to oppose Spirit, Word, Sacrament, and Law, I will try to coordinate all of them by starting with the very first one: the Holy Spirit is the gift of the risen Christ so that the Church might live from the gospel and become a spiritual sacrifice. My purpose is to propose a theological perspective of the whole, designated by the term "structured communion" and imbued with the idea of "institutionalized charism."

Chapter 5

Charisms of the Christian Life: Spiritualities and States in Life

Conversion is at the very beginning of Christian existence. It is an interior reality, the fruit of an understanding enlightened by the Spirit and of a freedom enlivened by the Spirit's grace, that results from listening to the witness to Jesus Christ by the Church. The Church's confession of Jesus Christ takes bodily form in the acts of Christian initiation, baptism and confirmation, i.e., in a person being incorporated into the death and resurrection of Christ and the permanent gift of the Spirit. The sequence of Spirit–Word–Sacrament is an indivisible one. Two sacraments impart a "character," a term that is meant to express the fact that the essential gifts of God, or one might say the double mission of the Son and the Father, are permanent, and that there is no need to repeat them since, at this foundational level, they will never be retracted. In a word, the Christian is "marked" by them forever. The Church is the paschal and pneumatic community of all those who have passed through this process of initiation, where interior movement and visible gesture in essence overlap one another.

The Christian act associated with this stage of initiation is the communal celebration of the memorial of the death and resurrection of Christ, which both stirs up and includes the spiritual sacrifice of Christians, i.e., their interior union with God and their concern for one another, manifested in mission, service, and compassion. In the one body of Christ, these are the contexts in which different spiritualities take shape and appear as various charisms, all determining the institutions proper to each.

It is important to speak about *spiritualities* in this context. Their various forms are not foreign to the constitution of the Church. On the contrary. A spirituality is a certain understanding of the gospel, so that by the process of selection and ordering of its values a definite style of life emerges. A spirituality is justified by the infinite richness of the gospel, so that no one form of evangelical life in time and space can measure up to it. And yet, the parameters of time and space condition cultures, so that it is from them that we grasp one or more aspects of the gospel which are receptive to, but also open to being purified and transfigured by specific states of culture. That is why the Spirit inspires "points of view" that are both contemplative and practical for the Church's understanding and implementing of the gospel in a given time or for a defined cultural space. In this sense, a spirituality is a charism that is sometimes given to a "spiritual master" and sometimes to a group of persons in the Church, so that an institution takes form, made up of Christians who feel at home in this spirituality and who desire to help one another along their common way.

The essence of the Church is given both in the Eucharist, where the spiritual sacrifices of Christians gathered for the memorial of the sacrifice of Jesus Christ are found, and in the Church's spiritualities, the unceasing movement of the Spirit in the hearts of Christians leading them in the way of the gospel. But this essence is lived out concretely in structured and ordered communities where the Spirit and the Sacrament are at work. It is incumbent on us now to turn our attention to such communities where we find the "hierarchical and charismatic gifts" spoken of by the council (LG 4).

Descriptive Account

First of all, regarding the holiness of the Church, we find the charisms which determine the *states in life* for Christians, viz., marriage and the "monastic state."[1] It is a matter of there being two different but mutually ordered ways for the same spiritual sacrifice of Christians, since in terms of their being fulfilled in the Spirit no distinction among the commandments of the Lord is possible. All Christians are called to live them out. The call to holiness is universal. The distinction is not on the level of the call or of the response in the delicate playing out of the Spirit and the Law, as we saw earlier. We are dealing with a twofold institution which, on the level of a person's sexuality, establishes a definite plan of existence that is ultimately left up to each one to choose.

Human Situations

Sexuality

We need to pause for a moment to consider the reality of sexuality, since when all is said and done it is the ultimate reason for distinguishing

---

1. I use the word "monastic" in the most generic sense to signify every state in life marked by a person's engagement with celibacy, whatever concrete form it takes and however more precisely the way of being engaged is defined.

among the states in life. Sexuality is the area of human life where we face the greatest mystery, where we have an immediate experience of desires directed toward another—the desire for love, for encounter, for communication; and self-reflected desire—the desire for pleasure, for tenderness, for recognition; and desire open to birth: the desire for children. In sexuality we have a certain perception of our own body as sentient and therefore as the place where all our human encounters occur, and perhaps too our encounter with the divine. For all its immediacy, the experience of sexuality remains obscure and evokes real fear in the face of a perception that seems so obvious but remains opaque. The origins of this propulsion of sexual desire remain hidden and we feel incapable of mastering and directing it because we do not know the coordinates by which it operates. The difference of the sexes, so obscure and so menacing, frightens us, even though it is related to what we feel intensely and is closest to us. We experience fear, too, in the face of encountering our self or another, since we learn the art of self-comportment only with great difficulty. Again, we fear the violence of our own desire manifested as the desire for another. But there is also fear of being deceived physically or humanly in our expectations of a sexual relationship. Even the fruitfulness of sexuality, the object of so much joy, shows itself to be a strange phenomenon that defies complete mastery. On the one hand, it is more profound than any form of human output or technique, because its fruit is another human being, but it is also terribly obscure, because we have so little control over its workings.

If we were to go deeper into our analysis, we could say that the mystery of sexuality comes from a close connection between sex and death. Can it be that they are related to one another like nature and culture? Sex enjoys the immediacy of meaning, of desire, of pleasure; death is a law imposed on this immediacy so that it might be humanized. How can we articulate these two so that sex does not remain savage, and death does not stifle and destroy our life but instead channels it?

All cultures have tried to articulate this paradoxical encounter of sex and death, or in more spiritualized terms, of love and law, though great care must be taken to avoid the process of spiritualizing sexuality and thus forgetting its truly sentient character. The forms of equilibrium that have been proposed are more or less stable or rigid depending on how far they extend into the milieu of one's sexual life: family, possessions, money, urban life. For more than a century, sociologists have tried to show the connections between all these domains and possibly their ultimate foundation in the difference of the sexes and its fruitfulness. In this sense, the famous title of Friedrich Engel's book *L'Origine de la famille, de la propriété privée et de l'État* shows the effectively close connection between these elements and human life, even if his effort at systematizing calls for considerable reservation. Nevertheless, if cultures have tried to regulate human sexual life and all that flows from it, each person needs to undertake his or her own long, and possibly never-ending education in this area.

Sexual Life and Human Existence

In the case of marriage, a couple is formed, including everything that leads to a certain style of living the gospel and to its place in society. In a family, through one's work, where one lives, one's country, the necessity of having resources, one's social relations, etc., all of this accounts for the way a person pursues the gospel, so that the process of discernment remains a constant encounter of the gospel with the concrete circumstances of one's life. In this state in life, the gospel both inspires and is in turn marked by one's use of time and space in the here and now, but also in the genealogical past one has received, as well as in the future that emerges from the creation of offspring.

In the case of "monastic" life, it is a matter of a solitary life, i.e., a life in which celibacy is determinative and in which spatiotemporal relations show themselves in a different way. The celibate brings a genealogy to an end and leaves behind no offspring to carry on. This colors in an essential way his or her present relation to the human and the cosmic milieus: residence, work, resources, social relations—all continue to exist but in a different way and with an evangelical impact that is formed differently. Experience works here in a double way: the one, more immediately spiritual, gives its undivided attention to awaiting the reign of God, in offering itself so completely as to include even one's body in the search for union with God, for life in God's presence. The experience of the Church, and maybe, too, of truly religious non-Christian men and women, e.g., Mohandas Gandhi (1869–1948), also shows the affinity of celibacy with a life spent in search of God. Then there is the no less real affinity between celibacy and the apostolic and missionary life, so that the sense of urgency in proclaiming the gospel, of being of service to humanity, of the Church's mission, etc., is so great that one cannot even imagine it without consecrating oneself to it exclusively.

Both states in life are marked by a spirituality, and experience proves that the greatest among them inspire both lay people and religious. However, the monk's more reduced place in the world opens up a certain immediateness of the impact of the gospel in this state in life and defines a proper way of being in relation—with oneself, with and for others, and with God and human realities. This style is in some sense objective, "corporal" according to the Fathers of the Church, so that we can acknowledge its relative "superiority" vis-à-vis the married state. What is really important, however, is to recognize that in both cases it is a matter of the "charismatic" character of one and the other, i.e., the Christian is invited to embrace the state in life God offers him or her and to live out of the grace proper to each vocation. Recognizing this fact is important from an ecclesial point of view: the whole Church is the People of God and the body of Christ, and that means that a naive sense of wonder on the part of the married for celibate religious on the one hand, and on the other hand a slight superiority complex on the part of the latter vis-à-vis the married, quite possibly tinged with a trace of jealousy, cannot help but hinder the awareness in the Church of this communion of charisms, and the fact that it is each one's task to find the way to become truly Christian and truly human.

The Choice of a State in Life

Vocation

A person's choice of a state in life corresponds to a charism, and we can better understand its meaning if we identify it with the more current term "vocation."[2] One's vocation is not a purely interior movement, something a bit nebulous. One's vocation is not a privilege of some Christians who feel themselves called to a life of celibacy for the gospel. No, it is a movement of the Spirit that attracts a person to a concrete state in life, corporally and socially determined, whether it is marriage or celibacy. Every Christian who has been initiated into the death and resurrection of Christ is effectively in some way "dead to the world" in which he or she must still live, and already participates in the new creation in a way that is incumbent on him or her to manifest and realize in the world. When St. Paul says that there is no more Greek or Jew, slave or free (see Gal 3:28), he is trying to express a sort of fundamental indifference to human situations or their neutral quality in regard to the work of salvation, in as much as they have not yet been taken up into the life of the Spirit. St. Ignatius of Loyola (1491–1556) joins such basic indifference regarding the states and conditions of life with the desire to discern what will contribute most to a life of service to the Lord, and makes them into a "principle and foundation" in his *Spiritual Exercises*. For Ignatius, the process consists of discerning, choosing, and consenting to the way God is calling a person, and thus the "charism" of one's state in life. In this sense, the two ways defined on the basis of

2. I am trying to imagine the best scenario, viz., when a person humbly searches for the will of God with respect to his or her life. I am quite aware that for many people the question is never asked, and perhaps cannot be asked, in these terms. A person marries often enough without really knowing why, and without even reflecting on the meaning of one's romantic inclination on the whole of one's life; or, as is becoming more and more the case in our world, a person remains celibate because no other alternative presents itself.

engaging in sexual activity or abstaining from it are on the same level: they receive their value from the fact that both are gift and vocation and come from the Spirit. Although in different ways, both are images of the union of Christ and the Church, and both are to be lived out of the reality of evangelical detachment and practice.

Freedom, Promise, Liturgy

Both states in life are marked by Christian freedom, because of the inspiration of the Spirit. In the beginning, freedom is signified by an act of a person's consenting, which has the properly human characteristic of engaging time and a priori fashioning its future form. This consent is a promise of fidelity. Ordinarily, far from imprisoning the person, it makes it possible for liberty to ripen, through life's joys and trials. Because the consent is Christian, marked by the paschal mystery of Jesus and bearing in its own way the image of Christ's relationship to the Father and to humanity, we can understand why the Church recognized the sacramental quality of marriage. But it is harder to understand why it did not do so for the act of consenting, vowed or not, to live out the condition of a monk. The latter, too, is a condition in which the gospel life is lived out, as indicated by Jesus Christ (who, in the gospel, speaks of marriage and celibacy together). The acts of consenting and promising are made in a liturgical context; and one can hope that the grace of the Spirit will accompany each one's calling and response. Jesus did not marry, and we venerate the *Virgin* Mary; thus, both the unique Mediator and the woman who is icon of the Church reveal and manifest to us the transfigured reality of virginity. Without calling into question the symbolism of the *seven* sacraments, I think it is incumbent on the Church to promote in a better way the liturgical significance of virginity in the Church, and not only in the canonical forms of religious life (and no longer bound to the priesthood either), but also the state of virginal consecration in the world, even without any particular canonical form.

Two Proposals

The council restored the possibility of the consecration of virgins, but only for women. Can we not imagine an analogous liturgy for men? The reason for such a liturgy fashioned for women makes some sense. If every human being knows a primal enclosure, viz., the umbilical cord, symbol of one's autonomy and the condition of communication with the other,[3] woman as virgin is even more sexually "cloistered." The liturgical consecration as it were seals this specific enclosure of the body, making her a sign of the exclusive openness of a woman consecrated to Jesus Christ. I think there

---

3. See Denis Vasse, *L'Ombilic et la Voix. Deux enfants en analyse* (Paris: Seuil, 1974).

is something quite accurate in this, something very human and really symbolic. I invariably feel ill at ease when the corporal aspects of the Christian mystery, be it the virginity of Mary, or the bodily resurrection of Christ, or consecrated virginity, are rejected when the expression "biological" is applied to them, thereby implying something that is judged to be inferior or insignificant. Corporeality is the mark of the human through and through, and the symbolism does not consist in negating it in favor of the "spiritual" which it serves to signify, but rather to directing it by employing the particular forms that transform it without excluding it. There is, therefore, a real "biological" foundation to the consecration of virgins, and I suppose that consecrated women know this not only in their minds and in their hearts, but also in their bodies. That said, we still need to reflect more deeply on what virginity represents for the experience of men. It is not a matter of sexual enclosure "from entering," as though keeping the physical space closed is the symbol of something being reserved for God; but rather of an enclosure "from leaving" ("continence"[4]), in as much as the retention of one's semen is the symbol of a change in the orientation of one's living forces. Why should this male symbolism, like that of female virginity, not be open to being solemnized liturgically?

Somewhat marginal to my arguing for its liturgical character, we should also foster the experience of temporary virginity, whether in the provisional form of monastic practice with a view to allowing one's understanding of the Christian mystery to mature, or as an overture to full-time apostolic and missionary activity. The exercise of certain charisms for the life of the Church and its testimony can make it possible for a person to give himself or herself exclusively to them for varying periods of time and in a form that can be repeated.

Institutional Elements

Persons engage themselves by becoming involved in a group: this is often true in the case of married persons[5] and almost always for religious. In other words, a person's charism–vocation leads to participation in a communal expression of this charism–vocation, unless it follows from it directly. Every charism of state in life gives rise to institutional forms, as we just saw in the case of a liturgical expression for one's engagement. I would

4. The author seems to be adverting to the fact that in French, and we can add in English, the noun "continence" is derived etymologically from the Latin verb *continere*, to keep or retain [translator].

5. Groups such as Marriage Encounter, various Franciscan and Dominican fraternities, and scores of other groups which meet in more limited circumstances such as a parish, a small community, a campus study group, etc., are just a few examples of this principle.

like to comment on two other sectors of human activity, which might be called "the understanding of the faith and action" and forms of organization.

Intellectus fidei et actionis

The charisms of state in life are not disconnected from the human reality in which they are embedded. If we do not ignore the sexual difference in which they are rooted and their provenance in a culture as a whole, it becomes clear that the concrete life of a charism in the world presupposes reflection in faith, an encounter with the culture, together with its growth, progress, and deviations. All this leaves plenty of room for what can be called the *intellectus fidei et actionis,* i.e., the reflection required if a person is to live out his or her state in life in a given set of circumstances.

I speak in this context of an *intellectus fidei et actionis* first of all to highlight the fact that the gift of the Spirit in the processes of discernment, welcoming, and implementation is primary in respect to any reflection the recipient can bring to developing its promises; and vice versa, that the gift of the Spirit includes a capacity to perceive, at the heart of the Christian tradition and in its openness to the further developments of a culture, the necessary solution to any problems that might arise. In other words, we can say that *doctrine* is found in the act of *giving witness* and not vice versa, or that *understanding* is given in faith and action and not the opposite.[6]

I will concentrate more on the state in life defined by marriage and life in the world, leaving to the next section a consideration of religious life. But the accent on the married state is not meant to be exclusive, though it is to some extent justified, as we shall see. If Vatican II, in article 31 of the Dogmatic Constitution on the Church, says apropos of the laity that "it is their responsibility in a special way to illuminate and order all temporal realities" in order to bring them into the kingdom of God, then it follows that they will meet their proper gift and inalienable responsibility in concretely *thinking through* human values and honestly *facing* the problems they pose. The state in life has its own autonomy, and those who live it out do not only have the task of doing something ("ordering" reality according to Vatican II), but even more of thinking through and talking about it ("illuminating" reality according to Vatican II). We will need to imagine (or give new life to) such institutions as well as their more precise norms, i.e., by determining the limits to welcoming a new culture (a welcome which with its limits necessarily takes forms that are pluralistic and so somewhat

---

6. We will have occasion to study this formula more closely later in chapter 7, pp. 195–97. References to the laity in the documents of Vatican II can be found in *Concile Oecuménique Vatican II. Constitutions. Décrets. Déclarations. Messages* (Paris: Centurion, 1976) 851.

antagonistic). *This effort of imagination and reflection will have to be conducted precisely by those who have received responsibility for the gospel and for the human in all the sectors it touches.* To react in this way is nothing more than having confidence in the Spirit who is responsible for the charisms of life in the world and who is also the Creator Spirit who does not deny inspiration to those called. It means no less than acknowledging the autonomy of created values which, as we saw in chapter 1, define an authentic modernity. This autonomy includes the *responsibility to reason,* whereas the gift of the Spirit facilitates the exercise of this responsibility in truth and not by whatever meets our fancy. A wonderful encounter takes place between the gift of the Creator Spirit and the inspiration of the Covenant Spirit. It is the same Spirit who creates the human occasions and then hands over the world to our power, who also inspires in us the way for their just use and, in the broken world we find ourselves in, for the progressive return to a truth that is practical and makes our history authentic.

In other terms, if the clergy were formerly the only ones who were literate and capable of dealing with complicated financial matters, such is no longer the case today. Something is askew when "matters of the Church's doctrine" in areas like sexuality, the family, economics, social justice, and political options are formulated by a magisterium that is clerical, episcopal, and papal, i.e., is exercised by persons who normally do not participate in these activities, who have no immediate experience of them, and who (and I believe history will bear this out) have demonstrated a practical judgment that was neither constant[7] nor relevant. My intent is not to deprive the ecclesiastical magisterium of its right to indicate the general lines that emerge directly from the gospel and that have been reaffirmed again and again by Christian tradition, but to suggest that, in those domains that are indivisibly human and spiritual, the process of reflection should stem from reason enlightened by the faith of those who are directly involved rather

---

7. In his encyclical *Vix pervenit,* Pope Benedict XIV (1740–58) did not seem to grasp the complexity of the problem of the use of credit in modern society. A century later, after taking the necessary precautions, Leo XIII (1878–1903) founded what can be called a bank within the Vatican, while he sought to control real estate in the neighborhood of St. Peter's. In principle, he did not act improperly in either initiative, but he clearly had a different perception of money and credit than his predecessor. In particular, the famous notion that money "by nature" was unproductive could no longer be held in all intellectual honesty without certain distinctions. The concept though, at least in principle, governed the official attitude of the Church up to recent times, and created many a crisis of conscience among Christians that could have been avoided if they had been given the responsibility and the challenge to think for themselves in their business dealings.

than from an "illumination" from above.[8] This procedure would better respect the economy of a Church that is structured communion.

In order to make my proposal more concrete, I would like to suggest that institutions that formerly flourished but have fallen little by little into disuse, especially those which were animated by the laity, including seminars, research centers, and curricula leading to academic degrees, should be resurrected and ways found for broadly publishing the results of their work.[9] In the area that has always been the subject of controversy, but even more so today, viz., sexuality, recourse to the laity can help resolve the problem of what might be called "double truth": on the one hand, the proclamation from above of one "doctrine" that does not take into account particular cases and so risks not only appearing impractical but of looking like it contests what it is even trying to express of the truth of the human condition; and on the other, the concrete advice, necessarily from clerics, that one receives in the semidarkness of the confessional or in the office of the bishop. To use the category of "law" in the way developed in chapter 3, the truth of an act issues from the law which determines its content and the law which prescribes relations, and the latter are always eminently concrete, never idealized. Moral truth, both as general definition and its concrete determination, can never be reduced to an abstraction in either of its dimensions. Perhaps those who struggle to live them out are in the best position to understand them and to talk about them.[10] I believe that in this domain, and in similar ones, the necessary and beneficial control of the hierarchical magisterium should be exercised first of all locally, since situations are not the same everywhere and therefore the application of principles cannot be identical. Without even speaking about general principles, the concrete elements for appreciating the moral law will be applicable in one situation but will not figure in another. Let us be clear: in the area of human existence more than in the domain of the evangelical faith nothing is ever simple. Christians need to be treated responsibly both in what they do and in what they say, and to learn to have confidence in the Spirit living in them. In the final analysis, they need the truth of the gospel.

8. Everything I maintained earlier about the Church and dialogue is important here. In all these areas, different ways of understanding questions can contribute to the probability of the justice of certain actions, or simply to seeing concrete realities better at any given time and place.

9. In fact, recently certain movements have been modestly resumed in France: "Concurrence et solidarité" (1991) and "Les médias et nous" (1993).

10. See the collection *Désirer un enfant. Enjeux éthiques des procréations médicalement assistées: des chrétiens s'expriment* (Paris: Centurion, 1994).

Organization

The third element that expresses and maintains a charism is institutional, viz., a body of rules. In the beginning, they have often been established by the authority of an individual or a founding group, tested in the common life of the group, taken up again and again, interpreted, and commented on by succeeding generations of men and women who received the same vocation from God. Such persons were truly qualified to continue the tradition, i.e., to bring about "negative reform" by eliminating abuses, attending to laxities, correcting directions taken that were not faithful to the essential charism, and by promoting needed adaptations without which the charism would no longer have any real impact in the world and in a Church that had changed.[11] Certain precise institutions, e.g., councils, chapters, assemblies, are established to institutionally test and promote the charism. Here is where we meet a characteristic aspect of life in the Church (even if in widespread areas it had unfortunately fallen into desuetude up to very recent times): the *rights* of a group (its rules, statutes, etc.) are elaborated and written by the members themselves.

Authority

If the structure of a community defining a state in life is organized by its members thanks to their charism, the community itself is animated by someone who has received the gift from the Spirit in a particular way. Institutional authority is spiritual in principle and in its exercise. For example, the responsibility of parents to educate their children is connected with their condition of being a family. But where it is a question of Christian holiness for a group, even more needs to be said about institutional responsibility. The normal mode of designating the persons responsible is *election:* they are chosen from the members of the community and by them. Only they have the spiritual, juridical, and human elements necessary not to make arbitrary decisions or even purely human ones, but to discern by way of reflection, exchanges of points of view, and votes taken in the communities, what the Spirit is suggesting and which persons the Spirit is designating.

Finally, the initiative of the institution and the elements of law which correspond to it, including authority, come from the spiritual charism that generates the institution. What is the role of other responsible persons, not of the communities this time, but of the Church, viz., the bishops and the pope? Simply put, to test, and if necessary modify (perhaps because of internal

---

11. The reader is referred to various works by Gerald Arbuckle on the process of refounding. See *Out of Chaos: Refounding Religious Congregations* (New York: Paulist, 1988) and *Refounding the Church: Dissent for Leadership* (Maryknoll, New York: Orbis, 1993) [translator].

inconsistencies, or in view of a better articulation of the community with other institutions in the Church), and finally to approve of official texts. It might include, but does not have to, the right to approve of elections.[12] Such acts give institutions born of charisms relative to a state in life a certain "public" character in the Church, but they do not constitute it.[13]

The Stability of the Charisms of State in Life: Considerations and Problems

In the case of persons and the appropriate institution, whether of married or the celibate life, the characteristic should be strict stability, or what is more technically called *indissolubility*.[14] I am going to plead my case that this institutional rigor be so reformed that it is *equally applicable to all Christians*. In the concrete juridical practice of the Church there seem to be various gradations of strictness, and this is especially true in the case of marriage, owing to the fact that the Church does not admit it has the right to dissolve an indissoluble commitment, and this both in regard to the natural law governing marriage and as a sacramental institution in the Church. It follows that divorced and remarried Catholics who persist publicly in

---

12. If elections are conducted with regularity and in accord with the community's rule and general law, we can assume that the Spirit has been active in the process, and further confirmation really adds nothing to it. The bishop's role is rather to be available as an instance of recourse should there be a case of abuse or of intervention should a community not be able to arrive at agreement. This is what St. Benedict foresaw for example in chapter 64 of the *Rule*.

13. Actual canonical language is much more "directive," since it comes from the Gregorian form of the Church, according to which it is inconceivable that "power" does not come from a "higher" authority. However, in the case of the form of structured community I have been developing, it makes more sense to distinguish between public law "by constitution" which corresponds to the global structures of the Church (which I will return to below), and public law "by confirmation." In the latter case, initiative is not due to the bishops or the Holy See, but to those whom God raises up for a definite form of life. I have examined these ideas in "L'Esprit Saint et le Droit dans l'institution religieuse," *Le Supplément*, no. 83 (1967) 616–19. Libero Gerosa, *Carisma e Diritto nella Chiesa* (Milan, 1989) develops similar thoughts. The *motu proprio* of Paul VI on the application of conciliar texts *Ecclesiae sanctae* (August 6, 1966) gave wide autonomy to religious institutes in the reform of their constitutions, but their full and effective recognition presupposes a non-Gregorian theology of the Church. The text of *Ecclesiae sanctae* can be found in *Acta Apostolicae Sedis* 58 (1966) 757–87. E. T. Austin Flannery, ed. *Vatican Council II: The Conciliar and Post Conciliar Documents* (rev. ed.; Dublin: Dominican Publications, 1987) 591–610; 624–33; 857–62 [Study Edition].

14. I will speak of the charisms of state in life from the Catholic perspective on sexuality. Nevertheless, at the end of the chapter I will make several remarks regarding some questions on these matters.

this situation which can be called objectively sinful do not have the right of access to the sacraments of penance and the Eucharist. Less strict, though still serious, is the case of priestly celibacy, since a dispensation may or may not be given, and in any case it implies that a priest desist from all priestly activity, i.e., from the effective exercise of the responsibilities tied to the sacrament of order. In the case of women religious and male religious who are not ordained, the strictness in application is practically nullified, since a dispensation from vows is almost always given within the ordinary time intervals. Isn't there something amiss and unjust in the way these different cases are handled? Isn't it possible that it could be less strict for married persons and even for priests, but should be stricter for religious?

Marriage

Indissolubility and Instability

With regard to marriage, there is no question here of my contesting its indissolubility in nature and in the Christian economy. The very least that can be said is that the record of the past century in the various states that legally permit divorce is not a positive one. The mentality of viewing marriage as a "provisional situation" has established itself to the point that cohabitation without any reciprocal public commitment of the parties has become widespread. The idea that divorce, even if it is to be regretted, is the normal solution to problems, has weakened the courage of spouses in those moments when they must face serious difficulties and when a spirit of extending forgiveness and reconciliation should be the necessary and beneficial rhythm of life together. But today couples choose separation for reasons that not too long ago hardly seemed insurmountable. Separation and remarriage do not always bring the stable happiness that eluded one in the first marriage. Doubtless, the struggle for fidelity and stability in marriage is a principal element in a person's building his or her personality, which cannot happen if one refuses to accept the difference of the other person, his or her mystery, and nontransgressible limits. Some such clash with others is necessary for knowing oneself and one's pain. When one consents to such a struggle, one discovers hidden resources in oneself— compassion, forgiveness, gratitude. As for the children of divorced couples, even if their situation is sometimes healthier than when they lived together in one household and where their parents remained together but led a life of hell, their affective equilibrium is rendered fragile and their conditions in life are disturbed, e.g., in school and in their upbringing. Their wound is always deep, their instability increased, even in those somewhat rare cases where their separated parents have made the utmost effort to lessen the tragedy that the divorce means for their children. Maybe the sentiments felt and the inevitable tragedy of the situation, tied to an understanding of marriage as "provisional," accounts for the later decision not to have children: why subject innocent children to such suffering, if one cannot be certain of assuring the family stability they need?

"Excommunication"[15] and Pastoral Work

I trust that I have explicitly and firmly made my position clear: I reject any ambiguous accommodation regarding the indissolubility of marriage. Now, I would like to examine two questions that are posed in this context. The first concerns the exclusion of divorced persons from the Eucharist and from the sacrament of reconciliation. The second, perhaps more risky question, concerns the procedures employed for recognizing the nullity of a marriage.[16]

Penance and the Eucharist

The practice in vigor flows from a general principle of moral and sacramental theology: if someone lives in adultery and will not renounce this state, that person remains in sin and cannot be admitted to the sacrament of reconciliation and consequently to the Eucharist as well. In other words, in the case of persons remarrying after being divorced, the couple is not united in the sacrament of marriage, since they are still bound sacramentally by their ties to the spouses from whom they have been separated. In this case they are considered to be living in adultery and are not admitted to the two sacraments in question. It is not possible to welcome to the celebration of the *sacrament* par excellence, the Eucharist, persons who are living their conjugal life outside the *sacrament* that has united them with a spouse from whom they are currently estranged. On the other hand, their other sins

15. I have put the word *excommunication* in quotation marks since in itself it has canonical significance that is not applicable in my treatment. The divorced and remarried are not excommunicated from the Church, and hence are not forbidden from receiving its sacraments. Nonetheless, they are not admitted to the sacraments of reconciliation and the Eucharist.

16. What I am going to propose here is along the same line of research and of solutions proposed by Bishop Armand Le Bourgeois, *Chrétiens divorcés remariés* (Paris: Desclée de Brouwer, 1990) and *Questions des divorcés à l'Église* (Paris: Desclée de Brouwer, 1993). See also the recent pastoral letter of the German Bishops of the Upper Rhine "Grundsätze für eine seelsorgliche Begleitung von Menschen aus zerbrochenen Ehen und von wiederverheirateten Geschiedenen in der Oberrheinischen Kirchenprovinz," in *Herder Korrespondenz* 47 (1993) 460–67 (see "Pastoral Ministry: The Divorced and Remarried," *Origins* 23 (38) (March 10, 1994) 670-73. —The study by Kenneth R. Himes and James A. Coriden, "Pastoral Care of the Divorced and Remarried," *Theological Studies* 57 (1996) 97–123, is well worth consulting [translator].

cannot be pardoned because they persist in what is considered adultery. This strictness, it must be said, only affects convinced Christians who yearn profoundly to participate in the Eucharist but at the same time are respectful of the Church's discipline. Indifferent Catholics are simply not concerned.[17]

However, today the persistence of the severity associated with the "excommunication" of the divorced is accompanied by real pastoral care. Such couples are invited and helped to pray, read the Scriptures, practice acts of charity and the works of mercy, and regularly assist at Mass, albeit without receiving Communion. With certain limitations, they are also invited to accept some responsibilities in the Church, e.g., administrative, "apostolic," or catechetical. Pastorally, everything possible is done to invite the divorced and remarried to participate in a truly Christian life, but the domain of the sacraments remains closed to them, because by their divorce they have put themselves outside its pale.

Even though this reasoning is understandable, one can still ask what a pastoral practice that is not effectively centered on participation in the Eucharist can mean in respect to the theology of the Church and the Eucharist. No doubt, in the Church there are many pastoral strategies that do not directly involve the Eucharist, because there are many stages of forming one's conscience and of conversion that have to be respected, etc. But in principle the Eucharist is the goal of these stages, since the spiritual sacrifice that is the object of such pastoral strategies is completed in the eucharistic sacrifice of the Church. In the case of divorce and remarriage, however, it is not a question of deferring something but of prohibiting it. Is there any theological sense in such an exclusion that is paradoxically coupled with a de facto recognition of the matrimonial and familial situation of the divorced and remarried couple and the effort to make this situation *holy and acceptable to God?* Christians are called to participate by their holiness of life and by the grace of the Spirit in the spiritual sacrifice of Jesus Christ. They are also called to the sacramental sacrifice of Jesus Christ which is the source of grace for all, but which some are not admitted to. How can we justify this unbridgeable gap between both sacrifices, spiritual and sacramental, in the case of the divorced and remarried? Or again, the open, pierced heart of Christ commemorated and made present in the Eucharist is the source of grace for all, and the Church's charge to administer grace and its pastoral strategy in behalf of the divorced tries to support them in every possible way: how, then, can we justify a separation of the divorced in the Church that only death can remove? Is this evangelically and theologically coherent?

17. Necessarily, though, they will receive Communion without any qualms of conscience, when at one time or another, or for one reason or another, they assist at a religious ceremony that includes the celebration of the Eucharist!

It needs to be said that one has the impression that in this case, as in so many others where the severity of the past is retained, the doctrinal progress made in the past century, and that the Church adopted at the council in particular, has not been taken into account. Thus, in the classical sacramental theology before the liturgical movement, the sacrament was considered in terms of its remedial value over the power of sin, and concretely in its helping the Christian avoid damnation. On the other hand, eucharistic practice was centered more on its sacrificial than its sacramental character. Its celebration before the faithful was not considered so important, and besides, up to the reforms of Pius X (1903–14), one received Communion only rarely. Today, the connection between the Church and the Eucharist, or between the spiritual sacrifice of the People of God and the sacramental celebration of the sacrifice of Jesus Christ by the Christian assembly is much more clearly perceived. Moreover, the invitation to live out the spiritual sacrifice and to "assist" but not communicate in the sacramental sacrifice appears to be lacking internal theological coherence and is perceived as something that is almost impossible to live.

Here is where the paradox lies: how can there be "excommunication" from the Eucharist (and the sacrament of penance), if there is "communication" in other areas of the Church's life? How can there be *true* adultery, if one deals with couples as though they are called to real Christian life and holiness, and if one does everything pastorally possible to help them? To put the question in more pointed terms: do we think of such couples as being "in the state of grace" or not?[18]

Evidently, there is no totally satisfactory solution to these issues. Nevertheless, in the framework of the ecclesiology of Vatican II and the place it gave to the particular church, we can imagine that the local bishop, who is in contact with his people, should be judged competent to determine the case. If, for example, a divorced and remarried couple, who seek to participate again in the Eucharist, have led a new and faithful conjugal life over a

---

18. To such paradoxes one can legitimately pose the opposite paradox: how is it possible that sacramental communion in the Eucharist takes place when the sacramental communion of marriage has been shattered? This point calls for a bit more reflection. We must remember the analogical character of the notion of a sacrament and not think that every case involves univocal identity. In reality, *the* sacrament is the Eucharist, the memorial of the paschal mystery of Jesus and the Church's perfect act of thanksgiving. The sacramentality of the other sacraments is taken from their relation to the Eucharist. It would be necessary to examine further to what degree this type of reflection can help think through the problem at issue here. —See the article by Walter Kasper, "Aspects of the Eucharist in Their Unity and Variety: On the Recent Discussion about the Fundamental Form and Meaning of the Eucharist," *Theology and Church*, trans. Margaret Kohl (New York: Crossroad, 1989) 177–94 [translator].

period of years,[19] and have been fruitful in all respects, and have rendered a genuine witness to the gospel to those around them, shouldn't the bishop, after having met with them and having requested and received appropriate testimonials, be able to publicly admit this couple to the sacraments? We can well imagine a formula that would not disguise the past matrimonial failure and would confide the situation to the mercy of God, but on the other hand would recognize the work of the Spirit and human fidelity in the present couple, and for this reason would admit them to the Eucharist. In this way, one neither dissimulates the ambiguity or the unsatisfactory character of the situation, and yet one resolves it in what appears prudently to be the best direction for developing the couple's well-being and the Church's. This represents no facile solution and offers no scandal, but is a humble recognition of grace in the very midst of what was weakness or sin.

The Process and the Declaration of Nullity

In the case I have just suggested, the bishop's declaration and his decision to admit a couple to the Eucharist does not put in question the validity of the sacrament which unites one or both parties of the remarried couple with someone else. That marriage perdures, but one judges that on the basis of a long period of testing the actual union of the sacramentally unmarried couple no longer points to the state of sin and separation from God, but henceforth is taken up into the world of grace and of the Church. I believe that the suggestion I have made is well founded and strikes me as both valid and acceptable, whatever one makes of a second proposal I want to make, a proposal that is more daring and debatable than the one I have just tried to make.

Today, the only method authorized for contracting a "second" marriage consists in demonstrating that there was no sacrament in the first case because there was no true consent. Only then can there be another union without committing adultery. The "process of the declaration of nullity" attempts such a demonstration. The procedure is centered on the past: on the basis of witnesses and documents, one tries to prove that genuine consent was never given since it was precluded by fear, deception, lack of maturity, etc. Competent judges render their verdict on the quality of the consent. Depending on documents and testimonies that purport to offer a sufficiently well-founded recollection of the event, the judges arrive at moral certitude that the contract never took place and that there was no sacrament, and they make their declaration of nullity in the bishop's name. The question I wish to pose is the following: is the process of declaration of

---

19. It would not be unreasonable to demand a period of about ten years, since perseverance takes time to grow.

nullity, which searches for the truth exclusively in the *past,* the only means for arriving at the recognition of nullity? Without too great a risk to the dignity and indissolubility of marriage, is it possible to imagine another way, especially when for one reason or another it is not possible to obtain the facts needed for a declaration of nullity or when they are inconclusive?

Epistemology of the Practical Judgment: Judgment, Criteria, and Procedures

In order to proceed with greater security, I need to make several remarks regarding the nature of the judgment brought in the area of matrimony: the judgment can be called probable.[20] Whatever de facto was their statement, it amounts more or less to the following: "It is morally certain that the marriage between N. and N. was [was not] validly concluded on such and such a date, and that given the present state of our knowledge, nothing permits [everything leads] us to call into doubt the freedom of consent mutually given by both parties." The reader will have noted that I am placing the *moral certitude* of the judges and the *probability* of their judgment side by side. I wish to say that, even though the object of one's judgment is not absolutely evident, a person can arrive subjectively at a sufficiently founded conviction that remains probable.

This probability is quite unobjectionable, since it is the condition of our judgment in practical matters. But this also claims that certitude depends not only on facts that can be gathered, but on the criteria used to interpret them. In the matter of marriage, it needs to be noted that the criteria for judgment have not always been the same.[21] In the Middle Ages, the question of impediments of kinship played a very important role in matrimonial life, especially for princes, and occasioned many an excommunication (not only sacramentally but canonically speaking) due to "incest" between spouses whom today we would qualify as "distant cousins." The degrees of consanguinity hardly ever play a role today in opposing the validity of a marriage. For reasons of complex cultural changes that go beyond the primitive taboos of incest, they seem rather to have fallen into desuetude.[22]

Another example is provided by the development of capitally important criteria of psychological immaturity, as much adverted to today as they were ignored in the past. In our troubled civilization, such immaturity is more frequent. However, we might ask whether there was ever a period in world history that was free of troubles capable of diminishing the

20. I am defining the term in precisely the way I indicated earlier on pp. 76–77.

21. A few pages ago, we employed a similar reflection regarding the morality in economics of "loaning at interest."

22. See the *Codex Iuris Canonici* (1983) Cann. 108–109.

clarity of one's reflection and one's will over desire. It is possible that the importance of nullity today arises from a more nuanced understanding of human existence and its fragility. It was probably always so, though formerly it was not adverted to.

On the other hand, just as the criteria for judging a case are better explained today, we can also point to the change in the process of nullity. Not too long ago, competence in this matter was reserved to the Roman Rota, the process took many years, and more often than not a negative decision was given. In the meanwhile, competence has been handed over to regional tribunals, where those who judge are also those who face the plaintiffs directly in their own familiar circumstances. To insure the gravity of the situation, there is an obligatory appeal, but the process is much faster than before and the result is frequently a positive one.

Toward Expanding the Criteria

Having taken into account the variability of the criteria and the changing character of a procedure that results in well-founded decisions, I ask whether the method can be expanded beyond one that searches for criteria of the validity or invalidity of a marriage that are focused *exclusively on examining the past*. Sometimes, it is not possible to demonstrate from documents and witnesses the real probability of the invalidity of the first marriage; the method in this case simply does not admit moral certitude. Would it not be possible to proceed in another way?[23] Once again I am posing an epistemological question. In Platonism's understanding of truth, with its demand for the purity and lucidity of truth, a probable judgment is an inferior act that must approach as much as possible the conditions of incontrovertible light. However, as I have already said, probability has an economy of its own in which objective criteria, interpretation, "engagement" of the persons who are making pronouncements, etc., form the truth arrived at. In this economy, truth is in part hermeneutical, i.e., it involves a process of interpretation, and performative, i.e., it is a constitutive action of human agents. The present and the future intervene in the constitution of probable truth and of the certitude that makes it possible. We are not talking about "truth on the cheap," but about another, indeed more frequent, modality of discovering and expressing truth.

Now let us try to apply this epistemological reflection to the case of a second marriage, and think, for example, of the frequent case where a couple

23. Of course, I have posed the hypothesis that the examination of the relevant documents and the testimonies of witnesses does not lead to the moral certitude that the first marriage was valid. Where the validity is morally certain, the process I am explaining here could not take place afterwards. In the latter situation, however, as I said earlier, they can still be admitted to the sacraments.

has obtained an early divorce after a first, unhappy experience, which they did not consider themselves bound to in conscience. For several years, they have led a new and faithful conjugal life and have continued along the path of the gospel. Can we see in the "success" of the second marriage, proved by time (i.e., by the grace of God and human fidelity), a sign that is sufficiently *probable* that the second marriage is the true one, and that the first was entered into far too quickly? It would be the bishop's responsibility in this case to acknowledge the "truth" of the second marriage as really the first one.

In another case, where the request for nullity has been made rather soon after the first divorce, but where the inquiry did not furnish sufficient elements to conclude to nullity, the bishop, being familiar with the couple and their situation, could impose a longer period of time, let us say about ten years, during which the proof would emerge of the will and the capacity to live a conjugal and familial life together. Could the bishop not judge that this will and capacity did not sufficiently exist for the first union? It is not a question of an "easy" annulment, given the probationary period imposed. On the other hand, the pastoral strategy for the divorced during this period would be ordered toward its sacramental goal, which is only appropriate in the life in the Church and which has a coherence that is both eschatological and sacramental.

In other words, I propose that the criterion for judging the nullity of a first marriage not be restricted to investigating the *past,* and so, primarily engaging our memory, but that it also employ a criterion of *duration,* i.e., of the present oriented toward the future. In both cases, the result is probability. But in Christian life, since it is a matter of harmony and fruitfulness, would God not be inclined toward our running the risk of error as far as the past is concerned, in order for the present and the future to better qualify for personal and sacramental holiness?

Uncertainties and Inquiries

Perhaps we need to justify this proposition by noting that its adoption, with all the necessary corrections that can come only from concrete experience, will not land us in laxism. I believe that we must humbly admit that in doctrinal and practical matters relating to matrimony, not everything is absolutely clear. Setting aside the fact that we could consider it statistically certain that historically some declarations of nullity were made when in fact the sacrament was valid, or vice versa, that other cases were not annulled, even though they were based on true reasons, let us instead examine three other areas of the issue, the first, theological; the second, cultural; the third, canonical.

First of all, a theological question. What is the sacramental quality of a marriage of baptized, but not catechized and probably not confirmed,

Christians who desire a certain sacred or religious character to the marriage, but nothing more. They are not really convinced by the prenuptial instructions they take; possibly they have no sense of being committed to their responses to the questions they are asked relative to the indissolubility of marriage and to the principle of their being open to its fruitfulness. Finally, even if they have some vague idea about what it means, they have no precise idea of the sacramentality of marriage, i.e., that their consent structurally orders them in the Mystery of Christ and the Church. Such cases are really very frequent today, especially, though not exclusively, in de-Christianized countries. Is their adhesion to Jesus Christ, real but latent, sufficient to transform their consent, serious or fragile, into a sacrament of union with Christ and the Church? *Can a free act—especially one that engages a life—take on a sacred and indelible force without the knowledge of the ones who pose it?* Can it be a sacrament of faith, if there is no faith? In a sense, this question remains academic, since hypothetically the partners are only marginally related to the Church. It becomes a burning issue when, after this "unconsciously Christian" marriage ends in divorce and one of the partners wants to remarry in the Church out of a better understanding of the case.[24]

Secondly, there is a question we will call cultural, for lack of a better term. Right about the time of the Gregorian reform a certain theological understanding and a system of law regarding sexuality was articulated: not that the elements were not already there, but the systematization was medieval and yet reaffirmed by the Council of Trent. In the Church's missionary mentality, this system of marriage, as well as celibacy, was imported in this specific form by countries with their own cultures, i.e., that had established a certain equilibrium between sexuality, family, property, and civil society. These evangelized societies did not have the time to switch from one state of equilibrium to another; they were massively encountered by a highly elaborated Christianity, whereas they continued to live much the way their ancestors did at the time of Abraham and the Judges, i.e., in other states of equilibrium that observed their own laws, exigencies, and sense of sin. However, I am not convinced that one can hurry time when it comes to the slow effort needed to create a worldview. Is the direct imposition of

---

24. The question of the sacramental character and its ontological meaning returns at this point. A baptized person is *really* marked by his or her belonging to Jesus Christ. But can this mark, mysterious and supernatural, extend to human natural acts without any present awareness of faith in the one who poses these acts and understands that the action of Christ changes its level? Must not the principle *agere sequitur esse* ["action follows being"] be subject to nuance when it is a matter of a person's Christian vocation? See Gaston Candelier, "Incroyance et validité du mariage sacramentel," *Revue de droit canonique* 41 (1991) 81–145, especially 128–31.

a family and social tradition, something that is a lot less self-assured than is evident, at least concerning practices and facts if not doctrine, really so beneficial? Are we sure that after only a century and a half of missionary evangelizing, questions of sexuality and family life have been resolved? Shouldn't we take up these issues in greater depth, risk other, less rushed ways of teaching about these questions, and fashion nonsacramental liturgies for marriage, etc.? Here we put our finger on the urgent need of decentralizing not only in what concerns theory but also concrete decisions. In areas that are so delicate, so intimately tied to human life, wouldn't it be better if our discourse was less exclusively interpersonal, as if it was only a matter of individual cases? Wouldn't it help if it was at least limited to restricted areas in a particular tradition, where solid development and profound conversion do not happen because general laws are applied, as if time and space did not exist?

The third question is canonical and envisions a certain number of cases where a legitimately contracted marriage which, even though it is sacramental in some cases and in others valid in natural law, is dissolved by the Church in order to permit another. I am thinking here of cases, well-known to canonists, of dispensations given *super ratum et non consummatum,* the so- called "Pauline" and "Petrine" privileges. Until very recently, in order to account for these cases, a theory of "vicarious power," entrusted by God to St. Peter and his successors, was constructed which permitted the popes in a "quasi-instrumental" way to untie a human bond, and which conformed to the natural law, and even the sacramental economy, and hence was indissoluble.[25] In the perspective outlined by Vatican II's ecclesiology, and because a theory of "sacred power" *(sacra potestas)* does not seem solidly grounded any longer, rather strong theological and hermeneutical objections can be lodged against it.[26] But the fact remains that dispensations and the privileges exist and so must be able to be justified in some way, even if the way of "power" is no longer available. But this supposes a change in the theological teaching.

I do not want to tarry longer on this. The three questions I have raised are meant to show that with respect to matrimony, probability and certitude are proper to them and both found them in reality and constitute certain obscurities. My conclusion is that it is possible and necessary to look

25. See Urbano Navarrete, "Potestas vicaria Ecclesiae. Evolutio historica conceptus atque observationes attenta doctrina Concilii Vaticani II," *Periodica* 60 (1971) 415–86; Antonio Abate, *Il matrimonio nell'attuale legislazione canonica* (Brescia: Paideia, 1982) 195–224; J. F. Castaño, *Il sacramento di matrimonio* (Rome, 1991) II:279–82; M. Nacca, "Indissolubilità del matrimonio" (doctoral thesis, Lateran University, 1993).

26. I will touch on this question again later in chapter 7.

more closely at their criteriology and at the process used to arrive at solutions which are doubtless just ones, or in any case constructive ones, in the area of divorced and remarried persons.

Religious Life

I have already indicated that religious profession has not been regarded as a sacrament, even though it has all the appearances of one. Is this why dispensation from vows is so easy to obtain? We need to examine the history behind such facility. St. Thomas Aquinas (1227–74) held that no one, not even the pope, could dispense someone from solemn vows.[27] What expedients led to the opposite solution? As in the case of consent to marriage, religious profession is a free decision that involves time. Like marriage, but even more so perhaps in practice, commitment to religious life involves a long process of discerning God's call. The religious community is also involved in the process of discernment. It is a matter then of a promise in response to what can probably be regarded as a demand and a gift of God. The ones entering into the contract, in the communion of the Spirit, are the living God, the human person and his or her freedom, and in a certain way the religious community. The Christian community as a whole witnesses to the existence of this charism as well as the public and liturgical response which the person called has given.

If this is the pattern of religious commitment, one can ask: in whose name does the Christian community or its hierarchical leaders, including the pope, untie the bond of a commitment a person has made under God's initiative and in a covenant solemnly entered into with God? Does the Church's mediation extend to the point of annulling something founded on the mutual commitment of God and a person, discerned within a religious community, and celebrated in the Christian community and ratified by it? It seems to me that the competence of the Church in this matter is not greater than in the case of marriage. I fully admit that one needs to examine and judge the effective freedom of the promise, and when the decision is a negative one, to admit that *there never was a charism or a promise* and that perhaps the discernment process was a poor one. But, and without necessarily bringing a defamatory judgment, one can also imagine that

---

27. *Summa theologiae* IIa–IIae, q. 88, a. 11. In reality, St. Thomas, who relied on the decretal *Quum ad monasterium* (Emil Friedberg, *Corpus juris canonici,* vol. II, 600), based his reasons more specifically on the vow of perpetual continence. It is interesting that the argument he favored had to do with *consecration* to God, a theme he treats more from the point of view of the virtue of religion and its "sacred" aspects, but in which today we can discern a certain sacramental import. On the other hand, the decretal mentioned above envisions poverty as well as chastity: the stress is on the totality of a state in life that is based on a rule.

a person can no longer, or no longer desires to remain in the state in life that has been the object of a divine gift and one's response to it. The fact does not call for an annulment. As in the case of divorced and remarried persons, one establishes procedures of access to the sacraments that do not prejudice the indissolubility of the commitment made. In effect, if the promise was really made to God it has become an element in the history of a man or a woman with God. If an agreement has been reached that questions the Spirit of God and the most profound freedom of a human being, what basis is there here to speak of an "annulment"? In the case of a professed religious, "indissolubly" bound to God by his or her profession but who has still departed from the community for another state in life, the question should remain open regarding how to proceed canonically, as far as ecclesial and sacramental life are concerned. Whatever measures are to be taken, and whatever is to be said of the Church's tolerance, for such a Christian as well as for others, one needs to ask whether the way of marriage should be immediately available to him or her. Will the person be more faithful in marriage than in the religious life he or she could not persevere in?

Conclusion

I think I have been able to disengage three elements in my exposition on the charisms of state in life, and by way of conclusion I would like to underscore them. First, the charisms of the Spirit for the gospel and the kingdom of God are modeled on the constitutive realities of human existence, even though they involve their transformation. They are not a substitute for the humanity of men and women, but presuppose it and order it in a particular direction of its accomplishment.

Second, putting a charism into practice assumes and nurtures an understanding and an organization, let us call it a practical theology and appropriate laws. The persons called to these states in life are also endowed with a sense of discernment and, let us call it, an imagination that has developed in the tradition of the Church but in an original way. Little by little, and not without mistakes and second efforts, it has defined the way to be a Christian in a given situation. Maybe the Church's leaders ought to listen more to what the Spirit is telling men and women, learn to respect uncertainty and temporizing without which we do not really grasp truth, learn to accept a certain measure of plurality, and consider that a "universal" discourse in matters of morality and law cannot fully enter into the specificity of personal situations. Error and sin are not fatalities that only forceful language and detailed prescriptions can correct; more important is the task of helping men and women grow in responsibility and thereby making them stronger, so that the Spirit can guide them into the fullness of truth.

Thirdly, stability in a state in life also participates in the gift of the Spirit. It is not a state of perpetual change or dissatisfaction, but a gift which gives a person the strength of continuing in a chosen direction. In a world that is particularly unstable and in transition, it is necessary to assure the fact that stability can be promoted and pursued in all states in life and with the same demands, without compromising the truth to satisfy human demands, but also without becoming inflexible in some cases and undervaluing it in others.

Chapter 6

Christian Service: Charisms of *Diakonia*

The Church is in evangelical service of men and women. Of course, this is true in the very heart of its visible body, but perhaps more so in its outreach to the world. This universal *diakonia* has specialized forms, depending on the tasks and the areas. To say that in all sectors this service begins with charisms signifies that the institutions which make this *diakonia* concrete find their origin and their development in the final analysis in the inspiration, the movement, and the assistance of the Spirit.

After saying a word about discerning the charisms of *diakonia,* I would like to try to reorganize them under three headings: service of the Word, the ministry of healing and compassion, and the exercise of administration. In conclusion, I will offer a brief reflection on the diaconate as an order.[1]

---

1. We need to recall what I said earlier in a general context, viz., that many of the observations and proposals made in the present chapter are already being realized in the churches. See chapter 4, p. 107, n. 20. One only needs to be somewhat familiar with one or another church or to read several diocesan, national or international journals on the spiritual life and the apostolate. But I am trying to articulate this ensemble under the rubric of the charisms of the Spirit and their appropriate institutions. I am deliberately avoiding the term "ministry" in favor of "charism" and *"diakonia"* in order to show the relative autonomy of the Spirit's charisms and to avoid completely their being considered "participations in the ministry of the priest" or as "taking up the slack in priestly activities," etc. Such expressions are implicitly bound to the Gregorian form of the Church and do not conform to the model of "structured communion" I am trying to describe. —See the highly informative essay by André Lemaire, "From Services to Ministries: 'Diakoniai' in the First Two Centuries" in Bas van Iersel and Roland Murphy, eds., *Office and Ministry in the Church* [Concilium 80] (New York: Herder and Herder, 1972) 35–49. See also Alfons Weiser, "*diakoneō*/serve; *diakonia*/service, ministry; office; *diakonos*/servant" in Horst Balz and Gerhard Schneider, eds., *Exegetical Dictionary of the New Testament,* vol. 1 (Grand Rapids, Mich.: Eerdmans, 1990) 302–04.

Discernment

Discerning a charism can originate from Christians themselves, who perceive a personal disposition and an interior call. It is their responsibility to accede to this movement by submitting themselves to the appropriate institution, or if none exists, to forming one. But the discernment can come from others: members of the Christian community and especially from the leaders of the Christian communities who might propose the task themselves ("Think and pray about . . ."), on condition that they watch over the formation and spiritually support the persons so engaged, since engagement in the final analysis comes from the Spirit. With this very brief note, I want to signal the essential connection between charism and institution.

Service of the Word of God

The first task of the Church is to welcome the "word of God," to understand it, and to proclaim it. I understand the expression "word of God" in its widest meaning, i.e., in the expressions of the Dogmatic Constitution on Divine Revelation, "everything the Apostles received—whether from the lips of Christ, from his way of life and his works, or by coming to know it through the prompting of the Holy Spirit" (DV 7). The Church is responsible for such an ensemble of which sacred Scripture is the primary witness and the Spirit constantly stirs up charisms that permit the Church to fulfill this task. These tasks are divided into different areas: missionary work where the witnessing takes on forms that are not necessarily easy to devise in the concrete and which themselves stir up distinct charisms: from the kerygmatic proclamation of the message, to dialogue with other religious cultures, indeed with totally secular cultures, and the institutions that give them flesh. Then comes organizing the liturgy, which is a service of the word of praise and of intercession. Next are the forms of instruction: preaching, catechesis, more profound instruction (mystagogy), theological research, and dialogue with cultures. In effect, evangelization is the result of the Spirit-led convergence of these different aspects of the service of the word, made effective and efficacious thanks to this very diversity of charisms.

Mission

When we think of mission, we can express it first of all in terms of evangelization properly speaking, i.e., of announcing the Good News of Jesus Christ. Here is a large field for charisms, and today we find ourselves

---

Though somewhat tendentious, John N. Collins' *Are All Christians Ministers?* (Collegeville: The Liturgical Press, 1992) is also worth consulting [translator].

before many different undertakings in this regard. It might be simple street preaching, bound up with a conviction of the immediacy of the Spirit and the power of the word, or proclamation in some other place apparently far removed from any religious influence, right up to the silent witness of one's life, of love, of a caring one doesn't even dare to verbalize prematurely but that one hopes will awaken in others a better sense of themselves. Between these extremes there is room for a real plurality of evangelizing charisms, and which we must take care to discern, train for, and foster their convergence as much as possible.

I will not insist any more here on this primary and fundamental level of the proclamation of the word, since I think it cannot become meaningful outside of a "reform" of the Church. This reform is what I hope my book will help it "imagine." We will undoubtedly find people who belong to Jesus Christ and the gospel, at least in some degree, and maybe they are more numerous than we think. But bluntly put, there are not many among their number who agree to enter the Catholic Church or to return to it by way of the sacraments and of apostolic engagement. The reasons for this reserve are due probably to the persistence of the memory of anticlericalism, and that even though today it is no longer aggressive, it nonetheless plays an unconscious role in a person's decision vis-à-vis the gospel and accounts for what one observes outside the Church regarding its conduct. Purging such a memory in society is a demanding matter and to some extent is beyond the Church's control. But the haunting question remains, Can the Church do something to present an appearance *that will make it desirable and lovable?* Yes, and very definitely so! The authentic mission results not only from proclaiming the gospel, but from the Church showing a face that reveals the tenderness of the "might" *(puissance)* of the word and the presence of the Spirit. Mission emerges from the spiritual and structured implementation of the Church as communion, and that is what this book hopes to contribute to achieving.

Liturgy

I am not concerned here with the question of celebrating the liturgy, which in itself is a holy and theological activity, for which the Christian is qualified by the sacraments of initiation and order. Instead, my interest concerns the organization of the liturgy, or one might say its programming: texts, music, gestures, space, and time. The Dogmatic Constitution on the Sacred Liturgy cleared the ground for reform in this regard. First of all, reform was conceived and then made possible thanks to two or three generations of Christians, who before the council saw the necessity of a radical renewal of the liturgical tradition, but thanks also to the generation that was up to the task of implementing the reforms immediately after the council. They possessed a critical understanding of the liturgical tradition and a spiritual and human ability to know precisely what needed to be introduced: the intelligent choice of scriptural texts and how to translate them, so that the text could speak to people today while remaining faithful to the letter; the composition of new Eucharistic Prayers that were doctrinally sound, mystical, and accessible; the composition of music which, even though it did not equal the power of Gregorian chant, expressed and supported the spirit of prayer, especially as it became more sure of itself in the light of experience; the reexamination of the whole realm of symbolism by purging it of historicist images, of needless repetition, of baroque accretions, and injecting new life into liturgical gestures and the symbols that support them; reconceptualizing the renovation or the construction of new churches with their decor, so that the assembled Christian community could find its true home, etc. All of this incredible work was done essentially after the council. However, two remarks are in order in the context of our study.

Experts and Creativity

First of all, the authors of these reforms have often been called "experts." The term expresses both competence and experience. But in using it we should not forget that it is also a gift, human of course, but a spiritual "charism" as well. Those who labored over this reform, before and after the council, sensed that they were called in behalf of the Church to provide a cult worthy of God and genuinely pastoral. They placed their intelligence in the service of their heart's intuition, since both came from the Spirit who animates the Church. The confidence we have invested in these "experts" rests as much on this call as on their theoretical competence or their juridical mandate to work for reform.

But in the history of this reform of the liturgy, which will probably never be written in full, mention must also be made of how all those Christians— men and women religious, and priests who enjoyed no particular formation in these matters but who had a certain innate sense of beauty and an appreciation of what human and Christian reality had to offer to prayer— contributed to provide direction and concretely implement what had been proposed in Christian communities. At the start of the reform maybe one or another point was made in too "intellectual" or too "ideological" a way; maybe, too, in some instances ways of doing things were proposed and imposed which were not based on sufficient knowledge or were not charismatically inspired; but with respect to the proposals made and their reception, on balance it was and remains the fruit of the Spirit in the Church. Moreover, in order for the reform to continue and develop, it is essential that we search out and promote this charism of the "creative expert."

Permanence of the Reform

In reality, the reform of the liturgy has not been concluded. First of all, it has only been done in the Latin Church.[2] But even in this rite, not everything has been done and there remains a long road ahead of us. The reform has to be taken up again and again, and what has been proposed for the Latin Church as a whole has still in large part to be applied in terms of differentiated practices in the particular churches, in parishes, and in other communities.

But there is even more that has to be done. The idea itself of reform is incompatible with a notion of an end or of closure. The only way not to fall back into a new ritualistic mindset is to keep alive a sense of initiative which either follows or anticipates temporal changes of a community, as it submits to or resists change in space, i.e., as a community that is definitely locatable historically, culturally, and geographically. Depending on each one's charism, creativity needs to be fostered in the particular churches by keeping its eye on the culture and also on current events. This is exactly why the liturgical books of the Latin Church speak of "contingent proposals": several formulas are available, and one is free to substitute other texts for those proposed, whether it concerns holy Scripture or certain parts of the Eucharistic Prayers. This applies to selection of feasts, too, and celebrations proper to certain communities but not obligatory for all. On the matter of building churches and sacred art, it is best for higher authorities to offer only very general instructions. In all of this, it is the Christian people that is concerned, or a definite group in its midst, that is animated by the necessary charisms, that urges attention to what needs to be done, that examines the possibilities, and that implements a liturgical program, with the help of "experts" and the authority of bishops and priests.

Such adaptations and transpositions have a real ecclesiological significance. The revised Latin liturgy was conceived and realized at a universal

2. The Oriental churches also need such liturgical reform, since in the present state of their celebration, they, no less than the Latin Liturgy, have not escaped the corrosive effects of time, and are as much in need of revision, whether reform, renewal, or emendation, as the latter. But first there must be a liturgical movement—I am tempted to say a "motion" or proposal—a kind of groundswell that will instigate theologico-practical reflection, but possibly too call for some experiments. I am thinking here of the reflections and proposals made by Alexander Schmemann with respect to baptism (*Of Water and The Spirit: A Liturgical Study of Baptism* [Crestwood, N.Y.: St. Vladimir's Seminary Press, 1974]), or those of Costi Bendaly with respect to fasting ("Jeûne et oralité. Aspects psychologiques du jeûne orthodoxe et suggestions pour une éventuelle réforme," *Contacts* 37 [1985] 163–229). The Oriental Catholic churches also have reservations about embarking on this kind of path, for fear that they will be perceived as attacking an ancient tradition and creating a gap between themselves and the Eastern churches not in union with Rome. Nevertheless, why shouldn't they become involved right here, out of a spirit of incentive service, while avoiding all arrogance or timidity?

level first of all, thanks to the activity of a board of experts—called the Consilium ad exsequendam Constitutionem de Sacra Liturgia—appointed by the Holy See.[3] It was the pope who promulgated the revised rites and published the authentic texts. It could not have been otherwise right after the council. But now, in conformity with an ecclesiology of "structured communion," the universal liturgy needs to move in another direction, that of the particular liturgies, i.e., liturgies inspired by the universal rite but largely autonomous in terms of their adaptation. To understand this better, it is essential to remember that the Latin Liturgy before the council was the liturgy of a particular Church—Rome—that had been adopted by other churches or was imposed on them. The extreme generalizing of the unique *Roman* Rite is of relatively late origin, dating from the time of what I will later call the "glorification of the papacy" in the nineteenth century. The postconciliar liturgy has lost this local footing: it is the *Latin* Liturgy, not the *Roman* Liturgy. It is imperative that the Church of Rome adapt its Latinity to its particular needs, so that everywhere, in Rome and elsewhere, there might be particular liturgies, common as to their *Latin* inspiration, but singular as to their local adaptations and transpositions. A liturgical charism is needed in the churches precisely to effect such a transformation from the scope of a universal liturgy to particular liturgies.

Instruction

Another sector of service to the word is instruction in the truth. My proposal is that education is fundamentally a gift of the Spirit that, like all other gifts, is at once stirred up, verified, and approved by those who preside over the life of the Church. By way of anticipating somewhat what I will have to say a little later concerning the bishops, let me say something about the distinction between the bishop's proclamation of the faith and its being taught charismatically.

In chapter 2, I distinguished three levels of the proclamation of the faith, or in other terms, in the transmission of revelation. Here, theology appeared as an intermediate stage between biblical and liturgical preaching and the authoritative, indeed obligatory, expression of defined truths. In all three cases—proclamation, theology, solemn definitions—it is a matter of teaching; only the manner is different. Clearly, the third level belongs to the bishops, but it is a very reduced teaching authority, one that indicates the limits of what may be taught, or that sets the framework within which

---

3. The makeup of the board of experts has undergone a number of changes over the years. From 1965–69 it was called the *Consilium ad exsequendam Constitutionem de Sacra Liturgia;* from 1969–75 it became the *Sacra Congregatio pro culto divino;* and from 1975 to the present the *Sacra Congregatio pro sacramentis et culto divino* [translator].

the teaching is to be conducted. The first teaching function is also specifically episcopal and presbyteral, when it happens as oral proclamation: in the liturgy of the Church, or when the pastor immediately addresses his people, or when it is communicated in writing as a reflection or a commentary. This, too, is a form of magisterium, wider and more important than the preceding one, and less marked by the quality of being "obligatory." What, then, is to be said of the intermediate stage?

Catechesis

I need to distinguish between catechesis, or to use the more ancient term, *didaskalia,* and theology. Catechesis can be defined as instruction in the fundamentals of the faith, that which is communicated to the catechumen or to the neophyte, so that he or she might know both the essentials of the Christian Mystery and the answers to the great questions posed by such issues as God, humankind, and the world. People thus catechized are equipped with points of reference which help them develop a Christian and a human life, personally and collectively, in a balanced way. The questions that arise in this context are the following: What authorizes a person to be a catechist? What determines catechetical programs?

As to the first question, we can doubtless say that the authorization is found in each one's personal gift, in communion with others, at skillfully and articulately rendering witness to one's faith. Here is where the *sensus fidelium* is realized in act, or where one "renders testimony to Jesus Christ by the spirit of prophecy."[4] It is frequently said that in countries where the faith was persecuted, it was Christian grandmothers who handed it on. It is also said, and rightly so, that parents are the first catechists of their children, not only by the example they give but by explicitly handing on the faith. If one is honest about what is happening in many places, catechetical teams are being set up according to families and neighborhoods. Each one does what he or she can to proclaim the faith, and each is in turn strengthened by this catechetical activity. These concrete examples show well that it is in the name of their being Christian, of their faith, of their capacity to communicate (and here one encounters both a human gift and a spiritual charism) that Christians teach catechumens, young and old. The role of the priest is often not to be the catechist but to establish teams of catechists, assuring their formation, and regulating the smooth operation of all the elements; in short, seeing to it that the charism of catechesis has a certain

---

4. See the Decree on the Ministry and Life of Priests, art. 2. This text speaks directly not about priests but about all Christians. —See also my article "*Sensus fidei:* Meaning, Role and Future of a Teaching of Vatican II," *Louvain Studies* 17 (1992) 18–34 [translator].

structure of verification that includes its content, its need for institutional forms, and its administration.

One can reply to the second question that the same theme of a spiritual gift plays the same role for "catechetical programs" that it did for the liturgical programs we just examined. Just as there was a liturgical movement in the first half of this century, there was also a catechetical movement which was often spearheaded by women. Their contribution consisted of elaborating methods of teaching that respected the pedagogy of children and that gave a privileged place to the symbolic and narrative dimensions of revelation, and this even though the leaders of the movement often encountered great resistance. They formulated a program of catechesis that was not a "dogmatics in miniature," but that strove first of all to be an initiation to prayer, to knowledge of the Scriptures, especially the Gospels, and to the concrete practice of fraternal charity. The question often put by the magisterium, and rightly so, was how such a presentation could safeguard the essential content of the dogmatic framework which the tradition of the Church guaranteed, in order to support what one sought to achieve by means of such a catechesis, viz., helping the Christian discover prayer, Scripture, and the love of others. Let us restrict ourselves to the following observation: whatever way one pursues to assure the dogmatic framework of catechesis, it would be harmful and highly prejudicial to the growth of the Church to allow a legitimate dogmatic scruple to obfuscate not only pedagogical research but also certain essential elements in the transmission of revelation: history, prayer, and the sacraments.

Theology

Among the gifts to the Church, we must certainly count an understanding of the faith among them. Earlier, I showed how the proposals of Vatican II gave new room to theological research, and I tried to spell this out by underscoring the particular importance which certain elements that were not directly demonstrative or rational gained in this form of interpreting the faith. Thus, the rediscovery of symbol and story at the head of theological knowledge left open in principle the process of "unending interpretation."[5] Neither timid nor ashamed, it is an explicit openness to the data of culture and the physical and the human sciences, that authorizes a method of searching for truth in communication with other competent persons, that invites one to a way of proposing the elements of Christian revelation as a source of light in the investigation of truth, and that, finally, elicits an effort of reinterpreting the faith with old and new cultural data.

5. I am alluding to the suggestive title of the work by Pier Cesare Bori, *L'Interprétation infinie. L'herméneutique chrétienne et ses transformations,* trans. François Vial (Paris: Cerf, 1991).

THE CHARISMATIC STATUS OF THEOLOGY

Our next question concerns the "charismatic" status of theology. The effort of reinterpreting and proposing the faith that is always more or less in process in the Church (and today definitely "more" than "less") presupposes a qualification that is both human and spiritual, which cannot result from a person's willing them, but which comes from the Creator God who lavishes these gifts on us and inspires spiritual gifts. In the patristic period, the beneficiaries of this twofold blessing were often, though not always, the bishops. However, not all bishops at that time were renowned theologians. The episcopal charism, including the charge to teach, is found elsewhere. St. Augustine's *On the Trinity* can be considered indirectly an act of his magisterium as a bishop, but it is essentially (like the work *On the Trinity* of the layman and monk Didymus the Blind) a "charismatic" work of original interpretation of the faith, accomplished in the framework of a specific culture and by a man who was profoundly spiritual, magisterially intelligent, and supremely sensitive. Moreover, there is no necessarily perfect agreement among the works of Augustine, Didymus (ca. 313–98), and the works *Against Eunomius* published by the Cappadocian Fathers.[6] They have different points of departure, diverse means and literary genres, and original conclusions that yield no single point of view. Sometimes, in his lifetime, the theologian—even a bishop–theologian—saw his innovations attacked. This was the case with Augustine himself for his positions on grace, which seemed to imperil the reason for the very existence of Christian asceticism and monasticism. In short, it appears that the charism of the theologian has a life of its own: it is more supple and more precise, more diverse than the episcopal charism that in its turn is tied to governing a Church as a body while observing "the rule of faith."

If we admit that among the theologians of antiquity there was a distinction between the proclamation of the faith connected with the bishop's charism of orders and the understanding of the faith connected with the theologian's charism of a deeper intellectual appreciation of the faith, then we should be willing to admit the same for later periods, when the bishops in general did not cultivate the theological charisms. Today, theological work is divided about equally between the clergy and the laity, and more and more between women and men. There are many examples of this mutual effort. In patristics, for example, the various volumes of the series *Sources chrétiennes* have been edited by academicians, without any regard shown to either their status in the Church or the lack thereof. The remarkable multivolume series on Church history, *Histoire du christianisme des origines*

---

6. See the discussion by Catherine Mowry LaCugna, *God for Us: The Trinity and Christian Life* (San Francisco: HarperSanFrancisco, 1991) 53–79 [translator].

à nos jours which continues to appear, is under the direction of a committee of professors which does not contain a single priest or bishop, and yet it
appears destined to become one of the major international reference works
in the history of the churches, and most particularly on the history of the
Catholic Church.[7] In those countries where the state of religious education
is such that laity are able to exist and support a family on their teacher's
salary, there are both lay exegetes and professors who are priests. Even in
the areas of systematic and fundamental theology the situation is the same,
regardless of ecclesial status. I cannot think of any more prestigious
thinkers in the area of "Christian philosophy" than Maurice Blondel
(1861–1941) or Étienne Gilson (1884–1978) in the first half of the century.
And let us not forget those Christian theologians who do not belong to the
Catholic Church but whose writings, whatever the theological discipline,
contribute so much to the discussion. Finally, one can say that theology itself is a "world" in which individuals, disciplines, and traditions intersect
and crisscross in service of its challenges; a world both passionate in itself
and indispensable for the effective penetration of the gospel in the lives of
men and women.

There remains one more discipline where the theological charism will
grow in importance in the future, viz., dialogue. Earlier,[8] I tried to situate
this mysterious field of searching for truth, both within the Christian confessions (ecumenism) and outside the faith in the dialogue with other religions
and even other cultures. The effective practice of dialogue presupposes a
number of competencies, an attitude and particular sensitivities in the encounter with others, an exact sense of the faith which good will alone cannot assure but which requires, in addition to special training, the movement
and the presence of the Spirit who, when all is said and done, guides us on
the way of encounter.

VERIFICATION AND ITS INSTITUTIONS

What is to be said on the issues of verifying theological charisms in
the Church and their corresponding institutions? First, let us note an inescapable fundamental conviction: if the Creator God gives understanding
and the Spirit of the Covenant bestows charisms, the basis for theology's
persevering in the truth is the gift of God. In the area of knowledge as in all
others, the infinite patience of God accompanies these gifts, directs their
deepening insights, and clarifies them, presupposing that the inquiry is
conducted in a spirit of humility. This divine accompaniment of theology
happens in individuals, to the extent that the theologian keeps his or her

7. Jean-Marie Mayeur, Charles and Luce Pietri, André Vauchez, and Marc Venard,
eds. (Paris: Desclée, 1990–). Fourteen volumes are projected.
8. See chapter 3, pp. 85–88.

spirit and heart centered on the Mystery he or she seeks to investigate, to speak about, and to understand. But today, as was always the case in the Church, theology happens collectively: in the course of discussions conducted, book reviews written, stances taken, even polemical positions, the theological community always ends up discerning and declaring what is at stake in terms of the discipline or the area of research. It ceaselessly corrects itself, not because it tries to produce a single and common discourse but because the positions taken happen to be situated in relation to each other and thus subject one another to further evaluation. Moreover, the theological community is located within the ecclesial community (even if it exceeds its boundaries) and the Church by its sense of the faith, which is the action and sign of the Holy Spirit, silently or energetically makes its contribution. We are talking here about the theological theme of "reception." And finally, there is a certain verification of the charism in the course of the very life of the Church, provided that we take care to respect the slow pace of time, an essential factor in discerning and assimilating truth. In a word, one could say that the rule of faith operates within the exchange of theological views.

Perhaps someone will object that this is all too rosy a view and that if anything history shows the very opposite: left to itself the theological charism leads to disasters rather than to remarkable accomplishments. I reply that the disasters in question, real as they have been and will continue to be, are not due exclusively to the uncontrolled fantasy of theologians. Let us be very careful, and begin with the contemporary research on heresies. Recent impartial studies show that in many of the well-known historical cases of heresy the condemnations and rejections were often excessive. Research has shown that Pelagius (ca. 360–420), the opponents of the Council of Chalcedon (451), Photius (ca. 810–98),[9] and scores of others were not exactly the evil monsters their enemies painted them to be. Often, these "heretics" sought to safeguard certain aspects of the truth (granted sometimes with excessive zeal) that in their eyes were not honored sufficiently by others. With the help of a polemical spirit they sometimes trespassed the limits of their positions, while for their part the condemnations pre-

9. On Photius, see Francis Dvornik, *The Photian Schism: History and Legend* (Cambridge [Eng.]: Cambridge University Press, 1948 [reprinted 1970]) —see also Dvornik's "The Patriarch Photius in the Light of Recent Research," *Photian and Byzantine Ecclesiastical Studies* (London: Variorum Reprints, 1974) chapter VI [translator]; on Pelagius, see Gisbert Greshake, *Gnade als konkrete Freiheit. Eine Untersuchung zur Gnadenlehre des Pelagius* (Mainz: Josef Knecht, 1972). The list could be extended *ad infinitum*. —See R. A. Markus, "The Legacy of Pelagius: Orthodoxy, Heresy and Conciliation" in *The Making of Orthodoxy: Essays in Honour of Henry Chadwick,* ed. Rowan Williams (New York: Cambridge University Press, 1989) 214–34 [translator].

vented a process of reconciliation within the bounds of legitimate diversity. Contemporary historiography tends more towards their rehabilitation. Not too long ago, Origen (ca. 185–254) for his general theological outlook, and Cassian (ca. 360–435) for his "semi-Pelagianism," were still under ban in the Catholic Church, and those who fifty years ago were involved in the effort to rehabilitate them were themselves subject to harassment. What would we give today to have, for example, the complete corpus of Origen or Porphyry (234–ca. 310), whose works were destroyed by the emperors with the support of the bishops?

It looks like we must always struggle in the Church and elsewhere to situate the precise status of truth. In an intellectualistic perspective tributary to Hellenism, there was the tendency to link truth (intellectual, speculative or practical) and concrete action, as if they were part of the process of cause and effect. Moreover, it is always difficult for human beings, at whatever level they are in a hierarchicized world, to be content with probability, just as it is hard to make room for other ways of looking at questions, ways that are legitimate but hard to reconcile with one another. One needs to be careful about falling into what might be called a "pathology of the truth": in the end and despite all appeals to the truth and to revelation (sometimes well founded), a certain anxiety concerning orthodoxy can arise from a preoccupation with the need for intellectual security rather than from a jealous love of the Word of God. This sense of security is sought more by way of excluding other positions than by the humble interiorization of the truth.

We might also ask whether the haste with which opinions were condemned or the rigidity of being on one's guard do not have bad effects today as well as then. This is undoubtedly true, but what is more important is to see a strategy at work regarding the truth whose principles are not limited only to the short term. When truly new perspectives emerge, they often cannot be worked out in the grid of the existing synthesis and one risks judging them (indeed even condemning them) in terms of the categories at hand. But the latter have to be integrated into a wider whole that is in the process of being built. Excessive caution, outright rejection or condemnation slow down and even hinder the process of refocusing. Now this attempt to delay or impede new expressions of truth also contributes to the disaster so bitterly regretted. It is not impossible to understand why Catholic intellectuals, given the constant reiteration of authoritative statements and eventual rejections of newer positions, lose all sense of responsibility for the faith and cannot continue their research out of a consciousness that they too are graced by a charism and helped by the light of the rule of faith. Instead of providing a point of orientation, the pretension of hegemony by the magisterium has tended to lessen, even in the eyes of theologians, the role of a powerful intellect or of language involved in theological effort. Because a person is not really responsible, he or she is tempted to practice a kind of "research without self-investment," where the meaning of the faith of the People of God is less actively involved than if a person sensed that he or she was really responsible in the Church for the task of understanding the faith.

THEOLOGY AND THE CLERICAL STATE

A concrete difficulty in recognizing the "charismatic" status of the theologian and of specifying the appropriate institution is connected with its clerical status and with its quality of academic instruction. Given his hierarchical status, and with the help of a special canonical mission, the priest–theologian is thought to be acting as an authorized witness to a defined doctrine. It is assumed that his proper charism as a theologian cannot be deployed in full freedom, even at the cost of the kind of error that comes with developing new perspectives and that cannot exclude clumsy first attempts. As a teacher whose public for the most part usually includes other clerics, the priest–theologian is considered to offer intelligent explanations of the doctrine he received, and so to be continuing a scholarly tradition more than searching for a creative encounter with his culture in uncharted waters. I think that these two statuses, that of the cleric (or religious) and of the teacher, have a real affinity with our question, since it concerns understanding the faith and transmitting a tradition. But teaching is a natural activity for any form of research, and so we need to distinguish further between institutes established for the education of pastors in their "occupation as priests," and universities which are by definition places dedicated to research and investigation where everyone works in collaboration with his or her colleagues, but fundamentally out of a responsibility that is proper to the Christian intellectual.

In conclusion, permit me to reiterate that the whole field of instruction in the Church is bound to specific gifts of the Spirit: first of all the gift bestowed on the bishops, with the help of study and prayer, to preach the gospel by way of introduction to the sacraments, so as to discern and to correct errors, with the help of the *charisma veritatis certum*.[10] No less important are the numerous gifts among the faithful, without respect to their sex or formation, which make concrete the *sensus fidelium* and render them

10. Note the interpolation inspired by St. Irenaeus of Lyons (ca. 115–90) and added at the last moment to the text of the Dogmatic Constitution on Divine Revelation, art. 8. On the meaning of the expression, see Louis Ligier, "Le *Charisma veritatis certum* des évêques: ses attaches liturgiques, patristiques et bibliques" in *L'Homme devant Dieu. Mélanges offerts au Père Henri de Lubac,* vol. 1 (Paris: Aubier, 1963) 247–68. —See also Jerome D. Quinn, "'Charisma veritatis certum': Irenaeus, *Adversus haereses* 4,26,2," *Theological Studies* 39 (1978) 520–25 [translator].

suitable for understanding and declaring the Christian Mystery, whether at the level of catechesis or theology. These charisms are organized by way of institutions that have an essential place in the structures of the Church and that might be modified or spontaneous, tested and when necessary promoted by the bishops.

The Ministry of Compassion

The forms of *diakonia* we have examined up to this point were concerned with the Word of God in its public expressions: liturgical, catechetical, and theological. But in the Church there is an ensemble of charisms centered on the hardships human beings must face, and which have to do with adversities intimately connected with the disorder found in civilizations, e.g., hunger, poverty, ignorance, etc. Others emerge from the darkness of the human condition, and affect the body or the spiritual condition of persons, and that call for a word of discernment, consolation and encouragement, of compassion and pardon.

By this ensemble of charisms of the Spirit, the Church more closely resembles the Servant of the Lord. It is the whole domain of attention to human suffering: physical, social, and spiritual.

The *Diakoniai* of Assistance

In this field of action, the Church's secular activity is directed at children and the sick, those whose condition has helped so many religious communities define their charism. But this field includes many more hardships, and I willingly admit my inability to understand them all. I admit that here I am not up to the task of "imagining" all that needs to be done. Let me only remark that in the practice of the churches, one can detect a twofold, almost contrary, movement. One must be able to analyze them theologically and without fearing the consequences draw out the theory and the practice of this type of *diakonia* that are imperative.

On the one hand, in richer countries responsibility for the institutions of instruction and health is being taken over more and more by the civil authorities, and that means that in fact as many Christian laity already work in so-called public institutions as in private ones, whereas the latter increasingly appear as real options in a world striving to be more pluralistic rather than totalitarian. Today, Catholic schools or clinics are much more motivated by a will to collaborate with the wider society than by motives of opposition, competition, or exclusivity. They defend their right to exist with arguments drawn from pluralism and complementarity. Without contesting the legitimacy of non-Catholic institutions, we are more concerned with the need to assure a sound education in the faith or religious assistance for those who need it. In regions where Catholic institutions are dominant, we no longer explain their existence as substitutes for civil or municipal establishments so much as for directly religious reasons.

Conversely, and I have no desire to be divisive on this point, we need to ask ourselves why in areas of great poverty the preferential option for the poor has so markedly taken on theological character, that we speak of the "theology of liberation." Isn't it the fact that there is a divine command, founded in revelation, not only to evangelize the poor but to defend and liberate them, i.e., to help them in the struggle for social liberty and political equality? The traditional help we have offered in the name of the gospel, viz., education and health services, are becoming irrelevant when the misery of these people is more structural to their societies. Genuine theological charity for persons and groups consists rather in working for structural changes than in the endless task of filling in the holes or the gulfs that arise from institutional disorder in the world.

And so, some see *diakonia* on behalf of children, the poor, and the sick as blurring the Christian dimension, at least to the extent that it is done in an exclusive way, while for others political and social action (even forceful action that is prone to use violent means) is seen as tied to an elementary demand for the gospel. In the latter perspective, the Church is understood as called to take a preferential option for the poor, and the bishops or priests who are openly committed in this way are seen as rendering a capital witness for the Church's credibility.

Spiritual Compassion

I want to emphasize something that is becoming increasingly evident at the moment, viz., concern for spiritual healing, for accompanying others, and for discernment: what might be called the Christian "relationship of being of help" and which many persons have received as a gift from the Spirit. The gifts related to this *diakonia* are distributed indiscriminately among priests and laity, men and women, married and celibate. History confirms this claim. Today's monks who return to the earliest sources are nourished by the teachings of Fathers who were not priests. St. Ignatius of Loyola (1491–1556), the initiator of what is undoubtedly the most widespread method of discernment in the Church today, began to write his *Spiritual Exercises* and to conduct workshops based on them while still a layman. The Church's spiritualities are nourished by writings that come equally from men and women. What would the interior life of the Church today be without a St. Theresa of the Child Jesus, Marthe Robin, and Charles de Foucauld? Less heroic and more hidden, but perhaps factually more important in today's conditions, are the growing numbers of "spiritual fathers" and "spiritual mothers" in the Church who are available for others who have set forth on the path of spiritual growth and who need to rely on some experience, i.e., to hear a word or ask to be heard (this too belongs to the process). There are those who visit prisons or hospitals, but there are also Christians who are capable of exhorting others and of practicing what is called "spiritual direction." There is a great need to recognize such gifts and to promote the education and formation of those who possess them, since the gifts of word and spiritual accompaniment are strengthened by formation. But we must also recommend such persons to others and support those who have a particular inspiration and a real competence. Here, again, we need to disassociate the ministerial priesthood and the gift of discernment. Even if it is normal that this gift is often recognizable among priests, they are not the only recipients, and we need to educate the Christian people in expanding their horizons when it comes to choosing a "spiritual director."

All charisms of service activate the Lord's second commandment, and from this point of view they manifest an essential relationship to the Eucharist as the Church's spiritual sacrifice offered in memory of the Servant Lord. Can such ideas lead to reflecting more deeply on a certain sacramentality that belongs to them? Often this is signified in a liturgy of prayer, of blessing, and of sending forth that goes hand in hand with the mission connected with the charism. But this would also be the place to study a sacramentality in the larger sense of actions bound up with charismatic activity.

An Example: Hospital Pastoral Care

In our perspective of examining the charisms of compassion and healing, we might consider the question of "reconciliation" worked by those members of a hospital chaplaincy who are not priests. It is not at all rare that in the course of a longer relationship between a patient and a visitor, the first expression of confidence leads to a confession of some evil in the past that is also a request for reconciliation. However, the patient might not be prepared to express the confession in a more formal way to a priest whom he or she does not know, and perhaps too because the patient knows little about the normal conditions for the sacramental pardon of sins. I believe that one could say that the exhortation, prayer, and even the evangelical assurance of reconciliation on the part of the visitor points to a real coming of Christ and disposes the patient for it. We could expand the reflection and ask whether it is the Church that reconciles and is reconciled in every act of reconciliation among Christians. The sacrament of reconciliation properly speaking, i.e., the ecclesial and personal celebration in the presence of an authorized priest, would be the form in which this economy of pardon is completed in Christ and by the Spirit who dwells in the Church in a permanent way.[11] An analogous question can be posed with

11. Apropos, it is a pity that, according to canon 960 of the new Code of Canon Law, the individual rite of reconciliation of sinners is considered the "only ordinary

regard to the sacrament of the sick (and maybe even more easily resolved): why is it not administered by those who visit the sick and are effectively responsible for their spiritual welfare? If they pray with and for them, if they contribute to the healing of their life, why can they not perform the anointing by means of which the Spirit of consolation comes? In this context, weren't the "elders" mentioned by James (5:14) precisely those Christians who exercised the charism of compassion in the Church?[12]

The Service of Administration

Another area for charisms is that of *administration,* which highlights the necessity of human life in the Church, but also the fact that the human must be directed by the Spirit. This involves the whole area of the Church's possessions, of its finances, not only in their use but in the way their use is decided. Apropos of this topic, one of the first examples of prayer and the imposition of hands in the New Testament concerned those who, having been chosen by the primitive community and accepted by the apostles, were set aside for the management of goods, and more particularly, for the care of the poor (see Acts on the choice of the seven "deacons"). Without doubt, a special abundance of the gift of the Spirit is needed for an administration of material goods that is both evangelical and fully human. The history of the Church bears this point out abundantly! Because socioeconomic questions undergo important changes in the course of time and according to place, it is necessary that the Church reflect on them, or better, it is imperative that it study the matter in order to define its Christian attitude at a given historical moment. In this way a tradition of social doctrine is formed which emerges from the charism of administration and strives to give a Christian testimony on the difficult issue of money.[13]

---

way" of administering the sacrament. In this way of thinking, we could say that communion devoutly received outside of Mass is the "only ordinary way" of receiving the Eucharist! It seems that one could set up a parallel between the celebration of the Eucharist and the celebration of penance. In both cases, we are talking about a celebration by the whole Church of the Mystery of Christ, and in the case of the sacrament of penance, with the added note of insisting on the aspect of pardon that is included in the Mystery. Just as each person seals his or her participation in the Eucharist by sacramental communion, so does each one seal his or her participation in reconciliation by the personal confession of sins.

12. See J.-A. Noual, F. Marty and E. Pousset, *Lectures théologiques d'un ministère en aumônerie d'hôpital* (Paris, 1989).

13. I speak of a "tradition" in the area of social doctrine, since this did not descend from on high in some fixed formula. In the papal documents there are developments in the positions taken, even in the vocabulary used. For example, it would be illuminating to show the growth in the appreciation of terms introduced by Marx into sociological

Conclusion: The Ordained Diaconate

Allow me to conclude this chapter on charisms of *diakonia* with a proposal apropos of the ordained diaconate. The restoration of the permanent diaconate effected by the council seems to have been somewhat disappointing. Some have remarked how almost all the tasks officially assigned to deacons can be performed by laypersons. On a pastoral team of celibate priests, a deacon who is married and the father of a family might experience trouble in finding his place, both because his state in life is different from theirs and because the current administration of the sacraments does not fall within his province. On a team of committed laypersons in a parish, he also has trouble, because he is a deacon! How can this malaise be resolved?

In a vision and practice of the Church founded on charisms and their institution—and not on the exclusive pluriformity of tasks of priests—the permanent deacon has the opportunity to retrieve the origins of the office. Couldn't we reserve the order of deacon to those who are responsible, in concert with the bishop, for the smooth running of the services of the Church, viz., those who stir up, organize, test, and above all promote charisms? Every particular Church has its central offices for the liturgy, catechesis, religious instruction, ecumenism, pastoral care of the sick, administration, finances, etc., and these offices usually have a priest, a layperson, or a religious as their director. It strikes me that the precise point is the need for close collaboration with the bishop, not with the direct running of a local community, e.g., parishes, movements, etc., but with managing the "services" (*diakoniai*) of the Church. The men and women who would be responsible for these activities should be the object of the Church's prayer and of a special gift of the Spirit; and those are precisely the elements of an ordination.[14]

---

vocabulary and the number of times they are cited in successive texts. Perhaps with time, after the process of fine-tuning necessary for everything that is assumed into the testimony of the Church, the theology of liberation will appear as a moment in this tradition.

14. If my proposal were followed, it would in certain instances revive old rivalries between the deacons around their bishop and the presbyters responsible for local communities. But all of this is more a matter of tactfulness. Those who strive to set down the grand lines or general orientations of a question (and this necessarily involves decisions concerning the allocation of funds!) will leave to those who are on the local scene the responsibility for implementation, which can never simply be the translation of theory. Those who are locally responsible need to be more appreciative than jealous of the help that they are given by those responsible for determining the lines of command and points of convergence. This kind of "conflict" or "malaise" existed not so long ago between the local bishops and the "cardinal–deacons" who were responsible for the Roman dicasteries and who were really priests, not bishops. Pope John XXIII tried to resolve this problem by ordaining the prefects and secretaries of the pontifical dicasteries bishops. Are we free to think that this solution was not the definitive one? In the

next chapter I will address the issue of the Roman administration established by Pope Sixtus V and which successive reforms made even stronger. But if, in another needed reform, the dicasteries really necessary for the moderate practice of the primacy of Peter saw themselves as *diakoniai* and not as "authorities," there would be no reason to be concerned that future cardinal–deacons would not even be priests. —Finally, I want to add that in the numerous writings on the diaconate I consulted, I did not find any deeper theological reflection in the direction of thinking of a "body of deacons" grouped around the bishop. I believe that on the whole we have tried to rethink the diaconate from the point of departure of the classical "ladder" without subjecting it to any criticism, viz., "bishop, priest, deacon." I am suggesting that we transform the ladder image into a triangle!

Chapter 7

The Diversified Charism of Presiding

We have finally arrived at the office of presiding over the community. First, however, I need to stress something we have run into at several points but which I have not lingered over: the extraordinary way that nature and grace correspond to each other. Authority belongs to the nature of politics, and which I am tempted to say is *hier*archic, as long as we do not understand the prefix "hier-" in the sense of something "sacred" that does not apply to the political order. However that may be, the Church, in so far as it forms part of a human social body, is not *an*archic and it has an authority whose purpose is to assure the governing of the People of God in its spiritual sacrifice, its witness and its journey toward the kingdom of God.

In my presentation, the theme of presiding or presidency in the Church appears at the end. My intention is not to denigrate the apostolic ministry but to situate it in its own truth, i.e., in relation to the Church and not vice versa. So, it was necessary to make more precise how the Church was structured by the charisms of the Spirit with a view to its end. Do we not instead need to consider the apostolic ministry also as a specific charism, whose particular importance is found in its task of encouraging the Church to remain faithful to the other charisms that permeate it? The charism of presiding is also a gift of the Spirit to the Church.

Presidency, a Charism and a Sacrament

Hierarchy is determined by the Church, since the members of the hierarchy belong to the Church too. In its origins and its nature, hierarchy obeys the charismatic character of the Church. No one establishes himself as president of the whole community or of a determined part of it without the calling of the Spirit, which is called a "vocation," especially when applied to priests. This is much more than a preliminary to sacramental ordination; it is the Spirit's proposing someone and supplying him with the appropriate gift, in order that he can function as a "moderator" in the Church. The whole of priestly formation is directed first toward discerning the gift's presence or absence, then with the formation of this spiritual charism, and finally with the ongoing formation that follows or should follow. It is even more imperative to speak about the nomination of a bishop, which can only be founded on the choice by the Spirit, since it too is the object of a process of discernment. This appears to be less the case than for a priest, since the present centralization and secrecy of the process, and maybe too of the criteria, do not make it obvious. It would certainly be clearer if we found a balanced way that permitted the churches to designate their own bishops, as we will see later on.

On the other hand, if the charism of being a pastor is the same for all who receive it, in a secondary yet real way it is also specified by those who receive it and by their taking their place in concrete time and space. Not every priest is suited to being a worker–priest or named a bishop to just any diocese. In other words, a canonical mission is founded normally in a personal charism, even if in the best scenario it also uncovers for the subject capabilities and a gift he was not aware of. But in many cases we are not dealing with the best scenario and the absence of an effective charism will mean that the sacramentally ordained priests or bishops will be wretched pastors. In this case, the sacrament functions in a vacuum, as examples too numerous to mention have shown throughout the Church's history. Vice versa, when the sacrament corresponds to the charism, it signifies to the Church, the world, and the subject himself the inchoate presence of this gift of the Spirit and calls for its confirmation and its fulfillment in the invocation of the Spirit *(epiclesis)* and the imposition of hands at the heart of the liturgy of ordination. By this fullness of the gift, the bishop is situated in the apostolic succession of the bishops, the guarantors and the persons responsible for the apostolic succession of this Church which "is" the tradition, according to the Dogmatic Constitution on Divine Revelation, article 8. As for the priest, he is under the guidance of the bishop in order to exercise responsibly the function of presiding among the People of God. When all is said and done, we must keep the charism and the sacrament together as the two faces of one continuous call of the Spirit, mutually supporting each other in order to permit an effective and useful response for the Church.

This insistence on the unity of the charism and the sacrament for the role of presidency in the Church, and the advantage to treating this charism at the end of our ecclesiological journey, is that they allow us to take into account some rather important changes initiated by Vatican II on how we understand the charism and the function. First of all, I will analyze these changes, moving from bishop to priest to pope. Then I will make some re-marks and proposals on the discernment of the charism under considera-tion and on the procedures for designating bishops and the conditions governing the access of priests to such a function. Finally, I will try to make more precise the function proper to this charism of presiding, viz., what one can call *episkopē* or the role of "vigilance" in the strong sense of the term.

Changes Initiated by Vatican II

Bishops

When it treated what it called the "Hierarchical Constitution of the Church" (an unfortunate way of referring to the matter, as I said earlier), the council first dealt with the bishops.[1] Concerning them, Vatican II teaches that "that the fullness of the sacrament of Orders is conferred by episcopal consecration. . . . Episcopal consecration confers, together with the office of sanctifying, the offices also of teaching and ruling, which, however, of their very nature can be exercised only in hierarchical communion with the head and members of the college. Tradition . . . makes it abundantly clear that, through the imposition of hands and the words of consecration, the grace of the holy Spirit is given, and a sacred character is impressed in such a way that bishops, eminently and visibly, take the place of Christ himself, teacher, shepherd and priest, and act in his person." (LG 21). For the Church (but also to anyone to whom it is addressed), the sacrament of orders sig-nifies, in mystery, that a Christian is signed by the Spirit in the image of Jesus, the crucified and risen Shepherd, and that he is appointed pastor in the Church. Made to resemble Christ the Shepherd by initiation, the bishop represents him and exercises that function in him. This spiritual-sacramental definition of the pastoral ministry, beyond retrieving the ancient tradition of the Church in speaking of the Christic configuring of every pastor by the Lord's sacramental action, is deeply in accord with the most classical theol-ogy of the sacraments as "effecting what they signify." On the one hand, that means that we must understand this theology in its plain signification, while on the other hand, we will have to reinterpret the whole of the doc-trine of ministry in light of this simple and self-evident Christian proposal. In other words, we must avoid trying to imagine it as a kind of "sacramen-tal addendum" to be integrated into the Gregorian form of ecclesial ministry.

---

1. See The Dogmatic Constitution on the Church, chapter 3. Nevertheless, at the beginning of the chapter, it mentioned what had been defined at the First Vatican Council (1869–70) on the papacy, in order to adopt and confirm this doctrine. But we will see later that this confirmation of the whole is not a dogmatic stance in the proper theological sense of the term.

No, we must rethink and reorganize the Gregorian elements at the very heart of this foundational sacramentality, whatever the practical consequences might be for the life of the Church. The primary form of pastoral ministry is therefore the ministry of the bishop.[2]

Authority and Community

The definition of the pastor in the image of Christ orientates the recipient of the sacrament directly to the community: he is the pastor of a community,[3] in order to hand on and help it in living out the apostolic heritage in its entirety.[4] Distinctions among the powers, i.e., of administering the sacraments, of proclaiming the gospel, of governing the body, etc., only serve to furnish a more global pastoral authority. But this does not prevent us from searching out an order (in the sense both of a "hierarchy" and the giving of "direction") among the various powers, which are the outpouring of the unique responsibility of Jesus Christ sacramentally communicated.

The Episcopal "Character"

I want to stress something that could be judged a trifling detail but which is in reality of capital importance in light of the axes of classical theology. If, as the Church thinks, the sacrament of order effects a "character," i.e., if ordination cannot be repeated in so far as Christ does not withdraw the mark he has placed on the man chosen for pastoral responsibility, this must be the case primarily for the bishop, something the council did not fail to mention (see LG 21). But how should we define this character? Though

---

2. In a sense, the whole question of the interpretation of Vatican II's ecclesiology is found here. Should power be understood from within the sacrament, of which it is an effect and by which it is measured, or is a sacramental nuance to be added to the heart of the sacrament? In the first instance, we would have to revisit entirely the question of authority—the bishop's, the pope's, the religious superior's, that of a lay leader—in the light of the double mission of the mysteries of the Incarnate Word and the Holy Spirit. Such a revision would have considerable institutional consequences, some of which we will examine in this chapter. In order to appreciate the "sensitive" character of the question, I refer the reader to Adriano Celeghin, *Origini e natura della potestà sacra. Posizioni post-conciliari* (Brescia: Morcelliana, 1987), in which the author lists no less than one hundred and forty authors who wrote about this topic in the twenty years following the council. Jean Beyer has given a helpful bibliography in his "De natura potestatis regiminis seu jurisdictionis recte in Codice renovato enuntianda," *Periodica* 71 (1982) 93–145.

3. The appropriateness of the title of "pastor" is self-evident when we recall the imagery employed by Vatican II in the first chapter of the Dogmatic Constitution on the Church: the community is a "flock" and a "sheepfold" (LG 6).

4. According to the Dogmatic Constitution on Divine Revelation, the very raison d'être of the bishop is to insure that the tradition received from Christ and the apostles will be handed on to everyone (DV 7).

the scholastic tradition dealt with character, it considered it from another point of view. To the scholastics, the sacrament of order was directly and essentially ordered to the celebration of the Eucharist; it concerned the priest directly, i.e., the one whom the liturgy calls a priest "of the second order." The episcopacy, which has no greater power over the Eucharist than the simple priesthood has, was not considered a sacrament in the strict sense of the term, and whatever "form" the bishop's "responsibility" assumed, it did not include a character. The latter was understood (at least by Thomas Aquinas, whose opinion became the traditional one) as the quasi-physical or "instrumental" power to celebrate the Eucharist.

The council's teaching on the sacramentality of the episcopacy and the affirmation that the sacrament of episcopacy confers a character necessarily expands the meaning of the latter: it cannot be reduced to an instrumental power over the Eucharist. Instead, we must understand the character as the "marking" of the bishop in the image of Christ the Pastor, dead and risen. We can say that the character, liturgically conferred by the sacrament of order, is an interior sign which confirms and consecrates a Christian's charism of presiding over a particular Church as given by the Holy Spirit. It is Christ's indelible imprint on this person that habituates him to act responsibly in the name and with the authority of Christ *(in persona Christi)* in the acts of his ministry. This is particularly evident when the bishop celebrates the Eucharist of the community, since in virtue of this global configuration, when the bishop speaks formally in the name of Christ in the sacrament, his word effects what it declares. Because the bishop is responsible for a community, he communicates to it the paschal mystery from which it lives, he nourishes it with the Body and Blood of Christ, and in the Eucharist he offers reciprocally the spiritual sacrifice of the community for which he bears responsibility.[5] There is no reason to continue to maintain St. Thomas's position on the character as *potestas,* since this is tied to a definition of the sacrament of order as essentially related to priests, whose priesthood would first and foremost be ordered toward confecting the Eucharist.[6]

5. The bishop, then, presides at the Eucharist because he presides over the Christian community. The council rediscovers explicitly the economy of the early Church's tradition. See the documented and convincing study by Hervé-Marie Legrand, "The Presidency of the Eucharist According to the Ancient Tradition," *Worship* 53 (1979) 413–38.

6. As I have said, because of the absence of his specific eucharistic ministry, St. Thomas did not admit an "episcopal character," and while he did acknowledge that the episcopacy was a "state of perfection," he did not think it was a sacrament. Moreover, in St. Thomas and in the classical theology, the expression *in persona Christi* had a meaning immediately connected to the Eucharist. When Vatican II uses this expression apropos of the bishop, what is it saying *exactly*? See Bernard Dominique Marliangeas, *Clefs pour une théologie du ministère. In persona Christi. In persona Ecclesiae,* Théologie Historique, vol. 51 (Paris: Beauchesne, 1978).

In saying this, both more and less is being attributed to the "character": more because we are saying that both the bishop and the priest in their ways are more representatives of Christ the Pastor than mere celebrants of the Eucharist and that the whole of this representation (and not only the strictly sacerdotal function) is in the image of Christ. But also less because the sacramental function itself must be thought of in terms of other functions and so differs only in terms of the specific degree in which it signifies and effects something: the sacrament celebrated is effective because of the priest's word, who is marked by the image of the Pastor and acts "in the power of the Spirit." There is no need to imagine a specifically permanent power *(potestas)*. But if one wishes to retain the category of instrument for the sacramental word, it would be necessary to apply it correctly to the *word* in so far as it is pronounced by the bishop and by the priest when they celebrate in the name and with the authority of Christ, and not to a power that is "physically" permanent. What is permanent is the configuration to Christ the Pastor.[7]

Collegiality

Later, in treating the topic of the episcopal ministry *(episkopē)*, I will try to locate its collegial aspect. What needs to be stressed at this point is the sacramental foundation of episcopacy. There is only one "Pastor and bishop of our lives" (1 Pet 2:25), with the result that all who are sacramentally conformed to him in order to make him present in the Church and the world today, are one with him. In other words, the unique and active episcopacy of Jesus Christ is rendered present in the body of bishops (and their assistants, the priests) and in each one of them singly. Concretely, this implies the setting up of institutions which serve the convergence of pastoral acts, if not their unanimity.

In order to offer a brief synopsis of what I've said about the theological change regarding the person of the bishop, it can be said that the apostolic ministry as charism and sacrament is to be understood as an image, a figure or type, a representation. The Spirit destines those chosen and what the sacrament expresses and confers is a *configuration* at once intimate and external of Christ the Pastor. Ministerial powers and actions flow from this primary reality: the one presented to the Church as pastor in Jesus' name

---

7. These observations permit us to surmount the opposition between the "ontological" and the "functional" ways of considering the apostolic ministry. The sacrament of order does not make the bishop more of a Christian than others, and in this sense nothing is added to the Christian's dignity thanks to the sacraments of initiation. On the other hand, the image of Christ the Pastor imprinted on a man, which is ordered immediately to ministerial acts, creates a holy and permanent foundation for the pastoral function.

receives by that very fact all the concrete authority necessary and acts effectively as pastor, as long as we take care to include the necessary bonds of communion bound up with collegiality and the primacy of Peter.

Priests

As with the bishop, the person of the priest is defined by his global responsibility with regard to a community. The priest is virtually the bishop's *lieu-tenant* (in the etymological sense of the term), exercising the pastoral responsibility of Jesus Christ in a portion of the particular Church.[8] Briefly put, this is his responsibility. Following the thought of St. Irenaeus and St. Augustine, the Decree on the Ministry and Life of Priests of Vatican II explains that they are ordained for the building up of a community of living men and women who offer a spiritual sacrifice to God by their mutual love and their witness and which the priest celebrates in the Eucharist. The latter is the liturgical place of the spiritual sacrifice taken up in the memorial of Jesus Christ and, thanks to the Spirit who flows from the pierced heart of Christ, is the source of the Church's Christian life. In virtue of the sacrament which the bishop confers precisely for this purpose, priests have authority that is doctrinal, administrative, and sacramental in the *ecclesiola,* i.e., the local community which is an image of the diocesan community, confided to them. Like the bishop, they are marked by a character which does not admit definition as *potestas,* and who like him act *in persona Christi* and *in persona Ecclesiae.*

Breadth of Change

What I have just said is simply the result of the ecclesiological inspiration of Vatican II. In reality, however, it implies significant changes that will require more time before they sink into our general consciousness. Earlier in the book, I underscored the elements that little by little have been stressed in the West to form the classical image of the priest: character and ministry.[9] The spirituality of the priesthood of presbyters that was current insisted first of all on the sacramental role of the priest, and on a certain understanding of character that made this role possible, while almost exclusively limiting apostolic and missionary responsibility to it.

If, according to Vatican II, the responsibility of the priest par excellence is "presiding" or the "moderating" of a community, it is not up to him to do everything in the Church. That the laity should become involved part-time, or for some even full-time, according to their own charism, is

---

8. This relation to a particular community is mentioned by the Code of Canon Law in the case of both the pastor (canon 519) and the chaplain (canon 564).

9. See chapter 2, pp. 59–60.

something normal and is in no way substitutionary because the number of clergy has declined and their assisting the clergy is limited to the current situation. In the mind of Vatican II, we must repeat, the ministry of the laity is not expressed theologically as their participation in the apostolic ministry. The latter is determined by the sacrament of order and hierarchical communion, and includes the bishops, priests, and deacons. The ministry of the laity rests on the sacraments of Christian initiation and their particular charisms. Practically speaking, we can say that the fundamental difference between the apostolic ministry and lay ministry seems to be that the latter is given particular form by the charisms imparted to perform this or that task, such as moderating youth groups, catechesis and the other levels of theological instruction, the ministry of healing or compassion, providing financial or administrative service, etc. The priest's mission is to stir up, verify, and coordinate these ministries in the Church and to gather them together in the unique sacrifice of Christ, whose mystery he proclaims personally in the homily.

The number of priests today would not seem so inadequate if, according to the mentality still found, we did not think that a man could not do anything important in the Church unless he was a priest. And as far as male religious are concerned, it is necessary that we give more weight to the fact that the essential charism that defines their foundation is most often not the priesthood. The parallel communities of women religious that sometimes have the same founder and that pursue the same goal by benefiting from the same charism and an analogous formation makes this amply clear. This fact would seem to prove that the ministerial priesthood is not of the essence for the corresponding institute for men. Why must one be a priest to accomplish the task of Catholic education, if, in a neighboring school conducted by women religious (who are not priests by definition), they are employed in the same work without benefit of ordination? Such a question seems to have nourished the claim to be ordained by some women. Now, in many cases, the solution to this disparity between men and women beneficiaries of the same charism is not the ordination of women to the priesthood, but rather changing the character of the male religious community in such a way as to restrict access to the priesthood. If it is a matter of religious life, the issue is the declericalization of a number of congregations in which the vast majority of its members exercise the charism proper to them all the better because it is not obscured by the "dignity of the priesthood" which in most cases is really not relevant.

The Age of Priests

If the priest is the one who presides, the one responsible for a Christian community, he must have attained an age at which he can fulfill his responsibilities. The Pastoral Epistles (1 Tim 3:2-7 and Titus 1:6-9) presuppose that to direct a community, the men chosen have attained maturity and have shown both by the quality of their Christian life but also by the quality of their human life, i.e., by their marriage and the upbringing of children, their capacity to lead a Christian community in a balanced and human way. Today, perhaps we can add that they have demonstrated the capacity to collaborate with others and to bring an important human activity to completion by the way they have exercised an occupation. The same elements apply for all Christians, even those who made the decision in their youth to give themselves fully in celibacy to the service of the Church and have matured in serving the community. In short, no one must be placed at the head of a community who has not manifested a real maturity, both on the human and the Christian plane.

An important question would be to determine how we are to discern such maturity. This is clearly not the whole, nor even the essential point, of a charism of presiding over a community, but maybe it should be its necessary condition. Once again, if there is no need to be a priest in order to dedicate oneself to tasks and activities that demand a certain youthfulness, ordination to the priesthood can be deferred until such time as the community can count on the human and Christian experience of someone to exercise the responsibility of presiding over it.

Celibacy

Evidently, the definition of the priesthood in terms of the charism of presidency and the hypothesis that the ordination of men should take place only after they have manifested a long practice both of Christian and human life, calls into question the general demand for priestly celibacy. I would like to venture several reflections on this important issue.

It is not my intention to denigrate in any way the state of virginity in the Church, whether for men or women, and I have spoken of its importance in chapter 5. Nor is it a question of discussing the real affinity that exists between the sacrament of order and the state of virginity, so that *whatever measures might be taken in the future, we can be sure that the celibate lifestyle will continue to be an option for many priests.* Given all this, it is still true that marriage is also a Christian state in life, and even a sacrament. It makes Christians, precisely as couples, the image of Jesus, the dead and risen spouse of the Church. It, too, is a spiritual calling demanding discernment, in the framework of life in time and space, and from this point of view is not at all inferior to religious life. It makes spouses witnesses of the gospel according to their charism, which can take on every form of *diakonia*.

I think it is legitimate to ask whether the Church would be well served if married men were also pastors of their communities. They have a certain experiential understanding of human existence that would give a particular tonality to the exercise of the charism of presidency: their relationship to sexuality and money is different from that of the celibate; their knowledge of youth is that of parents and not simply educators; and their professional relations of collaboration as well as their friendly relations with other families would impart a certain style of living with others. I think it would be preferable that both forms of life, married and celibate, be represented in the heart of the presbyterium. That would avoid a priestly spirituality that is too "other worldly," an attempt to identify the priest as too singular (and necessarily as setting himself off by a certain sense of superiority vis-à-vis others), but also by a certain unilateral approach pastorally, since de facto the pastoral ministry is directed exclusively by members of only one of the two states in life. I believe that pastors of both states can learn from each other and mutually support one another in effectively grasping *all* the dimensions of the kingdom of God.

I think the direction I am going is becoming clear. The priesthood is a matter of confiding a Christian community to a man who fully occupies a place in society, and so is not only married but also has an occupation or has exercised one. The Code of Canon Law makes provision for the case when the absence of a priest calls for the conferral of "participation in the pastoral responsibility" on a deacon, some other nonordained person, or a group of persons, so long as a priest remains ultimately responsible, even from a distance (canon 517, 2). Whoever they are, such persons clearly are engaged in life in the world where they are forced to live in a Christian way in their families and at work. Moreover, even if the Code of Canon Law in this regard speaks of "participation," in fact they exercise a real pastoral responsibility, i.e., they perform the work which defines the priest (according to the Decree on the Ministry and Life of Priests, art. 2): they form the community and each person in offering their spiritual sacrifice and their witness to the gospel. If they effectively fulfill this task, even though it is provisional and dependent on someone else, isn't this because God gives them this charism? From a doctrinal and a pastoral point of view, nothing stands in the way of (and I would even say, everything demands) their ordination: *if someone fulfills the priest's pastoral responsibility, why shouldn't he receive the sacrament by which God alone conforms a person fully to the image of the Son who is the dead and risen Pastor of his Church?*[10] But, on the other

10. Here is the very heart of the question of priestly ministry. If the priesthood is fundamentally pastoral, it is not an optional matter of giving the sacrament of order to those who are acknowledged capable of exercising the function in the Holy Spirit, because it is the sacrament which habituates them to act in the name of Christ in fulfilling them. Letters given by the bishops with a view to the nonordained fulfilling a pastoral mission are a juridical substitute, of dubious theological merit, for what should be

hand, such persons will not have surrendered their place in the world, especially if their other charisms have been well integrated into the community.[11]

If what I have tried to say is true, how are we to understand the "law of priestly celibacy" and its inviolability up to today? Undoubtedly mention must be made of the relationship between celibacy and the offering of a sacrifice.[12] But here, too, we must take into account the idea of hierarchy. In Pseudo-Dionysius, this idea is both functional, i.e., it is proper to hierarchies to hand on the symbols of union with God or the knowledge of God, and hagiological and ontological: Pseudo-Dionysius does not know how to distinguish these areas, even if he doesn't ignore them. Themes like freedom, which because of grace makes holiness possible for every Christian, and substance, which determines a creature independent of its freedom and spiritual knowledge, are not turned into problems by Pseudo-Dionysius. Also, the way of looking at the bishop is highly unitary for him: the bishop is at the same time supreme pontiff, accomplished saint, and the highest being in the initiatory hierarchies. On the other hand, the monks are the ones who are "perfect" among the initiated, and even if they do not function as mediators, they are situated at an unsurpassable summit in their order. In both cases, virginity is seen as the context and the condition of hierarchical perfection. From this point of view, the most worthy members of the Church are the bishop and the monk.

In the Western world, these ideas from Pseudo-Dionysius were applied to the priest. As the celebrant of the holy mysteries, he has the holiness of a hierarch, and without pausing to reflect on the difference, the virginity of the monk was also included. Finally, there was a third element, bound up with the Gregorian form of the Church, viz., "jurisdiction" could be given more easily to a man who had no other social ties. Since he had no

---

sacramental ordination. See the superb treatment by Bernard Sesboüé, "Les Animateurs pastoraux laïcs. Une prospective théologique," *Études* 377 (1982) 253–65.

11. I trust the reader understands that I am not pleading for married ministerial priests who will make pastoral or missionary work their exclusive occupation. I genuinely do not think that this form of the priesthood will contribute greatly to changing the form of the Church. I am pleading for men whose family and professional lives have demonstrated the maturity and the capability of directing a community, not all by themselves and not exclusively with the help of special assistants, but by implementing the diversity of the Church's charisms, wherever they are found (on condition that we seek them out and promote them).

12. See Hervé-Marie Legrand, "Bulletin d'ecclésiologie. Recherches sur le presbytérat et l'épiscopat," *Revue des sciences philosophiques et théologiques* 59 (1975) 645–724, at 658f. [explaining the thesis of Roger Gryson—translator]. Although I am referring to a detail of the author's presentation, the whole article should be read, as well as its sequel, "Le Ministère ordonné dans le dialogue oecuménique," ibid., 60 (1976) 649–92.

family and no occupation, he was more readily at the bishop's disposition. And if he was a religious, he was at the disposition of the pope. And so, the Church veritably "functioned" because of the clergy and almost exclusively because of them, up until very recent times.

The Pope

The doctrine of the sacramental character of episcopacy has also resulted in a change in the way in which the pope is seen as compared with his place in the Gregorian form of the Church.

Literary Changes

This change can be noted from the literary point of view in the text of Vatican II. We need to recall that Vatican I intended to write a complete constitution on the Church and that the supreme pontiff was to be treated in chapter 11.[13] Because of rather urgent circumstances, the bishops decided to anticipate the teaching on the sovereign pontiff, which gave rise to the constitution *Pastor aeternus*. Today, now that we finally have the full constitution on the Church that was only glimpsed in 1870, it should be mentioned, as the Second Vatican Council did in article 18 of the Dogmatic Constitution on the Church, that the bishops not only ratified and presented the teaching of Vatican I on the pope, but also that the earlier teaching now needs to find its proper, organic place in the constitution. It seems to me that that place would be right after article 22. The theological order unfolds in the following way. First, the council had to define the sacramental nature of episcopacy (art. 21). Next, it had to consider the unity of all the bishops in their pastoral responsibility in so far as it is founded on the one sacrament received directly from Jesus Christ (art. 22). Finally, it would have affirmed the special dignity of the Bishop of Rome, but would see him constituted a bishop in the Church by the same sacrament as every other bishop in the Church, and would understand that he is the first among the pastors and head of their college from the moment he is placed at the head of Peter's community, the Church of Rome. The natural place for this to be done would be in article 23.[14] In summary, it is necessary to understand the constitution *Pastor aeternus* of Vatican I as the anticipated text of a development on the doctrine of the papacy that can finally take its rightful theological place, viz., between articles 22 and 23 of the council's Dog-

---

13. See J. D. Mansi, *Sacrorum Conciliorum nova et amplissima collectio*, vol. 51 (Arnhem and Leipzig: H. Welter, 1926) 544–45.

14 Such a simple presentation would have avoided the almost obsessional repetition (I counted twenty!) in chapter 3 of the constitution that the bishop cannot do anything outside of communion with the pope.

matic Constitution on the Church. This proper place flows out of the council's efforts to do two essential things: first, to define the sacramentality of the episcopal office, and second, to understand the bishops as forming a college.[15]

Doctrinal Change

Such a literary change calls for a certain *doctrinal* change. When Vatican I defines the power of the Bishop of Rome, it characterizes it as "a full and supreme power of jurisdiction, [. . .] ordinary and immediate" (DS 3064) that is "truly episcopal" (DS 3060).[16] Now, Vatican II showed that such a *truly episcopal* power (and others) comes with episcopal sacramental ordination,[17] since it configures a man in the image of Jesus the Pastor, crucified and risen. The power of the pope is the universal extension, proper to the Bishop of Rome, of a truly episcopal authority that is sacramental in origin.

It follows from this that we cannot think of the pope's power as a fullness of jurisdiction that is self-constituting, received "directly from God," and not constituted by any bond with the memorial of the crucified and risen Jesus. We also cannot maintain, without very precise explanations, that this "jurisdiction coming from God" is the indirect source or obligatory channel of the more limited jurisdiction of the bishops. And, finally, we cannot say it is the source of every other jurisdiction in the Church. In denying such "autonomous" conceptions of jurisdiction, bound as they are to the Gregorian form of the Church, we are certainly not diminishing the authority of the pope. To the contrary, this opens up the way for another practical distribution of episcopal and other powers in the Church. To the

---

15. Apropos, note that the Prologue to *Pastor aeternus* is almost an outline that anticipated the Dogmatic Constitution on the Church, or at least as the summary of the fuller constitution that Vatican I wanted but was not able to complete. In the Prologue, we find the following order of topics: the People of God, episcopacy, the office of successor to Peter. See Mansi 52, 1330.

16. On the teaching of Vatican I on the Roman primacy, see the excellent study by J.M.R. Tillard, "The Jurisdiction of the Bishop of Rome," *Theological Studies* 40 (1979) 3–22, and the article by John P. Galvin, "Papal Primacy in Contemporary Roman Catholic Theology," *Theological Studies* 47 (1986) 653–67 [translator].

17. The constitution *Romano pontifici eligendo* (no. 88) of Paul VI took note of this point by deferring the ceremony of a pope's imparting the papal benediction *urbi et orbi* only after his episcopal ordination, in the case of the election of a pope who had not been previously ordained: he must be consecrated Bishop of Rome in order to become pope and to be addressed as such in the Church. *Acta Apostolicae Sedis* 67 (1975) 644. There was nothing similar in the earlier constitution *Vacantis Apostolicae Sedis* of Pius XII. A comparison of no. 101 of the latter with no. 88 of the former constitution is highly revealing of the theological change that occurred in the time between the appearance of both texts. See *Acta Apostolicae Sedis* 38 (1946) 97 for no. 101 of Pius XII's constitution.

extent that the whole canonical system of the Church from the time of the Gregorian reform rests on the theme of a primacy of jurisdiction totally distinct from the sacrament, we cannot effectively reintegrate this primacy into a sacramental model without reconsidering the whole of the Church's law. Taken in its entirety, current Church law proceeds from the Gregorian form of the Church and not the sacramental form of Vatican II. It is not a matter of rejecting something but of taking up the whole all over again and giving it a new form.

Pastoral Change

If he is the successor to Peter because he is Bishop of Rome, occupies the see of the Prince of the Apostles and governs the Church that Peter governed, and where he died and is buried, shouldn't the pope effectively and first of all exercise his particular episcopal responsibility precisely there? Succeeding to Peter is not something timeless, without any local roots. Like any form of apostolic succession, it is connected with time and space. The church of Rome is not an abstract, universal entity; it does not live on only in its past monuments which reflect a long tradition. It has to do with a living church, one confronted today by all the problems any church in a large metropolis has to face: population growth, inadequate housing, expanding suburbs, the absence of places of worship outside the city limits, decline in the number of clergy, missionary problems connected with large numbers of domestic and foreign immigrants who have been uprooted from their cultures and their traditional forms of religion, Christian or otherwise. One might sum up Rome's situation, like that of all the large cities of the world, with the formula applied to postwar France for its shock effect: "Rome, a mission country?" There is no intent to insult Rome. Wasn't Rome a mission territory when Peter governed the Church? Thus, the pope is not a universal administrator without immediate and concrete responsibility. His responsibility over the universal Church is exactly the same as that over the church of Rome: the latter determines the former. To exercise local pastoral care effectively can make the pope attentive to the real needs, which are both different and identical, of his universal pastoral mission in all the diversity of its realizations.[18]

---

18. Perhaps an anecdote will be of help. In the course of a recent *ad limina* visit, a French bishop who had a delicate pastoral problem shared it with Pope John Paul II and asked for his opinion. The pope said: "When I was in Krakow . . ." and shared his past experience on the subject. Now, whatever solicitude the Pope shows toward the Diocese of Rome, he was not in the position or thought of saying: "In Rome this is what we do . . ." A pope without previous episcopal experience could not even say anything, except for some theoretical observations, possibly very helpful, or by making an appeal to the experience of others, something good in itself but less relevant.

In other words, one could say that this definition of the pope as essentially the Bishop of Rome calls for a certain pastoral way of acting, like one encounters with certain great bishops whose international influence is vast, because of their words, their writings, and their trips, but is found also in the limitations of governing a diocese that remains personal, even though they are often widely assisted by competent auxiliaries, i.e., by bishops or other persons. The question is knowing whether a redistribution and a rearranging of the pontifical function and its services is possible, so that the concrete task of the pope remains simultaneously directly pastoral and truly universal. I will offer a few suggestions a little bit later.

I want to add a remark that, though it is not strictly relevant, is not totally pointless either. The geographical location of the primacy of Peter in Rome is open to receiving a negative connotation. It could be asked why the Bishop of Rome, the capital of a once great empire and today the capital of a country of moderate influence, is the head of the universal Church. Why not the Bishop of the Holy City of the Old and New Testaments, Jerusalem, where Jesus and not Peter founded his community, and where he died and was raised, where his tomb is venerated, the sign of his death as well as his resurrection? In Church history, the Church and the formation of the great patriarchates, Jerusalem did not occupy the first place. Far from it! Beyond purely historical reasons, we might ask if that is not a spiritual sign. Jerusalem is the city of Christ; the Bishop of Rome does not govern it but goes there on pilgrimage! As if, in the place of his passion and resurrection, Christ cannot be replaced. Peter is not Christ, but his *lieu-tenant* (again, in the etymological sense), and Jerusalem remains the place that polarizes views and the place where the Church waits while preparing for Christ's parousia. From this point of view, Rome is a city like any other, a community like any other, except that Peter, who was its bishop, gave it a particular mission for all time. In a sense, Christ is always the only bishop of Jerusalem, whatever one makes of the succession of bishops who preside today over the diversity of Christian communities.

Election of Leaders

Introduction: The Roman Model

The Responsibility of the Community of Rome

In the apostolic constitution *Romano pontifici eligendo* (1975), Pope Paul VI mentioned how the election of the Roman pontiff belongs to the Church of Rome, represented in this case by the cardinals.[19]

---

19. *Acta Apostolicae Sedis* 67 (1975) 611 [609–45]. See *Origins* 5 (23) (November 23, 1975) 360–67 for a partial English translation.

It seems to me that in this statement of the responsibility of the church of Rome for the election of its pastor, there is the forceful realization, in spite of all the historical vicissitudes of canon law, of what is a creative intuition of Vatican II and a central fact of the Christian tradition, viz., that the Church exists first of all as a whole, that it is the subject of a gift of God, and that it bears the responsibility for holiness and witness. When it loses one of the members essential for its life as a church, its duty and responsibility is to provide for his replacement. Two remarks are in order. First of all, this duty and responsibility are spiritual; it is not a matter of a purely human process, to be accomplished according to purely sociojuridical procedures ("conversations," "candidates," "election," etc.). It is a matter of discerning who possesses the necessary qualities and can be considered as designated by God from among those Christians available. In other words, it concerns the discernment of the *charism of the Spirit* wherever it is, and the sociojuridical procedures exist to facilitate the search for and the designation of the one who is considered "the choice of God." The specific character of such an "election" helps to determine the appropriate climate of the choice. Second, it is incumbent on the Church of Rome to seek out and to designate the one who will be its bishop, but it cannot constitute him in the episcopal order. Only those who already have this responsibility in the Church are capable of ordaining a bishop, i.e., of marking him in such a way that he resembles Christ the Pastor, as I have already explained.

The proper responsibility of the Church in the election of its pastor can be elucidated by a fact that should be noted: whatever might have been the vicissitudes in the election of popes over the ages, e.g., political pressure, internal corruption, etc., it never dawned on the pope to nominate a "coadjutor with the right of succession." In terms of a certain understanding of the papacy, such a nomination appears theoretically possible: if a pope decided, *per impossibile,* to make such a procedure canonical, who could effectively oppose it? If someone thought to invalidate such a designation after the pope's death, couldn't the pope while still alive resign, so that his coadjutor could become the Bishop of Rome, head of the college of bishops, the true pope and pastor of the universal Church "with full rights"? If no pope has ever done so, it is undoubtedly because he sensed spontaneously that it did not belong to a functioning bishop to provide for the time following his death. The question does not fall within his province but the Church's. Still, one could imagine a case where a pope, desiring to resign after a certain time, informs the Church of his intention, invites it to gather in conclave but without having an active voice in it himself, and remains in charge for some time in order to provide a period of transition for the successor that the Church has given him.

Proposals for the Composition of the Electoral College of the Bishop of Rome

Having made these refinements, we can ask if the College of Cardinals, according to *Romano pontifici eligendo,* is truly representative of the church of Rome and if the position which it seeks to provide for is truly the head of this church. The reply to both questions is clearly negative. The cardinals, taken from all the continents of the earth, in reality represent the universal Church, the ensemble of Christians. The wide diversity of origin of the cardinals allows for the representation and expression of all the possible sensibilities: of the different continents, nations, and ethnic backgrounds. The cardinals in question do not function in the college as bishops of local churches; they are not members formally in terms of their office as bishops,[20] representatives of the episcopal college. On the other hand, they are concerned with the universal Church and it is the primate of this Church whom they seek to elect and not directly the Bishop of Rome. In other words, the election as it actually unfolds corresponds to the time, still very recent, when, to employ an expression of the canonist Klaus Mörsdorf, "as Supreme Pastor of the Church, the pope is also Bishop of Rome, and not vice versa."[21] But today we have seen that it is as "Bishop of Rome that the pope is also Supreme Pastor, and not vice versa." This cannot be without consequences, both for the exercise of the pontifical function, and for the election of an incumbent.

If, as I have tried to show, the Bishop of Rome should ordinarily have real local pastoral care, it would be normal that the members of the Church of Rome, the priests, deacons, and laity who are the subjects of this solicitude, would participate with full rights and in substantial enough numbers in the electoral college that designates their future bishop. We must reexamine the composition of what is called the "Sacred College" and imagine what pertains to the representatives of the Church of Rome, what to the principal bishops of Italy, and what to a certain number of presidents of episcopal conferences. Moreover, it would probably be better if these members of the electoral college of the Bishop of Rome were themselves, at least in part, elected to the position. For the members of the Church of Rome, I refer to what I will have to say about the election of local bishops. Regarding the electors from the presidents of episcopal conferences, I suggest that,

---

20. Until quite recently, the "cardinal–deacons," who participated with full rights of election, were not bishops. Some were not even priests. History has known conclaves in which cardinals have participated who if they were not laymen, at the very least were only tonsured, i.e., nonordained clerics.

21. *Lehrbuch des Kirchenrechts auf Grund des Codex Iuris Canonici* (11th ed.; Paderborn: Ferdinand Schöningh, 1964) 347.

on the occasion of a synod of the presidents, they elect the necessary number of representatives, and when one of their number retires or dies, they can elect his replacement at the next such synod. There are not many reasons why the pope should intervene at this point, since it is his successor that is at issue, and hence the head of one Church, particular and universal, whose pastor he will no longer be.

The Election of the Local Bishop

The "Nomination" of Bishops

If the principle recalled by Pope Paul VI, according to which the church of Rome should elect its pastor, is true, why should the election of the pastor of every other church not observe the same principle? Or to put it differently, does the pastoral universal function of the Bishop of Rome *ordinarily* include the right to name bishops? It seems not. On the one hand, my earlier considerations regarding the church of Rome are evidently valid for the whole Church; while on the other hand, there are plenty of historical precedents, past and present, for canonical procedures based on the principle of the right and duty of the particular church to provide for itself a pastor who is worthy and capable of leading it. The direct nomination by the pope of virtually all bishops of the Latin Rite, and of some others as well, is the result of a long history, which I cannot even think of summarizing here,[22] and which form part of the logic of what I have called the "Gregorian form" of the Church. Responsibility passed from entire ecclesial communities to the clergy and eventually to an influential part of their number. In other juridical and political circumstances it was granted to lords and princes, or was claimed by them, and little by little the pope found himself the only one who could limit their autonomy, and for that matter maintain, with difficulty, the essentially religious character of the nominations. A new stage in this history was constituted by the concordats ratified by the Holy See and secular princes from the sixteenth century, of which the nomination of bishops formed an essential part of the transactions. When in contemporary history the old concordats lapsed and new ones were concluded, the Holy See claimed as much autonomy as possible in the nomination of bish-

---

22. There are plenty of studies on this topic. Without excluding others, I refer to J. Gaudemet, J. Dubois, A. Duval and J. Champagne, *Les Élections dans l'Église latine des origines au XVIe siècle* (Paris: Lanore, 1979). —See Giuseppe Alberigo and Anton Weiler, eds., *Election and Consensus in the Church*, Concilium 77 (New York: Herder and Herder, 1972); Peter Huizing and Knut Walf, eds., *Electing Our Own Bishops*, Concilium 137 (New York: Seabury, 1980); and Jean Gaudemet, "The Choice of Bishops: A Tortuous History" in James Provost and Knut Walf, eds., *From Life to Law*, Concilium 1996/5 (Maryknoll, N.Y.: Orbis, 1996) 59–65 [translator].

ops. The last step in this direction is article 20 of the Decree on the Ministry of Bishops of Vatican II, which calls for the complete independence of "the competent ecclesiastical authority" vis-à-vis all civil authority in the naming and appointing of bishops. It discreetly invites those states which still enjoy some right over episcopal nominations to renounce it of their own accord.[23]

In order to concretize what follows, we can ask the following question: in 1905, when the concordat between the Holy See and Napoleon Bonaparte was abrogated and the separation of Church and state in France was proclaimed, why didn't the Holy See hand over to the churches the responsibility of electing their bishops, and why didn't it establish a canonical procedure that would permit the election to be vetted and ratified by the Holy See or by some other competent ecclesiastical authority?[24] The answer undoubtedly is that it never occurred to anyone, so embedded in their minds was the idea that the nomination of bishops came from above and that the churches have no say in the matter. Moreover, even if one had thought of it, it certainly was not the auspicious moment, both because of the unfavorable historical conditions and because the freedom to elect a bishop presupposes a gradual education of Christians for the task that had not even begun. It would be possible today, given the theological and ecclesiological decisions taken at Vatican II and the consciousness in the churches of their own coherence and their prayerful responsibility for mission.

Proposals

In what follows, I take my inspiration from what exists already in the Church. As a matter of fact, there is a large area in the Church's life that is

---

23. Even the *Nota praevia* does not say that the pope has the exclusive right to name bishops. The opinion of Christian governments was the last vestige of intervention by the People of God. On the *Nota praevia*, see Jan Grootaers, *Primauté et collégialité. Le dossier de Gérard Philips sur la 'Nota explicativa praevia'* (Louvain: Leuven University Press, 1986), and the reviews of this book by Giuseppe Alberigo, "L'episcopato al Vaticano II," *Cristianesimo nella storia* 8 (1987) 147–64; Carlo Colombo, "Appunti a un'opera di ecclesiologia conciliare," *Teologia* 12 (1987) 161–67; and Gianfranco Ghirlanda, "Riflessioni sulla *Nota Explicativa Praevia* alla *Lumen Gentium*," *Gregorianum* 69 (1988) 324–31.

24. When the concordat was signed in 1801, the monastic orders were suppressed in the French church and their property nationalized. The issue of the nomination of abbots, commendatory and regular, of monasteries as powerful or important as bishoprics was also not discussed. If certain monasteries survived the French Revolution, it is because Napoleon had demanded the right to nominate abbots as well. When the concordat was broken in 1905, the Holy See would doubtless have claimed the nomination of Benedictine abbots, which from the point of view of the stability and the truth of monastic life would have been harmful. I cite this example to show that a de facto situation, arising out of quite definite historical circumstances, can determine a law without one even being aware of it and that this is not the best situation.

regularly conducted by the use of elections, viz., religious life. If the election of *all* superiors seems to be practiced only in the different families of St. Benedict and among the Dominicans, it is still a fact that the *superior general* and most often the *superiors provincial* in all religious families are elected. The major staff members of religious communities accede to their functions by way of election by their religious families.[25] Such a canonical procedure in general operates well and is considered normal. Aren't the religious who have a definite charism and tradition more apt for discerning who among them is capable of leading the congregation? The superiors elected not only provide for the well being of the religious confided to them, but also for the apostolic life of the order and the life of the universal Church, whose general direction has been set by the Holy Father.

Since the experience of religious orders shows that a process of election is both possible and beneficial, is it not possible that today this process can inspire the election of bishops by rediscovering there or elsewhere certain constants in earlier law founded on the nature of the Church? Let us imagine a scenario that is in part inspired by monastic experience. When an episcopal see is vacant, one or two bishops, e.g., the archbishop of the province, the president of an apostolic region, or even a bishop from a commission of the episcopal conference who has been elected to attend to such elections, come to the diocese, possibly accompanied by one or two priests or laypersons from other churches. They gather the Christian people in the cathedral for prayer, and they invite the parishes and various diocesan movements to assemble also to pray, after which they are asked to indicate the name of a candidate or the characteristics that the one elected ought to have. Sometime later, the bishop and his associates return and gather an electoral college, made up for example of the Presbyteral Council and the Pastoral Council of the diocese and possibly others whom law would provide for. They would make a three-day retreat to pray, invoke the Holy Spirit, and be disposed for making a spiritual discernment. Discussion would follow, either with the candidates the church indicated or about the direction to be taken. One could imagine that in the course of the discussion the bishop, knowing which persons are worthy of the episcopal ministry in the church, proposes one or two names of candidates who are invited to meet with the assembly.[26]

25. The elections of major superiors are made at chapters, general or provincial, but the members of the chapters are elected by the communities, and so by all the religious. Even the members who attend by law and have not been elected, for the most part have been elected at some other time to the function that gives them active and passive voice at a chapter.

26. It could be objected that if a candidate visits with such an electoral college and is not elected subsequently, his reputation would be damaged. At least, it seems that this question of a person's reputation is one of the reasons for the secrecy kept during the cur-

At the end, after prayer, they would proceed to the election by qualified majority of two-thirds of those voting. If the election was conducted spiritually and canonically, the presiding bishop would confirm it and, having participated in the spiritual experience just lived, would be the most likely one to ordain the one elected bishop several days later. In the meanwhile, the candidate would have sent letters of communion to the Bishop of Rome, the head of the episcopal college, to the bishops of the episcopal conference to which he will henceforth belong, and to all the bishops whom he wishes, and to which they will respond with greetings of peace.

Two remarks seem to me to be important at this point. First, the experience of religious life proves that when persons are given responsibility and are introduced into a process of prayer and discernment, they give their best. Why should it not be the same in the churches? I believe very sincerely that there is no reason to fear an election conducted in a spirit at once prayerful, liturgical, and reflective. Without a doubt failure can happen and sometimes will happen in the course of an election or following one. It is inevitable, but if we have confidence in the Spirit working in the churches, failures will be few. Are there not also failures in the centralized system of nominations?

Second, there is the issue of those who inevitably are discontented. Here perhaps is the difference between Christians in general and religious. The latter have a certain formation in the rule and in obedience, and there must be really weighty reasons to contest an election before a superior authority, since they know from experience that it is more beneficial to try to work with someone in charge than to pursue a process that results in division. On the contrary, it may happen that during an episcopal election there are dissatisfied persons among the Christian people who venture to complain everywhere and do not stop until they have had recourse "to Rome."[27]

---

rent procedure of nomination by Rome. Can't we rely on good Christian sense and simple humility in this matter? One can be an excellent priest (or, why not, a layperson?) without necessarily being the one deemed the best candidate at a particular moment in history.

27. I can write what I have because I am French! Between the two world wars, it appears that Bishop Maglione, the apostolic nuncio in France, in the course of the painful affair of the "Action française" said: "Among two French catholics, there is always one who is packing his bag in order to go to Rome to denounce the other." One has the impression that since the council, the privilege of delating someone to Rome is unfortunately not exclusively French, and that is a shame. In any case, misfortune would have it that the Catholic who "packs his bags" is probably rich enough to pay for a trip to Rome and educated and intelligent enough to present his or her cause in the best light possible, while the poor in terms of financial resources or education remain silent. To denounce someone successfully, a person needs to have "influence." On the other hand, a delation gives central authority the occasion to intervene, and if, often enough, it has

It is imperative, then, that the "higher authorities" of whatever level, be extremely prudent and reserved in the face of manifestations of dissatisfaction apropos of a decision made in prayer and discernment. In this way, a *tradition of life* can develop that, after a period of time, will be assured for all and by all.

Visits

An elected and ordained bishop is not protected from faults and mistakes, and the church for its part can respond poorly to its pastor. In any case, even when things are going smoothly in a church, it might be well to take stock from time to time. At the moment, this happens especially because of a direct connection of the bishop with the Holy See: every five years he personally goes to Rome and delivers a report on the state of his church. On the other hand, a judicious permanent control exists thanks to the presence of the apostolic delegate who may or may not also exercise diplomatic responsibility as nuncio. In principle, this control is not directed toward the internal life of the churches.[28] In line with what I have said, we can imagine a procedure that involves the local church much more. Here, too, several suggestions might come from religious life. The latter is not so particular in the Church that what derives from it cannot be taken up and reworked.

I have in mind what is called the "canonical visit," viz., at regular, fairly close intervals of three or four years, as fixed by particular law, a superior (alone or with another) visits a house and verifies its observance, apostolic zeal in conformity with the institute's charism, and, of course, the financial records. He receives and listens to the local superior and all the members, if necessary talking with them to encourage them, calm them, and bring them to reflection. At the end of several days of concrete, interpersonal contact, he can gather the community and give a talk that opens the way to continued progress along the way. He can also, and in certain cases must, write a report that can serve as a point of reference for the next visit. The essential thing is not in what is written down, but in the encounter and in the religious experience it elicits. Thus, one can imagine that a church might also be visited regularly by another bishop, alone or accompanied. He should be informed of the life of the church, of its liturgy, its undertakings of giving apostolic witness, the state of religious life, and he should have the opportunity to listen to those who want to meet him, to encourage, appease,

the wisdom not to do so, in many other cases it does, and that is not always for the good of the churches.

28. However, it seems that in the churches of the Third World, the nuncios or apostolic delegates have real authority much greater than in Europe, for example.

and when necessary reconcile, but also to take up and indicate paths to be pursued. More specifically, he can communicate to the bishop and his collaborators certain remarks that can encourage them, but also remarks that can help correct certain attitudes, reduce conflicts, and move things forward. The advantage of such visits is that they look at a particular church as a whole, and not like the present method, which is directed toward the local bishop's going to the Supreme Pastor and his associates to render an account of his administration. Instead, it is more a matter of helping a whole church to continue in harmony, peace, and zeal for prayer and mission. In a word, it concerns a "pastoral visit,"[29] not of parishes by the bishop, but of the whole church by another pastor or another church. It might have beneficial results.

Why not make this experience of visits more general? Why should the church of one country not be visited every ten or fifteen years by the president of the continental episcopal conference, or by a patriarch, and in certain cases, by a legate sent by the pope?

"Episkopē"

We now come to the exercise of the charism of presiding. We will examine successively the areas of its exercise and its different "styles": concrete, personal, collegial, and pontifical.

The Areas of the Exercise of *"Episkopē"*

In the preceding chapters, I tried to imagine a form of the Church that would be founded on the power or "might" of the Spirit, who is expressed in the diversity of charisms (and which implies their organization, institution, and verification) and finds its completion as well as its source in the celebration of the Eucharist. I have had occasion to give several indications on the charism of presiding: from the point of view of directing the Church, we have seen the figure of a bishop emerge that is marked by a resemblance to Christ the Pastor, is relayed to the communities by a body of priests, and is assisted by a body of deacons who moderate the various charisms.

---

29. At the moment, as far as dioceses are concerned, there is only an "apostolic visit," but this only takes place when there are extremely serious problems or grave difficulties. In terms of the daily life of a church, no provision is made for avoiding the emergence of smaller or less urgent problems. I add that such visits do not imply any moral fault on the part of the bishop; they do not reflect any doubt in principle of his competence or his zeal. A bishop who is aware of his limitations and those of his church should normally rejoice in any help given so that they can live the gospel better.

Modalities

If we must now determine precisely how *episkopē* is to be exercised, we can appeal to two fundamental attitudes, viz., listening and speaking.

LISTENING

The church precedes the bishop, who arrives there and finds in place the organs of the sacramental life and the institutions that support the charisms of the Church. This chronological priority is the sign of an objective priority, forcefully underscored by Vatican II: it is the Church as a whole that is the subject of the holiness and mission of the Church. It is in this sense that listening "to what the Spirit is telling the Church" is a primordial element of *episkopē,* for the one who stands in the name of Christ the Pastor for this church. It is not a passive listening, but attention brought to bear on the divine movement that animates a particular people through what they have and what they lack.

The bishop, pastor of his church, promotes the coordination and the unity of the local communities confided to the priests. He is the moderator of these charisms of the church, as I tried to describe briefly in earlier chapters. It is a matter of verifying which charisms correspond to the needs of the life of the church. In certain cases the charisms themselves will reveal them, since sometimes one does not see the real needs, and so the charism makes them clear. There is a place for insuring that the internal structuring of the charisms is correct and suitable in order to both guarantee the well-being of those who share in a charism as well as to contribute to the effectiveness of their service. Those who bear a charism must also be helped to find their place in the life of the Church and when necessary to modify this or that direction in order the better to meet others who are also engaged in the same task.

In order to accomplish such a task of verifying and nurturing, the bishops have the tradition and the traditions of the Church at their disposal. We cannot keep inventing the Church for each generation, and so there are traditions available, authorized, efficacious for today, and guaranteed by the presiding function in the Church. It is the bishop's job to recognize them, to respect them, to adapt and to demand adaptations, so that order among the charisms reigns in the life of the Church, so important in the eyes of St. Paul (see 1 Cor 12).

SPEAKING

It is not enough to listen, verify, promote; one must also speak. I want to insist first of all on the word in the liturgy. The summit of the bishop's work is the celebration of the Eucharist, the source of the Spirit for the Church and the place where the spiritual sacrifice of the Church is offered to God in Christ. In the course of the Eucharist, as in the celebration of the other sacraments of initiation, the bishop proclaims the word, commenting on the liturgy or on Scripture. As I said earlier,[30] this is the moment par excellence of the prophetic and the apostolic functions. We can ask if it wouldn't be appropriate for the bishop to celebrate in the cathedral more often than is ordinarily the case today, and in the parishes, avoiding embarrassing his priests, and that he proclaim the word of God. When heard in faith, the bishop's discourse can form little by little an "ecclesial attitude" which prepares the people truly to *be* the sacrament of the encounter of God and mutual love for men and women. In this way, the bishop will lose some of the image of being a distant administrator, which today is often the impression he makes.

Speaking also means determining the general lines and pastoral orientations for the Church's holiness and mission. Such words, both because they emerge out of his attention and listening, and because they arise from the authorized initiative of a bishop who is capable of imagining the present and the future, will confirm the dynamism of the communities and various institutions and set a common direction for them.

Sectors

In talking about the various charisms in the preceding chapters, I had occasion to sketch what pertains to verifying, promoting, and correcting charisms. I will not repeat what I've said on the various sectors in view. A few suggestions on one or another particular sector will suffice.

LITURGY

If the organization of the liturgy redounds to those who have shown a capacity for it, under the final direction of a deacon who has this responsibility for the Church, it reverts to the bishop and his priests to celebrate the liturgy for the people whose pastors they are. It must be the business of the bishops to define the practice of the liturgy that is better adapted to their people. Of course, for the most part matters are determined by the liturgical traditions of the Church. But from a theological and ecclesiological point of view it is not evident why a bishop should be prevented from composing a Eucharistic Prayer that meets the precise needs of his church, or from borrowing a text composed elsewhere and which seems to him to be pertinent given the actual pastoral practice, or of modifying a translation, etc. If the liturgy is the prayer of the local community, it means that the texts and gestures which constitute it are the true carriers of this prayer, and as such can both give birth to it and express it. It gives birth to it since

---

30. See chapter 2, p. 41.

the liturgy expressing the Christian mystery provokes the prayer of the Christian marked by this mystery: it gives the Christian the words and proposes the gestures that correspond to his or her unconscious or implicit waiting on the Lord. It expresses it, since the Christian in whom the Spirit dwells must find the words and gestures that permit him or her to speak the praise of God in Christ, together with the community. Ordinarily, the forms of the liturgy must be good instruments for achieving this goal. With respect to both engendering and expressing the liturgy, the Christian and the community are humanly and culturally situated, but also historically, since human life consists of events. It is healthy for liturgy to be the actual encounter of the liturgical tradition with concrete situations. The bishop, with his local councils, and/or in collaboration with his neighboring bishops, must be the judge of what is opportune in this matter.

It also redounds to the bishop to define the practice of the sacrament of reconciliation, of course, in light of the situation of the broader Church. All human liturgies, religious or otherwise, know moments of penance and making amends and have defined their rites. With various degrees of success, these combine external symbols, confession, and communitarian and interpersonal reconciliation. In the Church, Christians are capable of sincerely entering into a liturgy of reconciliation without attaining the point of confessing their own sins (though participation in such liturgies can act as a gradual pedagogy of personal penance that can reach the point of effectively acknowledging one's own sinfulness). Vice versa, as in the case we noted in the previous chapter, some people can be led to the knowledge and the confession of their sin, without understanding the need for the sacrament properly speaking. The situations are so diverse, especially perhaps in a world that is both distant from the Church, guilt ridden, and in search of symbols that would make personal and collective reconciliation possible. As the pastor instituted by the sacrament of order, in particular for the work of reconciliation, the bishop must be able to see what has to be done to assure the infinite mercy of Christ for those who thirst for it, but without necessarily demanding that each and every one satisfy all the requirements of the sacrament.[31] Naturally, the bishop will do this in con-

---

31. In order to deepen our appreciation of these questions, we should pay greater attention to the development of the theology of penance, from the time when the practice of having only one opportunity for forgiveness after baptism was either called into question by some or recognized by others, to the current practice of penitents, in the secrecy of an encounter between them and a priest, who confess sometimes extremely serious sins and receive pardon thanks to a "penance" that in the final analysis is very light given the gravity of the sin. We need to reflect on the evolution of the corresponding liturgies, on the qualification of the minister (bishop? judge? father?), and on the idea of God and the gospel that undergirds these different conceptions and practices.

sultation with the priests and deacons of the diocese and after consulting with his fellow-bishops in the neighboring churches.

We should extend our reflections apropos of the liturgy to other domains, in particular to catechesis and theology. In the preceding chapter, I ventured a number of reflections on this subject, but I am not going to develop them further at this point. I will take up this topic again when I treat the question of the "magisterium" later. Instead, I would like to say something here on a point that strikes me as capital: the proposing to the churches of models and intercessors—the saints.

HOLINESS

The Christian people need models and intercessors. They must be able to contemplate the image of Christ and the form of the gospel reflected in real human beings and not just in general but for each cultural and historical entity. We need saints from our families, our country, from our humanity generally, in whom we can recognize ourselves. Such models are certainly not lacking, since the Spirit lives in the whole Church, old as well as new. Sometimes, in the stories and the testimonies which the evangelizers and the educators of new Christian societies told, one could trace the profile of admirable figures, quite worthy of being proposed publicly to their church or the neighboring churches, as models and paths of sanctity. Evangelization drew immense power from the presence of such native models.[32]

Unfortunately, in the present canonical situation, no local bishop or episcopal conference is entitled to beatify persons.[33] Moreover, the young churches do not have the resources in terms of time, personnel, and money

---

See Groupe de la Bussière, *Pratiques de la confession. Des Pères du désert à Vatican II* (Paris: Cerf, 1983). —On the history of penance, see Karl Rahner, *Theological Investigations,* vol. 155, *Penance in the Early Church,* trans. Lionel Swain (New York: Crossroad, 1982); Ladislas Orsy, *The Evolving Church and the Sacrament of Penance* (Denville, N. J.: Dimension, 1978) 27–51; and Kenan B. Osborne, *Reconciliation and Justification: The Sacrament and Its Theology* (New York: Paulist, 1990) [translator].

32. This is certainly the reason that motivates Pope John Paul II in his multiplying the number of beatified Christians, particularly in the churches of the Third World that he visits.

33. The reservation of the right to proclaim sainthood to the Holy See goes back to the Middle Ages, and is another manifestation of the Gregorian tendency toward centralization. See André Vauchez, *Sainthood in the Later Middle Ages,* trans. Jean Birrell (Cambridge [Eng.]: Cambridge University Press, 1997) 22–32 ["Towards Papal Reservation of the Right of Canonization (Eleventh to Thirteenth Centuries)"]. Perhaps it was justified at the time, to avoid certain abuses and superstitions. But aren't the bishops and episcopal conferences competent today for such a discernment, a task after all that belongs intrinsically to their ministry?

that would allow them to pursue the course of a beatification. Finally, the criteria for the process of discernment are not in all their characteristics the most suitable for today, since they are more characteristic of other times and places, e.g., the Middle Ages or even Benedict XIV (1740–58). What results is that, with few exceptions, the churches of modern or recent foundation, even if they sometimes have beatified or canonized martyrs, have practically no *confessor* saints, i.e., persons whom the Church recognizes as having lived their uniquely personal lives according to the gospel and died, as the saying goes, "in the odor of sanctity."

This absence of acknowledged confessors is rather tragic, even if one doesn't think about it every day: the particular church does not have a concrete awareness of the holiness that is present in it, of its capacity to cause saints to burst forth, in its poverty and the whole Church's. Holiness, as a real note, is outside its perspective and its discourse. This certainly does not prevent the Spirit from working, but this work itself is helped the more if it can stress the fruits that the Spirit brings to the men and women of this church. Conversely, the old churches, already possessing a large gallery of witnesses to the faith, continue to beatify and canonize new ones. European Caucasians and whites of European descent are still in the majority among recent beatifications and canonizations (again, with the exception of martyrs).

It would seem normal to restore to the local churches their right to beatify their own saints. In effect, even today, when a Christian is beatified his or her cult is not proposed for all that to the whole Church; it remains local. If it concerns a local proposal, why shouldn't the beatifications be made in and by the local churches? That is why I think it would be good to return to these churches the right and the task of *beatifying* their own saints and proposing them to their faithful for imitation and intercession. If possible, the task of determining the criteria for a beatification should even be left to the local churches, gathered for this purpose at the supranational and even continental level. Since it is not a matter of proposing saints to the universal Church, we could be less stringent and not proceed from theoretical principles but from concrete observations based on the lives of individuals, on the influence of their reputation for holiness that they continue to exercise, perhaps at their burial places. The Holy See would continue to reserve to itself *canonizations* at the level of the universal Church. In the case of these canonizations, too, there would be greater possibilities of drawing the attention of the Church toward important saintly persons. Without doubt, sanctity knows no borders and a St. Theresa of the Child Jesus speaks to everyone; but this would give the Church the means that it actually lacks right now of proposing to the old churches also the St. Theresas of the Child Jesus of Africa, of South America, and of Asia.

In short, shouldn't we return to the practice of the early churches, with discernment and prudence, of course?[34] None of the saintly Fathers of the Church was ever the object of a canonical procedure aimed at declaring his holiness; some of them, and some great ones, undoubtedly would have been refused, such as the irascible and tormented St. Jerome (348–420). Moreover, many locally venerated persons became saints by virtue of the saying *vox populi, vox Dei*—which voice the bishops of the period obeyed. Time, too, has made its selections, leaving some saints to fall into oblivion, while highlighting others, up to the recent past, when their canonical situation was regulated by the Holy See, in particular in the second half of the nineteenth century. But were such confirmations really necessary?

I am quite aware of the fact that such a proposal of returning beatifications to the churches in order to allow them to honor their saints remains very general and that it demands further study in terms of its concrete implementation. One could probably test its foundation and the possibility by reexamining the historical circumstances and the theological reasons

---

34. It is a source of joy to see that the authors of the *Nouvelle encyclopédie catholique théo*, eds. M. Dubost, X. Lesort, S. Lalanne and V. Rouillard (Paris: Droguet-Ardant/Fayard, 1989) have dedicated the opening chapter of the volume "Des chercheurs de Dieu par milliers . . ." to holiness, and from the very start, without saying so, proceed to a kind of impromptu beatification: "Today who does not know of Mother Teresa [1910–98], Martin Luther King [1929–68], Helder Camara [1909–99], Abbé Pierre, Oscar Romero [1917–80], etc., and some figures a bit more remote in time: Edmond Michelet [1899–1970], Tom [Thomas A.] Dooley [1927–61], Madeleine Delbrêl [1904–64], Teilhard de Chardin [1881–1955]? These men and women are points where all of humanity meet" (21). Further on, they add Marcel Callo (1921–45) (since beatified by John Paul II), Madeleine Daniélou (1880–1956), Raoul Follereau (1903–77), Joseph Folliet (1903–72), Charles de Foucauld (1858–1916), Jean Girette (1899–1979), John XXIII (1881–1963), Raïssa Maritain (1883–1960), Marthe Robin (1902–81), Jean Rodhain (1900–77), Robert Schuman (1886–1963), Albert Schweitzer (1875–1965), Edith Stein (1891–1942) [since canonized by John Paul II—translator], Franz Stock (1904–48). See ibid., "Des témoins pour aujourd'hui," 125–33. The churches of Latin America have also published their recent "martyrologies." —It might not be impertinent to add the names of Mary Ward (1585–1644), Pierre Toussaint (1766–1853), John Henry Newman (1801–90), Orestes A. Brownson (1803–76), Cornelia Connolly (1809–79), Damian de Veuster ("Damian of Molakai" [1840–89]), Matt Talbot (1856–1925), Dorothy Day (1897–1980) and Peter Maurin (1877–1949), Maisie Ward (1889–1975) and Frank (Francis J.) Sheed (1897–1981), Dietrich von Hildebrand (1889–1977), Dietrich Bonhoeffer (1906–45), Thomas Merton (1915–68), Joseph Louis Bernardin (1928–96), Henri Nouwen (1932–96), Jean Vanier (1928–), and Bernard Häring (1912–98). See also Elizabeth A. Johnson, "Saints and Mary" in *Systematic Theology: Roman Catholic Perspectives*, eds. Francis Schüssler Fiorenza and John P. Galvin (Minneapolis: Fortress, 1991) 145–77, and idem, *Friends of God and Prophets: A Feminist Theological Reading of the Communion of Saints* (New York: Continuum, 1998) [translator].

that led the Holy See to reserve exclusively to itself the declaration of saint-hood. One could also carefully study the decisive work of Pope Benedict XIV on the matter, in order to see what in it is outdated or superannuated in order to stress what pertains to the unfailing tradition of the Church. But we should not wait until the final returns of such indispensable and partially completed studies, to take certain provisional steps in the direction I've indicated. These works can help in fine-tuning the perspective and the legislation, but they cannot be absolutely prerequisite. If holiness is the first note of the Church, it means that this be recognized and proclaimed *quickly*. A church that knows itself to have been faithful to the Spirit to the point of producing saints receives from this new dynamism and enthusiasm. In fact, aren't the young churches *nolens volens* put in the situation of the servant who hid his talent (Matt 25:18), since they do not have the means to recognize that some of them have brought forth the fruit of two or five talents?

The Style of "Episkopē": Personal, Collegial, Universal

Earlier, I brought out how evidence from the sacramentality of epis-copacy explains its collegial character.[35] If episcopacy is the sacrament of Christ the Pastor of the Church, it is clear that all those who receive the sacrament are one, to the extent that they all reflect and make present the one Pastor of our souls, Jesus Christ. It follows that the exercise of this pas-toral mission is both personal and collegial. The spacial determination of a particular church is a fact of positive law that we have tried to establish on sociogeographical grounds, and that makes possible in practice the mission of *episkopē* of a pastor. But the borders of a diocese are not the Berlin wall of yesteryear and Jesus the unique Pastor is not divided: the exercise of *episkopē* must normally take account of the neighboring churches. The provincial, national, continental, and universal levels are drawn for the pur-pose of communications, exchanges, and decisions.[36] It is natural that, pru-

---

35. The bibliography on collegiality, like every other point of the council's ecclesi-ology, is immense and the positions held run the full gamut of what is possible. I refer only to the proceedings of the Congress of Salamanca (January 3–8, 1999), eds. Hervé Legrand, Julio Manzanares, and Antonio García y García, *The Nature and Future of Episcopal Conferences* (Washington, D.C.: The Catholic University of America Press, 1988). —See also Thomas J. Reese, ed., *Episcopal Conferences: Historical, Canonical, and Theological Studies* (Washington, D.C.: Georgetown University Press, 1989) [translator].

36. The existence in the Church from early times of archbishops, patriarchs, pri-mates, etc., demonstrates the normal nature of intermediate steps in any institution. In the Latin Church, these titles have tended to become mostly honorific, but there is no reason why they cannot be invested with new meaning, just like the synods and assem-blies which correspond to them in tradition.

dently evaluated, this forms part of the local *episkopē*, while the latter forms a reciprocal part of the *episkopē* at all the other levels of the Church's life.

Retrievals in the Spirit of the Gospel

I believe that, if one looks at things in an uncomplicated way, what I have said above and what I have maintained regarding their implementation through intelligent institutional reform does not pose any theological problem. Looked at theologically, collegiality only becomes complicated when it is exercised out of its proper context, viz., when it is defined in terms of "jurisdiction" exercised at the various levels of the Church's authority. Whether we choose to accept it or not, we Latin Catholics spontaneously understand the Church's institutions out of a mentality of "jurisdiction" and have become habituated to a papacy that intervenes frequently in affairs, either directly in the person of the pope or through the organs of the Roman Curia. In order to understand *episkopē* theologically and institutionally, and in particular to discover the effective forms for the exercise of the papal office, I believe it is indispensable that we bracket out, at least provisionally, this mentality of jurisdiction.[37] Several observations are in order on this topic.

Obedience

The understanding of authority in the Church in terms of "jurisdiction" leads, as far as obedience is concerned, to a highly formal and in practice unreal view that stunts it instead of allowing it to grow, by tying it too closely to the idea of obligation. Some explanations would have it that the Christian needs to obey only his or her local bishop and the pope, since all intermediate instances do not enjoy the same kind or degree of authority.

37. In recent discussions concerning the exercise of collegiality, one gets the impression that the mystical and prudential sides of a collegial style of life in the Church have not been stressed enough. Already back in 1965, I was taken aback by the haste with which the new episcopal conferences set about writing their bylaws. The sacramentality of episcopacy and the collegiality that flowed from it were scarcely defined, and yet they were renewing rather profoundly what could be called the "spirituality" of an episcopate shared in by various Christians, in the perspective of a Church as the body of Christ and People of God understood as entirely liturgical and missionary. Shouldn't the experience of living together, based on a clearer belief in the mystic reality of charisms and sacraments, have been acknowledged first, before moving on to the process of codifying and organizing it? Wouldn't it have been better to have had the experience of more informal encounters for treating certain more or less concrete matters, in order to see what new style of being Church was emerging and how it could best be advanced? Didn't we move on to systematizing the law before experiencing the life on which it would be based? And didn't we sometimes forge unhelpful or inept administrative shackles?

In the Church of Vatican II, it seems to me that prayer and mission are areas of life and responsibility for all Christians before being areas of obligation and power, and that by reason of the charisms that each person possesses and the place he or she occupies there. The Church's life is the object of reflection, prayer, dialogue, and a way of discerning God's will. It is a matter of supernatural prudence, both for those who exercise the role of presiding as well as for those who have other functions. Of course, it is reasonable to propose orientations at the start, just as it is reasonable to put an end to research or to deliberations, and these times are the bishop's responsibility. And so, there is time for obedience, but exercised with prudence and discernment.

At all levels, proposals, dialogue, obedience operate in a way that advances the mission of the Church and out of a discipline that is spiritual. That is true of the pope's authority, the bishop's, and that of the episcopal college in its meetings, be they more limited or more universal. It is a matter of establishing a climate—prudent, human, supernatural—for the exercise of *episkopē*. No doubt, there will be unfortunate or difficult circumstances, when it will have to give proof of its authority in a more marked, affirmative, and imposing way, in a word, of "obligatory authority," and perhaps at these times the competence of the local bishop and of the pope is more weighty. However, it would be contrary to the spirit of evangelical mission to understand the Church's life and law from hard cases and possible failures. I have already said that the temptation of centralized, martial law based on fear of certain excesses is, in the final analysis, a poor counselor and the fruits of its harvest, over the long haul, are disappointing. Let us try to understand obedience in terms of a docility that is free, and let us ask that those who possess ecclesial authority nurture this docility rather than impose obedience.

Authority

A mentality of jurisdiction also whittles away the genuine understanding of authority by treating it precisely in terms of an imposed obligation. Authority is really much more diversified than this; it is less compulsory, but asks for more. At every level of the community, authority exists and must exist, and must be effective. For example, if there is an episcopal conference, it must have a president. In other words, someone must direct the preparations for assemblies and, after consulting the members, must ultimately determine what will and will not be on the agenda; someone must direct the deliberations and bring them to a conclusion, all the while respecting proper procedures, etc. Absent this authority, there can be no peace and no effective work; but where there is an institution, there must be a minimum of law and authority. Once decisions have been made, are they "juridically obligatory"? Possibly not, but is the problem there? A bishops' conference is not a "club" where freewheeling discussions take place and a bishop is free to ignore directions taken by the group if they do not please him. But it is also not a scull, where the only thing a bishop has to do is row in sync with the others. It cannot function without a minimum spirit of collaboration and agreement, of "docility" one might say, and of discernment, all of which permit a particular church to profit from common provisions, adapted with intelligence.

The pope's authority is "truly episcopal" and it is final. It is absolutely necessary that in certain urgent or very grave cases it be exercised immediately and authoritatively. The idea of "primacy of honor" makes no evangelical sense, and I suggest that the East developed this idea less because it wanted to express a privilege given by Jesus to Peter than because it felt the need to reject the centralized understanding and exercise of the office by the Roman pontiffs since the eleventh century. But this truly episcopal character of papal authority does not of itself require its constant intervention, nor does it signify that everything the pope says or does is the object of blind obedience to obligatory decrees or proposals that are beyond discussion. What I want to make clearly understood is that the attempt to impose the obligation of submitting, etc. (to the pope, of course, but also to others) diminishes rather than increases the effective reach and the benefit of authority, because it makes it both less human and less spiritual: there is no place for understanding and discernment. Vice versa, if one finds the sense of evangelical docility, one must be able to respect its subsidiary forms and better recognize an ultimate authority.

Collegial Institutions

Having made more precise the spirit in which collegiality takes place, we must recognize that this is only a word if it is not accompanied by institutions that give it effective life. There can only be two kinds of institutions here: synodal and diaconal. By "synodal" I mean those meetings that formerly were called "councils." They were named after the cities where they were held, and gathered the bishops of a province, of a larger region, or of a nation to discuss urgent matters.[38] Even before Vatican II these councils were resurrected, on the national level, and given the name of Assemblies of Bishops (but utilizing the primitive terminology, for the situation in France, one can speak of the first, second, etc., council of Lourdes). They

---

38. Important collections of their proceedings and decisions have been edited and published over the years. One of the most helpful is that of Johannes Dominicus Mansi, *Sacrorum conciliorum nova et amplissima collectio,* 53 vols. (Arnhem and Leipzig: Verlag H. Welter, 1901–27).

can exist also on wider regional levels, or even as a continent. Their primary purpose is to offer the bishops a chance to meet and exchange experiences; the second is to examine together the problems they face and the decisions they need to make. One might only ask whether the bishops meet too frequently today and whether their agenda is too heavy. A more fundamental question might be whether such assemblies might also invite other persons to attend them. If the churches as a whole are in the final analysis the ultimate subjects of holiness and mission, would it not be opportune on occasion to hold assemblies of churches at which laity, religious, deacons, and priests would be represented?[39]

By diaconal institutions, I understand permanent administrative organs that assure communication (which currently in France are called secretariats or bureaus and are generally run by priests). Nothing stands in the way of their being entrusted to deacons who are ordained for this very task. It is necessary that these offices not be characterized by a lack of a meaningful charge, just as this is true with regard to episcopal commissions that are formed for one or another sector of Church life. I have no experience to point to beyond a few concrete suggestions, but I believe that just as an administration is needed here, so too must one constantly guard against its becoming an end in itself. I also think that it must protect itself against producing "documents." It is natural that a commission does its work, arrives at certain conclusions, and then writes them up and publishes them. Taken one by one, such documents are justified in the eyes of their authors and of their recipients. For all that, the Church today is staggering under the weight of printed documents, too often neither read nor reflected on.

I have tried to underscore two things regarding collegiality: doctrinally and in reality, it is incontestable, since it is founded on the unity of the sacrament of order which establishes certain men pastors in the Church who make present Jesus Christ, the unique Pastor and Bishop of our lives, as St. Peter says (1 Pet 5:4). If, on the other hand, this collegiality is real and

---

39. On the level of Europe, the ecumenical assembly of Basel, at Pentecost 1991, is an image of what I have in mind, but with the added complication that it would involve all of Europe and all the churches and Christian confessions. (Let me note on this point that delegates of the non-Catholic communities would be determined on the basis of their *Church* affiliation, while Catholic delegates, including laity or priests, would be determined on the basis of their respective *episcopal conference,* so difficult is it for Catholicism to accept in principle the incontestable reality of national churches, cohesive among themselves and in communion with Rome and its pastor.) It would be advantageous to develop an institutional plan for the Catholic churches akin to the German *Katholikentag.* See *Rassemblement oecuménique européen de Bâle: Justice et paix pour la création entière. Intégralité des textes et documents officiels,* ed. Conference des Églises européennes et le Conseil des Conférences épiscopales européennes (Paris: Cerf, 1989).

not simply abstract but de facto instituted by the Lord, then it must be able to express itself effectively, as it did from the beginning in the churches. The condition for its effective implementation might be termed a reform of our attitude toward it. Both among Christians and the clergy, it must rediscover the true meaning of authority as obedience (and not as jurisdiction and obligation) in its character as truly Christian and human. It must be able to recognize the various areas where the dialectic of authority–obedience operates in order to avoid useless power struggles or harmful refusals of obedience.[40] Ordinarily, in the framework of one Church which knows itself to be the body of Christ and the People of God, animated by the Spirit's charisms, the service of personal, collegial, and universal authority must appear more collaborative and harmonious than conflictual.

The Magisterium of the Faith: Proclamation, Theology, Defense

In both my presentation on the "Gregorian form" of the Church and in my efforts here to sketch a new ecclesial form inspired by Vatican II, I have given priority to the question of truth. I believe that this is what in reality governs the question of the Church and its institutions, even if not always in an explicit way. The result is that the charism ordered toward presiding over the churches implies a special responsibility vis-à-vis the truth of the gospel, and which is designated today, somewhat reductively, as the "magisterium."[41] I have alluded to the question of proclaiming and especially defending the truth above apropos of the Inquisition.[42] When I treated the charisms of states in life, I suggested that the proper responsibility of

40. I sometimes ask myself if, when certain Christians attack the bishops "who do not obey the pope," they are not defending an ideology or their own will. After all, the pope is named by these bishops, and if he has their confidence, why not have the confidence he has in them? But the pope is far away and the documents of the Holy See are so numerous that it is not hard to find some citation or other that supports one's own point of view. Referring to the pope often seems to me a convenient excuse for withdrawing from the effective life of the Church as one finds it. It is true that participation always demands sacrifice, which can be avoided by forming small groups of "those who are faithful to the pope." The truth becomes clear when the pope, after drawn-out silence, commands something they do not want to admit or do.

41. We should mention the resonances in St. Augustine's work in Latin, the *De magistro*, which implies the restoration of the order of magisterial actions and which we spoke about earlier. See Yves Congar, "Pour une histoire du mot 'magistère'" and "Bref historique des formes du magistère et de ses relations avec les docteurs," *Église et papauté. Regards historiques* (Paris: Cerf, 1994) 283–315. —The first article has appeared in English as "A Semantic History of the Term 'Magisterium'" in *Readings in Moral Theology*, vol. 3: *The Magisterium and Morality*, eds. Charles E. Curran and Richard A. McCormick (New York: Paulist, 1982) 297–313 [translator].

42. See chapter 2, pp. 44–45.

the laity included the task of reflecting on and speaking about the truth of their lives. Finally, I spoke about theology in the analogous perspective of a responsibility connected with a charism.[43] When I made several suggestions above apropos of the different areas of *episkopē,* I deferred until now the presentation of several points of view on the question of proclaiming and verifying the faith. If this mission belongs to the episcopal charism as a whole, the Petrine mission includes its own responsibility, viz., "Strengthen your brothers" (Luke 22:32), a task all the more emphasized today, following on the proclamation of the pope's infallibility in 1870 and its extensive interpretation in Roman circles. As a result, it is the Roman magisterium which has occupied center stage. That is why it is opportune to treat the magisterium at this point—between our treatment of the *episkopē* of the bishops and that of the Bishop of Rome.

I indicated above the three episcopal tasks relative to the faith: biblical and mystagogical preaching, theological research, and the correction of errors, and I underscored that the last sector has assumed greater importance at the expense of the other two. This was particularly true when theology properly speaking, but also when the bishop's and the pope's preaching, fell into the background. In an attempt to "imagine the Catholic Church" in this sector also, I believe it is important first to evaluate the evolution of the situation in the last hundred years or so (let us say from 1878, the year Leo XIII assumed the papacy).[44]

Points of Reference for an Assessment

The Return of Theology

Whatever spirit personally motivated him, the initiatives of Leo XIII were a point of departure culturally for Christian thought and action, and their value as intellectual initiatives in the areas the pope touched on, but in others as well, should not be minimized. Catholic theologians and philosophers felt liberated by these gestures of openness and set about thinking and writing, in order to resume the patient effort of understanding the faith of the first Christian millennium and of finding their way in modern epistemologies. They did so according to their own genius and by using the intellectual instruments at their disposal; they frequently opened up or resumed fruitful paths, but sometimes, too, were misguided. Furthermore, their work did not remain purely speculative to the extent that the fields of knowledge they developed were often connected with practices in worship,

---

43. See above pp. 116–18 and 142–48.
44. See my *Histoire théologique de l'Église catholique. Itinéraire et formes de la théologie* (Paris: Cerf, 1994) 341–84 ["Le Retour de la théologie catholique (de 1878 à nos jours)"].

ethics, politics, and society. Their knowledge involved concrete undertakings, and theologians became promoters and agents in all sorts of encounters and engagements. In this vast enterprise, they were far from being unanimous, but their conversations, and even their polemics, often opened a moderate way to engaging the "disputed questions" of the day. After a century, today we can take stock of the extraordinary contribution this biblical, liturgical, patristic, ecumenical, and philosophical work made in forming a new spirit in the Church—ours today—and thanks to which research can continue to vivify faith and culture.

The Tempered Permanence of the Primitive Form of the Magisterium

Here, however, a kind of misunderstanding or, even worse, of contradiction emerged little by little. In the medieval tradition of truth and its assiduous defense, the Holy See has long become habituated to guiding the life, or lack thereof, of Catholic thought, of controlling the institutions of the Church, and of judging in practice the relevance of political and social enterprises, in a word, keeping thought under the control of the epistemology of "illumination." It even seems that on this point Leo XIII and his successors did not disagree, whereas the new intellectual they were in part responsible for creating could no longer be answerable to this system. Here is the constant problem we must now examine more closely.

In the thought of Leo XIII, neo-Thomism was held to provide an intellectual structure of the Church and the criteria for detecting errors that were sometimes quite real, but more often only represented the inevitably imperfect state of research which had to grope towards results, but which was conducted in good faith and in an apostolic spirit. Theological effort largely surpassed the neo-Thomist framework and the criteria of judgment it proposed were seen as inadequate to the task of evaluating the new developing disciplines.

The Holy See was forced to work in the newly reopened sectors of the theological world, and for its part it did so by doing what the earliest bishops and popes had done in their day and who were themselves the object of research. It did so often in an interesting and convincing way, but both then and now it presented this theology in a normative way, which has led to new difficulties. The "understanding of the faith" *(intellectus fidei)* does not belong to an order that can be regulated by law but to reflection that is accountable. Nevertheless, the growing number of documents emanating from the Holy See for a century now, and of which only a small part were signed by the pope (the others remaining anonymous), do not admit their character as theology. They offer practically no citation from a theologian other than St. Thomas. They do not admit their methodological yet real dependence on the results of contemporary fundamental theological or philosophical research, even in cases where they are justifiably criticized. They use terms and thought forms that come from secular authors without explicitly entering into dialogue with them, and no references to persons or academic institutions that have helped in their composition are ever cited.

Although they often depend on research conducted in other ways, these documents do not distinguish between the tasks I indicated earlier, viz., the bishop's duty to proclaim the faith, to present it theologically, to point out dangers to it, and to condemn errors. They are published as though the doctrine proposed descends from above, with the intervention of the pope or some Roman congregation believed to speak in his behalf, and in itself clothed with an obligatory character. They aim at obedience before involving a person's intelligence, and they are presented, not as authoritative theology (even though that is what they are) but as doctrinal truth both by reason of their source and the intrinsic quality of those who pronounce them. These documents would enjoy greater influence in the eyes of a responsible reader if their character as "authoritative theology" were admitted and the insistent proclamation of an "obligatory magisterium" were downplayed. The latter tries to speak authoritatively in every area of the culture and is forced to expand its impact thanks to the modern means of communication. The media allow the magisterium more and more to address directly the whole People of God, and even all of humanity, while the bishop's mediation tends toward becoming purely formal and limited to presenting and disseminating Roman documents. Furthermore, when the bishops try to bring up delicate matters in the contemporary world, they are regarded with suspicion and are closely monitored by Rome.

The theology which professional theologians engage in is subjected to what can be called the "task of commenting." When it tries on its own, with all its attendant risks and dangers, to clear the way for something truly new and tries to use different language, it is quickly judged to be arrogant. In the past, even the very recent past, the magisterium has too often condemned theologians' truly creative and beneficial ideas, only to take them into account years later. (One gets the impression, too, that the magisterium tends to abstract from the fact that doubts and errors are inherent to any form of research.) It has then proceeded to integrate their insights into its own documents, without explicitly admitting its debt to them or acknowledging past injustices done them.[45] Simultaneously, in this way theology is theoreti-

45. We need to nuance this statement today. John Paul II, like his predecessor Paul VI, in certain circumstances or given certain facts, recognized the error of the Catholic Church, e.g., concerning the condemnation of Galileo. See John Paul II's address before a group of scientists in *Origins* 13 (3) (June 2, 1983) 49–52. It is rumored that on the occasion of the new millennium in 2000, the pope would like to acknowledge in general the responsibility incurred by the Church during these two thousand years and to

cally promoted, secretly used, but strictly surveilled, and the same is true of the magisterium of the bishops. As for the responsibility of the laity for thought, it is not really taken into consideration as a normal instance of examining secular reality.

An instance of this difficulty, which can be called constitutive, opposed to any change in thought in the Church and of dialogue with other cultures, can be found in the internal workings of the Holy See itself. Upon consideration, sometimes we note the presence of discreet but real differences between the Pontifical Councils created after Vatican II to advance dialogue (e.g., the Secretariat for Christian Unity, the Pontifical Council for Interreligious Dialogue, etc.) and the congregations set up after the Council of Trent. The respective tasks of these institutions arise from two different dynamisms. The one lives in a world of dialogue and emerges from what I called above the "communional structure" of the Church. It is essentially in contact with men and women, and sees itself as "mistress of humanity" but also as a "disciple" of the seeds of the Word wherever they may be found. The other, and again we are in the "Gregorian form" of the Church, lives in a Neoplatonic world, where there is one God, one Christ, one pope. This perspective implies a Christian people marked by sin and intellectually underdeveloped, as it was represented in the late Middle Ages, a majority Church in society, and one that is under attack and must be defended. In this ecclesial understanding, the moment the pope agrees to his election he receives all power in the Church directly from God and his

---

ask for forgiveness. That is certainly something that honors truth and would be both beautiful and moving. However, it could be asked whether the confession should not be quite precise, naming names and indicating the precise reasons for the injustices. So, for example, in order for the Galileo affair to be truly closed, wouldn't it be necessary for the Prefect of the Congregation for the Doctrine of the Faith to go to the Church of the Minerva in Rome and solemnly proclaim the error and maybe the evil of the condemnation pronounced there in 1632? And shouldn't he also annul in writing the document of the Roman Inquisition that memorialized the deed? Until just such an act takes place, can one say that this error and this evil have *truly* been confessed and atoned for? I sincerely believe that an act of this sort, far from diminishing the Church in the eyes of Christians or non-Christians, would profoundly renew the credibility of its ministry of giving witness and teaching, and thus strengthen the docility of believers and attract everyone's attention. To act in this way, on the other hand, would be for Rome to recognize that in the future there will be greater flexibility and discretion not only in its activity but in the theology of the magisterium. And isn't this perhaps the sticking point, since it would necessitate renouncing a certain theory of truth and consequently of the effectiveness of a single institution of proclamation and control? But these very theories cannot support the hypothesis of an error and would leave it intellectually and practically disarmed in the face of error when it happens. In the perspective of the "epistemology of illumination," it could just never happen.

teaching is regarded as having no source other than this divine primacy. Even if there were other mediations of his teaching, there is no need to mention them. On the question of a plurality of theologies, they are regarded as something dangerous.

Verification of the Faith in the New Contexts of Truth and of Communion[46]

In raising the "thorny question of the magisterium," I am not disputing the task of teaching that is connected with the episcopal ministry by the sacrament of order and which pertains to the Bishop of Rome in a very specific, but not exclusive, way. But the question I am posing is the following: if the system of the "epistemology of illumination" is no longer appropriate to a proper verification of the faith, what can one "imagine" in this area, so that the spiritual charism of thinking and of research can flourish, and that inevitable deviations can be identified and corrected? Over more than a century, I mentioned, the Church opened itself up to all the avenues of knowledge and Christian practice. It strove to nurture broad dialogue with contemporary learning, so often marred by a modernity suspected of despair, but also with other churches and other religions. The Second Vatican Council confirmed this new openness and encouraged it for the future, since it realized that it was the price of the salvation of humanity *today*. The Church's pursuit of its mission in this perspective of reconciliation, of evangelization, and of dialogue simply is not possible if we maintain the form of the magisterium that corresponds to a Neoplatonic understanding both of truth and of the Church and its hierarchy, when it comes to matters of defending the faith, of orthodoxy, and of controversy. In other words, the perspective agreed to and confirmed by Vatican II is one of *undertaking some high risks*. But the implied wager was that the Holy Spirit would not be lacking to the Church at this important juncture.

The question then is: what might be the form of the prophetic function of the episcopacy and the papacy (including the aspect of necessary vigilance) in order to take this risk, so that each time a danger looms on the horizon or when this or that theologian, and maybe even a particular church, seems to have embarked on an unpromising or even dangerous

---

46. Research and proposals on the theme of "Magisterium and Theology" are numerous, and what I am saying here is not anything that has not already been said. I am simply trying to emphasize the deep roots of the conflict, which is found in the opposition between two conceptions of truth and authority, both of which are theological and not strictly speaking a matter of revelation. Among many studies, I refer to J. Pfammater and E. Christen, eds., *Theologe und Hierarch*, Theologische Berichte 17 (Einsiedeln: Benziger, 1988), where one can also find excellent bibliographies.

path, we will not recoil from it? The question is not *the* magisterium but *which* magisterium. Perhaps today we are at an historic moment, which rehearses other such moments. Is the audacity of a Thomas Aquinas to prevail or the timidity of the authors who condemned him in 1277? Is Christianity to be interpreted according to a Neoplatonism in which the tendency of the "Alexandrian School" and its "proclivity to Monophysitism" reigns supreme, or a Christianity that in its own way, including its institutions, rediscovers the inspiration of the early Church in waiting for the Lord and practicing love and understanding? Not only the future of Catholic theology, but also the credibility of the Church and hence the service of salvation of men and women, depends on the reply given to this question.

The Christian Community, the Place of Truth

In the perspective that I outlined briefly at the beginning of this part, the knowledge of truth is always in the process of happening—up to Christ's parousia, and its definition makes no *sense* except in so far as it results from this "happening" and promotes its further development. It *exists* only in the heart of a community maintained by the Spirit of God in the state of testimony, of reflection, and of discovery. As a result, theological expressions of the faith are verified because the life of the community constantly verifies it and because it takes place in the community. In other words, the question first of all is to know if the liturgy continues to constitute the community, if the word of God is being read and reflected on there, if the language of witness and reflection flows naturally among brothers and sisters in the community, if their commitment to one another and their service to the world around them is strong—all are signs showing that the Spirit is alive in the Church. This fundamental verification flows from spiritual discernment: the *sensus fidelium* is found only where the breath of the Spirit is welcomed. Conversely, when a community struggles to remain faithful to the Spirit and the Word that is proclaimed and celebrated, and to its commitment to the many forms of charity, we have reason to believe that truth dwells there, even if it does not always find the words to express itself and even if the Spirit is always working to purify it of sin—that is how the Spirit leads it to the truth. This is the fundamental level on which the *sensus fidelium* operates and where the bishop's primary ministry to the Word is exercised: to proclaim the gospel by preaching and announcing the Mystery of Christ in the Spirit. The reciprocity is constant: the bishop announces nothing that the community does not believe, and it is essential that he listens to the community even while speaking. But he must also listen in order to speak. For its part, the community receives the authentic statement of its faith from the bishop, since this is his charism: to proclaim the Church's faith and so establish and confirm it.

Doctrine in Testimony

If this is conceded, we must still try to give an initial response to the question of what precisely is the right place of "doctrine" in the Church's testimony and what means need to be employed to assure this place. The need for doctrine arises when faith's testimony must be expressed in the language of the culture, i.e., when, with a view to understanding the faith and to accomplishing its mission, Christian faith must find the right way of interpreting the Bible or of expressing its belief in human words.

It strives to undertake this effort with theological hope and intellectual courage. If we believe that the Spirit really does guide the Church, every encounter between faith and culture should normally be beneficial for both. The God of covenant and forgiveness is also God the Creator. But if we undertake this effort in a spirit of controversy and fear, as though eventual error is a priori stronger in itself and in its effects, we will not achieve any positive results. What is worse, we contribute to the genesis and development of error, because we do not have the means of firmly and peacefully establishing the truth.[47]

After defining and sincerely defending our basic mentality, we must try to interrelate three groups which have responsibility in this effort. First, there is the Christian community, where the Spirit, source of all understanding lives, but which must necessarily remain open to today's urgent problems, even if they often do not understand them. Next are the men and women who have the charism of theology, those members of the community whose intelligence enables them to study how we speak and understand. Finally, there is the apostolic ministry which must be knowledgeable about today's problems, keep apace with them, and even orient the research and learn the proposed solutions, all the while avoiding becoming unduly frightened by real or apparent mistakes, and knowing how to let time do its job. *We must not stop trying to lessen the distance separating the Christian people, the academy, and the hierarchy.* There are difficulties here. Some arise from the infrequency of interpersonal contacts, and some from the explosion of knowledge (whether the printed word or computer-generated knowledge), with the result that one often encounters conflicting ideas and

---

47. In his discourse of November 15, 1980, in Cologne, John Paul II masterfully recalled the real coordinates of the relationship between "science and faith," and encouraged further scientific research without fear. See "An die Wissenschaftler: Neue Verbindung von Wissenschaft und Glaubenskraft" in *Herder Korrespondenz* 35 (1981) 30–33. E. T. *Origins* 10 (25) (December 4, 1980) 395–98. Perhaps we should add that these reaffirmed principles, which are those of St. Thomas Aquinas, have validity not only for the delicate matters raised by astrophysics and the theories of the origins of the universe, but also for the human sciences and technology and their ethical implications.

yet does not have the possibility of discussing them face to face with another person. However, if we are persuaded that in this area of proclaiming the faith, of understanding it better, and of the Church's mission close cooperation between the faithful, theologians, and bishops is necessary, we will find the ways to realize it.

Signed Documents

Should one or more bishops judge it necessary to write a document and invite several theologians to collaborate with them, why shouldn't the names of their collaborators be noted? If a committee of theologians that may or may not include bishops prepares a document for a given episcopate or for the Holy See, or if the final version is written by a specific person, why not say so? What is at stake here is the rejection of the myth of a teaching that owes nothing to human sources. Shouldn't we believe that the Holy Spirit has been active throughout the process and that there is no need to conceal the ups and downs of any human endeavor? In any case, this myth correlates with the theme of obligatory obedience, as though the latter can happen without exercising intellectual and spiritual discernment. There is a certain "Monophysite" tendency in this process, or at any rate an overly juridical one, which does not correspond to the facts of the matter. Most of the time it is a matter of an *authoritative teaching,* which the Holy See or the bishops have good reasons to think can serve the Church's goal of testimony, of formation and of mission. In a more or less forceful way, it attracts the attention of the churches whose primary duty is not to obey but to believe and understand.

Definitions and Condemnations

Sometimes more than an authoritative teaching of doctrine is needed. It would be naive to think that error never happens or that it will not work harm. There are times when a precise definition of truth and the condemnation of error are demanded. I will first mention several precautions to be taken in this area, and then I will say a word about the formulas themselves, before addressing the question of the ones who issue the definitions or who bear the condemnation.

I spoke above of the temptation to give more importance than it deserves to the conception of truth proper to the "Parmenidean culture." In expanding on the topic, I want to say that it is also necessary to guard against what might be called the "pathology of unity" as much as against the "pathology of truth." Not all unity is Christian unity or even genuine human unity. Effectively, in the idea of the One there is an essentially negative element that we must recognize, if we are not to naively consider all unity as something positive and absolute. We need to exercise constant discernment in order to be sure that the authentic search for Unity is not perverted into the inability to accept an Other that is also part of the condition of being a creature. We must test to see whether such a search is not a desire to realize here below an absolutely full communication that would lead to the "unity" of all difference. Such a desire is truly eschatological: in desiring here below to fully realize it, one is led to combinative and totalizing mind sets that establish only superficial unity and that shatter the differences that belong to the very reality of creatures. "Unity" obtained in this way is the opposite of the fear of losing oneself, and is tied to the inability to welcome the diversity of the other and to move with the other toward true unity. In this case, the unity in question is nothing more than the unity that is totally limited and imaginary of someone turned in on himself or herself, or the unity of a community paralyzed by its fears. We could say that in itself every form of magisterium is tempted by this type of unity. The greatness of the Catholic magisterium consists in rising above this temptation.

In the same way, a legitimate desire to do the truth and to remain in it can be perverted by searching for formulas that do not vary *(ne varietur)*, because we forget that they are never more than approximations, and that paradoxically it is their limits that represent their value. I would like to return here to a point I mentioned earlier apropos of the "weak" objectivity and the character of "probability" of an expressed truth.[48] In a Platonic world, only what is free of all approximation, untarnished by any opinion, and that dazzles a perfectly purified mind with its blinding light can be true absolutely. In the Cartesian and post-Cartesian world, the criterion of the absolutely true is what is subjectively certain. The victorious resistance to methodic doubt is the sign of truth; what refuses to resist or resists weakly cannot be qualified as truth. As far as objective truth is concerned, in what pertains to moral, historical or religious knowledge, it can never exceed the probable (i.e., Aristotle's "opinion" and the *"scientia quia"* of the scholastics), and subjective certitude arises in part from the decision of the will (necessarily directed by grace) to "hold as true" that which is not evident, all the while contenting itself with sufficiently objective guarantees. Such truth can never be evident, however much one insists on it in theory or practice. We must admit that a statement of the faith does not show a "strong" objectivity that would ground it, and that faith's certitude is not subjectively evident. And so, if the formula is only true in an approximative way, and if the certitude is not only a matter of the understanding but simultaneously of help coming from the will and grace, a certain maneuverability of interpretation always remains, so that one must hope (in the

48. See above, pp. 75–77.

strong sense of the term) that the Spirit is guiding the process and uniting the believer directly with the very "object" of faith by means of the "authority of God revealing" *(auctoritas Dei revelantis)* and the "interior instinct of faith" *(instinctus interior fidei).*

When all is said and done, if it appears truly necessary to define a point of the faith or to forcefully correct an error, one can ask if the ancient practice of the Church was not the better way, viz., to write a short creed *(symbolum fidei),* pronouncing a certain statement to be false and indicating its degree of error, and if possible doing it in irenic terms. It should strive to keep the future open, since history shows that new insights can nuance a statement that would then appear absolute without them.[49]

The Need for Time

Years ago, it took a long time for a formula to reach its addressees and for their reaction to become known to the sender. One had to write out by hand many copies and then send them using the means of transportation that were time-consuming and precarious. Now the time spent waiting that human conditions imposed had a certain value, allowing thought to mature, agreement to be reached, rejection or reservations to be expressed, etc. Today there is none of that, which does not mean that in matters of doctrinal formulas we must renounce all the modern means available to us, but that it is absolutely essential that we provide for moratoriums, i.e., that we allow for time. *Actually, the formulation of truths transcends time and space on the one hand, and interpersonal communication on the other.* We need to be conscious of this simple fact and try by all possible means to remedy it, since otherwise the formulas are hypostatized. One is tempted either to consider them so divine that the conditions of their being communicated seem hardly human, or to contemn them because time had not been taken to humanize them.

The Universal Episkopē *of the Bishop of Rome*

We shall now attempt several observations on the concrete forms of the universal *episkopē* of the Bishop of Rome. Here the task of imagining is

49. As Paul VI reminded Patriarch Athenagoras, the ecumenical practice of certain Fathers of the Church might serve as a model here. Moreover, the recent mutual recognition by Paul VI and the Coptic Orthodox Patriarch Shenouda III of the orthodoxy of the christological formulas of both the Coptic and the Catholic Churches gives us occasion to reflect: how much secular discord, how many undying hostilities, how much spilt blood between Chalcedonians and non-Chalcedonians might have been avoided! On this subject, see my article "Le Document de Lima et l'Église catholique: interrogations et perspectives" in *Il ministero ordinato nel dialogo ecumenico* (Rome, 1985) 217–28.

difficult because we are not accustomed to think of *episkopē* in this context but of centralized administration, highly organized after the Council of Trent to combat heresy, to defend itself against more or less hostile civil authorities, whether Christians in name or in fact, and because it was distrustful of local government. In the Middle Ages, the Church of Rome was familiar with the College of Cardinals, which then was a kind of synod of neighboring bishops and of the pastors and deacons of the city. It was also acquainted with "particular councils," which consisted of the bishops of Italy or those living in Rome, whom the pope assembled to consult. The Curia, though, is neither the synod of the Bishop of Rome, nor a permanent particular council; it is not even a "government" whose "ministers," i.e., the prefects of the various congregations, are convened by the pope (or when necessary, the Secretary of State) to assess matters in general and to determine what needs to be done to enliven the life of the Church. Whatever Sixtus V (1585–90) intended and whatever adaptations have been made over the centuries, the Curia is the administrative organization of a primacy that itself is considered to be immediately present at each level (which in principle does not imply a "horizontal" communication with others) and which acts in its own name and with its own authority. Two echelons in the Curia are more central and more powerful: the Secretariat of the State and the Congregation for the Doctrine of the Faith. Gradually, due to the ever-growing prestige of the papacy, this organization has taken on an almost sacred character that leads it to be suspicious of the slightest questioning of its authority. Everything I've said so far, however, shows how necessary it is for us to rethink the concrete exercise of the primacy of Peter, so that it will remain strong enough to accomplish its proper task, without relying on an outdated political theology. By reason of its long tradition, which Vatican II paradoxically seems to have reinforced and enlarged by creating new central agencies, the Church scarcely has any experience of what might be an effective exercise of collegiality around the pope. On the other hand, we cannot imagine what the more modest "diaconal" services would look like which will assist the Bishop of Rome in organizing his universal responsibility for the gospel. I will limit myself to a few very general observations.

The Primacy of Peter in the Context of Collegiality

We can imagine an *annual synod of the presidents of the episcopal conferences of continents* around the pope. It would consist of a maximum of eight to ten persons, i.e., the ideal number of individuals for working together effectively. It could discuss the situation of the churches in all parts of the world in order to detect any urgent problem that exceeds the resources of one or more particular churches; but it could also discern any impulse of universal value that can be proposed to the churches in the actual world situation. Holding such a synod would be all the more effective because it would convene the optimum number of participants for fruitful discussion, discernment, and action.

The practice of holding regular synods of bishops (canons 342–48) needs to be continued, so important are they for the effective consciousness of collegiality and co-responsibility in the Church. But must they deal with a single topic? Can't we imagine the presidents of certain episcopal conferences reporting on their churches? And can't we imagine that the bishops at such a "summit conference" will meet each other and share their ideas regarding the major aspects of the *episkopē* of the Church? It would be well if a concluding short document were written by some of its members, at a joint working session with the pope, of course.

Likewise, the *apostolic visits* which the pope makes to the other churches should be continued. But maybe their pastoral character could be enhanced and they could be held in greater simplicity and respect for poverty. Because the bishops will no longer have been named by the pope and the collegial responsibility of the local churches will have been developed, mutual contact between the pope and the bishops would be possible. A papal visit would be the time to hold a local council at which bishops and other members of the People of God could be present. At such occasions of meeting one another, speaking and listening to each other will be more balanced. The pope would celebrate the liturgy and preach on the Scriptures, and possibly make other interventions, at the request of the bishops or as a result of what he has observed during the visit. It would represent a human and supernatural presence of the successor of Peter, whose "visit" would take on the character of resolving issues rather than issuing reprimands. Conversely, from time to time the bishops could travel on pilgrimage to visit the tombs of SS Peter and Paul and use this occasion to "pay a visit" to the Bishop of Rome and to take advantage of the service of his universal primacy, should there be a need.

If the pope cannot go everywhere himself and there are circumstances that demand the intervention of the successor of Peter, he might think of *sending legates for a specific purpose* who would be charged with looking into a situation, passing a judgment, promoting solutions and general approaches to the issues, and reconciling estranged parties, i.e., with doing everything needed to "maintain the unity of the episcopacy." Visits of a legate, or when circumstances warrant it, several legates, would last only as long as necessary to address the gravity of the problems and the need of the churches. At any rate, there would no longer be any need for the permanent presence of an "apostolic delegate" of the Holy See in foreign countries, since the majority of questions could be resolved locally, regionally, or nationally.

The Diaconal Organization of the Primacy of Peter

Just as we can imagine a body of ordained deacons around a bishop acting as moderators of the various sectors that the Spirit animates in the life of a particular church, so too can we imagine a diaconal organization on the national and continental levels of the churches and an ensemble of diaconal services necessary for maintaining the continuity and the cohesiveness of the Petrine primacy. This is the role which the Roman Curia currently fulfills in the framework of a highly centralized Church. In the perspective I am trying to sketch, we can reserve for the needed diaconal agencies the rather modest name of "secretariat," which were the agencies created just before or right after the council, of which the most famous was the Secretariat for Christian Unity. This would truly be a service of deacons, viz., to administrate but not to decide matters. It could be simpler and less top-heavy than the current Roman offices which spend much time verifying, approving, and discussing the actions of bishops and of churches, as well as drafting instructions and documents. From the point of view of a Church structured along the lines of charisms and their institutions, the majority of these functions can be left to the less universal competence and the more proximate familiarity of persons and groups in the churches. For each of the areas of the bishop's *episkopē* that the secretariats deal with (in contrast to the permanent "congregations" of today's structure), we can imagine regular meetings of several bishops, not to replace the local bishops or collegial structures, but to discuss what is necessary and to examine what should be brought to Rome. The person responsible for each of these encounters could give an account at the following synod of bishops, which would permit the latter to better grasp what is happening in the Church.

In what I have said thus far in this chapter and in earlier ones, there is the germ of what might be a replacement for the centralized organization currently governing the universal Church. I say "replacement" and not "reform": we give another form to what is deformed or poorly adapted to situations, and reforms of this type occurred in the Curia of Sixtus V (1585–90) and others by Pius X (1903–14), Paul VI (1963–78), and John Paul II. But what is at stake in a Church viewed as "structured communion" is the discovery of new operational structures, less top-heavy, more supple, of service to the various charisms and their respective institutions. Several examples might prove helpful.

If the task of verifying the faith takes into account that ordinarily the charisms of reflecting on the faith and teaching it function well, and that the episcopal task of teaching retrieves its greater responsibility for preaching and the search for the "understanding of the faith," then we need to imagine an institution for verifying the faith that is truly new, not "Gregorian" in form, that will replace the current Congregation for the Doctrine of the Faith. If the bishops are elected by the churches and if the churches receive regular visits, there is no place, at least not in its present form, for a Congregation of Bishops, since the latter exists to nominate bishops and to examine the quinquennial reports sent to the Holy See for the *ad limina* visits. If the clergy essentially consists of mature men, some of whom are married and engaged in secular occupations, and the diaconal ministry in the Church is much more diversified, there is no place for a Congregation of the Clergy, at least not in its present form. If religious life is organized essentially thanks to the charisms that belong to it and that permit a spirit of vigilance and interior reform, there is no need for verifying it so closely by a Congregation for Religious. And if the Bishop of Rome is more concerned in the future with his own diocese, he would have less time to control the activity of those who act only in his name, even if they never meet him, and there will be no need to multiply administrative positions. These are only a few examples of possible changes. We would probably have to enlarge their number, but this is hard to predict before some steps have been taken in the direction proposed here.

Finally, we must necessarily provide for legal agencies, to the extent that some local tribunals (whose activity will undoubtedly be extensive) will not be able to solve one or another problem and to the extent that some problems will completely escape their ability to deal with them.

Church and State

The relations between the Church and nation-states is a special area for the exercise of Petrine primacy, to the extent that only the latter are in a position to defend the liberty of the churches because of their inclusion in political entities. A special responsibility of the primacy of Peter might be the defense of the liberty of churches and conversely helping them to find an advantageous position in a politically difficult situation where they have few options for responding. Vice versa, the Church's mediation can be helpful in a difficult national or international situation.

Nevertheless, we can ask to what extent it wouldn't be better to rethink the legal bases of this primacy of the pope. From the perspective of a Church as "structured communion" these foundations cannot be the same as in the system of "pontifical Christendom." We must be very careful to avoid anything that smacks of the pretensions of the medieval popes of world supremacy, of the "jurisdiction over the whole world" (*jurisdictio supra totum orbem*) that even the apostolic constitution *Vacantis Apostolicae*

Sedis spoke of in 1946.[50] But the problem of the relations of the Holy See with other states also cannot be based on the same foundations as when the Church was considered a "perfect society."[51] The relevance of such a concept is questionable nowadays, even on the level of sociological or political theory, at a time when we must recognize that terms such as "perfect" and "absolute" are not even used to describe "national sovereignty." The notion of the "sovereignty of the Catholic Church" as it receives concrete form in the "Holy See"[52] cannot be exempt from possible revision.

Without going to the heart of these matters—a study still to be undertaken—we might ask whether we can imagine the closing of the permanent nunciatures of the Holy See, both as agencies of diplomatic representation, because they would no longer have such a reason to exist, but also because there would no longer be the need for the presence of a permanent pontifical delegate in a national church. Certainly, the political independence of the Holy See is something absolutely essential, and that symbolically makes possible the existence of the Vatican State. But the Republic of San Marino, the principalities of Liechtenstein or Monaco do not maintain official delegations in all the states of the world and do not become entangled in the business of recognizing new states and new governments. Without doubt, the Vatican State can do the same and thereby gain greater liberty vis-à-vis nation-states. If it is argued that diplomatic exchanges do not take place between the Vatican and the states, but between these states and the Catholic Church, in so far as it is a "sovereign power," such an argument is valid only if the two concepts "Catholic Church" and "sovereign power" are compatible, and that seems doubtful today. In fact, it might be argued that the existence of the Vatican State guarantees the liberty of the Church as the body of Christ and People of God by reserving for it a certain symbolic independence. However, I do not think that it acts as the foundation of any such thing as the "sovereignty of the Catholic Church."[53] Whatever the reason, the existence of a permanent diplomatic

50. See *Acta Apostolicae Sedis* 38 (1946) 97. No doubt, the Holy See no longer has the means, if it ever had them, of exercising such political supremacy over the whole world. But, once it lost it, the temptation could arise to hold on to a sort of intellectual supremacy over the world, by pretending to sovereignly dictate the only legitimate ways of thinking and acting, even though the Church's every word is found at the heart of the humble witness it gives to Jesus Christ.

51. See Patrick Granfield, "The Church as *Societas Perfecta* in the Schemata of Vatican I," *Church History* 48 (1979) 431–46 [translator].

52. See Rolland Minnerath, "Siège apostolique" in G. Mathon and G. -H. Baudry, eds., *Catholicisme hier, aujourd'hui, demain,* vol. 14 (Paris: Letouzey et Ané, 1994) 26–42.

53. It seems that the idea of "sovereignty" is tied in reality to the papacy's political past and to the existence of the Papal States. The same could also be said of the Order of

representation today can harm the liberty of the Church both particular and universal, since too often it makes diplomatic gestures obligatory that are disputable and can be interpreted in one sense or another, with scarcely any advantage to the gospel or for world peace, or which appear, and sometimes unfortunately are, veritable compromises.

On the contrary, we can and must imagine the sending out of legates, each time that the liberty of the Church is under attack in a country and must be defended by the Holy See, or when a grave disagreement between Church and state necessitates serious discussions that cannot result in success on the local level alone, or even when the state believes it has a justifiable complaint against the Church and asks for arbitration. It might be asked whether it is really necessary for the ambassador to be an archbishop. It might even be better if it is a deacon, as when St. Gregory was sent to Constantinople as the delegate of Pope Pelagius II (579–90).[54] Conversely, the Bishop of Rome, primate of the universal Church, would receive politicians when they desire it, in order to establish or maintain contact with the supreme head of the Catholic churches.

Malta, also called "sovereign," because in a certain way it serves as a reminder of the time the order owned the island of Malta. Conversely, other international organizations that exist for humanitarian purposes, like the Order of Malta, but which came into existence after the reign of princes in Europe (e.g., the Red Cross, the Food and Agriculture Organization, or UNESCO) are not called and not considered "sovereign." They do not send out ambassadors, and if they do so, it is in view of regulating economic, not political, problems.

54. On this incident in Gregory's life, see W.H.C. Frend, *The Rise of Christianity* (Philadelphia: Fortress, 1984) 883–84 [translator].

Chapter 8

Conclusion

At the end of our investigation, it might be well to return to our point of departure. It is essential that the effort to "imagine the Catholic Church," as I have tried to do in the final chapters, avoid being closed in on itself and that it not ignore the thrust of the whole project. This alone can render the act of "imagining" desirable. If the current crisis of civilization has the character of a *kairos*, how can the Catholic Church best fulfill its mission under this condition? The question can be divided into three areas.

First, what face would permit the Church not only to give witness to the Good News of the gospel, but also would be recognized as the place where the Good News can be found and that it is something to be desired? Both witness and place are essential if the gospel is a principle of salvation for humankind, an agent of renewal after a long history of suffering, and a source of humanization for each person, each social and political group, and for humanity as a whole.

Second, which structures might the Church adopt, so that the face they present can help human communities discover their own proper organization in service of unity arising out of their diversity? In the current grave crisis of a modernity gasping for breath under the weight of its pretensions (and this to some extent because of the past refusal of the Church to do its part), what model can the Church modestly offer? Which communities can it propose that are both open and vigilant, and that can articulate the human desire for relationship and the thirst to know? How can it show that it is not afraid of proposing certain limitations which alone can free human beings so they can develop to their fullest? How can it show that it is capable of combining authority and freedom, while still respecting human autonomy relative to the different domains of thought and action?

Third, in order to contribute to healing the wounds of separation among the Christian churches that go back a thousand years and so effectively bring about the unity Christ prayed for, how can the Church rethink the historical forms and the theological treatment of its institutions, while keeping intact the institution of the Church founded by Christ, viz., respecting the sacramentality of the apostolic ministry and the Petrine primacy? Though certain expressions were useful at different historical moments, these institutions are not definitively bound to any particular form.

I thought that in order to respond to these questions it was necessary first of all to venture a diagnosis of the situation, which would include both the present evil in modern civilization and the banefully uniform and exclusive form of government of a Church that accompanies this same civilization and seems not to have contributed much to warding off this evil. Of course, the situation is not absolutely desperate either for the world or the Church: planet Earth has still not imploded under the weight of its vaunted technology, the gospel continues to be proclaimed and welcomed, and finally the Catholic Church, with greater or less skill, has remained steadfastly faithful to Christ. And still, the fundamental search remains. Even if the world is unaware of it, the dialectic of Christianity and world, Church and human communities, is constitutive of God's plan. The search continues, even though appearances seem to contradict it and the Church increasingly appears marginalized, while the diversity of religions and systems of wisdom seems to open up an unlimited pluralism. It is of capital importance that the Church rediscover its significance for humanity.

In this grave but not hopeless situation, it seems that the Church must accept the need to free itself from what I have called the "Gregorian form," bound as it is to other cultural conditions and arising out of a different equilibrium of faith and reason, Church and politics. It is imperative that it try to imagine how to incarnate what is constitutive of its Mystery in a tangled and troubled situation today. Allow me to try to summarize the essential points of the book's approach.

Summary

Christian revelation concerns the reign of God, which will come to us and which we will enter when Christ, the Son of God, born, crucified, and risen for us, will come again. The Church is before all else a community that *awaits*, that must give witness of its prudent impatience for Christ's parousia. A concrete point of practical ecclesiology would be to know how to revive this eschatological "impatience" that alone gives time its positive meaning and that no philosophy or culture seems to give a place of honor.

In the meanwhile, the Church is the community of men and women who keep the *memory* of Jesus Christ, *give thanks* for the salvation already given and whose completion they await, and finally live *according to the Spirit* they have received. It is a "eucharistic" community if it is true that the memory is kept alive by the story (used here in its strongest sense, since the event evoked is also somehow made present), and which gives rise to a spirit of gratitude and spiritual offering. (After all, isn't self-giving the expression of gratitude?) As eucharistic, the Church is also a "scriptural" community, since in the Scriptures it preserves the document that must be interpreted again and again by its memory of Jesus Christ. Finally, it is a "pneumatic" community, since it lives concretely from the Spirit of Christ who is its interior law, helps it understand the Scriptures, and gives power and efficacy to its Eucharist.

Upon this constitutive foundation, the Church's activity is first of all to give *witness* before all men and women of salvation in Jesus Christ and the coming kingdom. This testimony presupposes a *life in community* that is at once marked by the threefold commandment of love—of God, self, and neighbor—and by a *charismatic* organization, since it lives and gives witness by the various gifts of the Spirit. This witness promotes our humanity, either by contributing to the forgiveness of sins and the healing of injuries, or by liberating all our powers of sensation, imagination, understanding, and love. The true love of the Spirit results in our *humanization*.

Before all else, the Church must become more powerfully aware of the presence in it of a Spirit that is truly divine and that guides and animates it. The Spirit hands on to Christian communities the tradition of the word, of Scripture, and of the Sacrament left by Christ to the first apostolic community. Thanks to the diversity of sacramental and institutional gifts, the Spirit brings the communities to a state of spiritual sacrifice offered to God in the eucharistic sacrifice of Christ, and of effective witness before humankind. Paradoxically, the stress put on the presence of the Spirit frees our humanity. The gifts of the Spirit are correlated to the existentials of human existence and educe a constant mutuality of faith and reason, of grace and freedom, of revealed truths and human study, of divine counsel and intelligently prudent action. We are in a world of docility and discernment, both advanced by exchanges that are of human proportion, by institutions and laws whose purpose is to sustain the impulse of the Spirit.

Nothing can come of any of this if *institutions* are not established and provision is not made for the intervention of *authorities* without which there would be only anarchy. But, coming from the same Spirit, these must be diversified, reflected on, and articulated among themselves. They must not be reduced to the institutions that are bound directly to the apostolic ministry. I have tried to describe these flexible spiritual structures and institutions in some detail, but without being able to go into precise details that can only come from lived experience. They are based essentially on the sacraments of initiation and take their place thanks to greater attention to the Holy Spirit, the gift of God to the Church which awaits Christ's parousia. The central idea which dominates my presentation is that *the gifts of the Spirit determine the institutions and that they have a real autonomy with respect to the double responsibility of reflection and organization.* It is important that we find ways to develop these particular exercises of autonomy, while coordinating them with other autonomous institutions, in a communion of which the eucharistic community itself is the sign and the center. In this global context of the Christian community celebrating the Eucharist and bearing witness, the general administration is entrusted to a *charism of presiding, consecrated by the sacrament of order,* and bearing the succession of the apostles to the extent that they guaranteed the witness of Jesus Christ. Those who preside must try to maintain contact with each other, with the help and under the authority of one of their number, the Bishop of Rome, the administrator of the community where Peter and Paul gave their lives for the gospel.

Thus, the global task of a practical ecclesiology that must imagine and then realize the Church in the wake of Vatican II will be as follows. With regard to the particular churches, it must articulate the various Christian institutions defined by the states in life and the services *(diakoniai)* in such wise as to persevere in the way of holiness and witness, and, please God, succeed in realizing a new evangelization. With regard to the communion of the churches in the universal Church, it must foster the collegiality of the bishops, of course, but also of the communities by rediscovering forms of conciliarity, and by finding appropriate institutions in conjunction with the Church of Rome, the center of communion and its bishop, that are less centralized and oppressive. Instead, the latter will advance the convergence of all the churches on the way toward the kingdom and will help those among them that cannot find their way out of momentary difficulties because they lack the means.

The hypothesis I have formulated is that such institutional reform would render more credible the witness of the gospel in the contemporary world, which does not assume a hierarchicized order. It can modestly offer certain models to secular societies badly in need of reconciliation and unity. Negatively, I have underscored that when it comes to knowledge, an ecclesiastical organization founded principally on an "epistemology of illumination," and when it comes to action, founded on a theory of "power," no longer seem capable of effectively sustaining the Mystery which is the object of evangelization. The same needs to be said when it comes to action, when the Church constantly opposes the autonomy of cultures and their proper responsibility, because it understands itself in terms of a theory of "power."

In ecumenism, the chief task of the Catholic Church is to be found in the same general direction. It must undertake an institutional reform that rises to the level of the Spirit's desire manifested at Vatican II, or in other terms, to extend to the whole of its life and its structures what the council did with audacity. And might we not hope that the same daring will continue with respect to liturgical reform? Here is where we will find the *witness* of the Catholic Church: in showing a new face—older and yet newer, thoroughly humble yet quite audacious; the "older" needs to become more approachable, so that "her sisters" might not fear to approach her and themselves tend to the business of the appearance they present to each other.

From Utopia to Reality

I have presented this study as an "imagining" or a kind of "utopia." Can we now risk several hypotheses on how such an imagining might become reality? I would like to speak succinctly about the possibility of its implementation, about the authority that can seize the initiative, about the conditions necessary for its realization, and about possible obstacles and how they can be removed.

Possibility

Institutional reform of the Church of the kind I have proposed can be found along the lines drawn by the reform of the liturgy begun at Vatican II, and its realization is no more impossible than was the latter's. The reform of the liturgy[1] was prepared by years of reflection and experimentation at the heart of the liturgical movement undertaken in many countries. Endorsing and acting in accord with what was learned in this vast effort, the council laid down the principles of reform. The latter went largely beyond the premises it determined, since there is a certain logic in the work of liturgy that cannot be completely understood before they have been implemented. In fact, liturgical reform returned to the sources of the Latin Liturgy, and evaluated them in themselves and as confronted by the ecclesial and human reality of the time. It produced a body of texts and practices where the new and the old seem to be mutually reinforced, and where much was left open to further adaptation, with a view toward the particular communities and cultures. This reform can serve as an example. It illustrates perfectly the effective content of the notion of tradition, which is

---

1. I am trying to complete in this section what I indicated earlier in chapter 6, pp. 137–40.

not repetition pure and simple or the obstinate holding on to obsolete elements, but a profound retrieval that permits, thanks to thoughtful changes, the deep reality of the spiritual cult of the Church to continue.

The reform of the liturgy not only points to the possibility that an effort of the same scope is possible with regard to the institutions of the Church, but that it is necessary. The liturgy is one of the Church's institutions and its reform cannot, over the long haul, be sustained in the Spirit who dictated it, if other ecclesial structures arise from a different inspiration. At the heart of the liturgy one finds a language, a lived perception of the relation between truth and love in the spiritual cult, placing the diverse Christian charisms under the presidency and the guidance of the bishop, but also a relationship that is lived among the particular churches and between them and the Church of Rome. All of that cannot help but be extended to the other canonical levels of the Church and receive their mutual support in sustaining this liturgical life. But if planning for the ensemble of Church structures remains apart from liturgical reform, the latter will soon come to grief in a new ritualism, little by little losing contact with the Spirit who animates it.

Just as prior to the reform of the liturgy there was a long process of returning to the sources, of theological reflection, and of practical proposals, so too before and after the council, slow but steady work has not been lacking on sketching the possibilities of institutional reform. What I am proposing in this book is a "synthesis" of these possibilities.[2] Whatever piecemeal efforts have been made to date, the difficulty in undertaking global reform undoubtedly is connected with the fact that the "Gregorian form" remains firmly rooted in the Church, and not only in the very long canonical tradition,[3] but most concretely in present structures. It follows that resistance to profound institutional change remains stronger than the resistance to liturgical reform.

Authority

When we stand before a system that is highly structured and centralized (as is the case with the Catholic Church), effective reform can come

---

2. See above, chapter 4, p. 107, n. 20.

3. We must remember that the tradition of collections of canons, begun at the outset of the Gregorian reform, bears the profound imprint of the papacy, and that it found its form (more or less definitive at the time) in the *Codex Iuris Canonici* of 1917. Particular canonical proposals made in the course of history always took on (or had always been considered as taking on) an anti-Roman, sometimes schismatical, cast. It is this Roman–anti-Roman dualism that we must surmount by seeking out new forms of achieving equilibrium.

about only with the initiative and persistence of the central power. The convoking of the Second Vatican Council was due to Pope John XXIII and his peaceful tenacity; and the undertaking, pursuit, and completion of the liturgical reform were due to Pope Paul VI who supported them with unflagging determination at every stage. The same pope also undertook the reform of canon law, which resulted in the Code of Canon Law of 1983, and was promulgated by Pope John Paul II. However, it seems that Paul VI did not see the indissoluble link between liturgical and canonical reform. We know that he gave instructions that the future code should remain as faithful as possible to the spirit and organization of the code of 1917.[4] It was not to be a question of a profound retrieval, going beyond the medieval canonical collections (without for all that denying their contribution), as was the case in the liturgical reform that reached back before the ninth and tenth centuries, but all the while conserving elements from these centuries in a new form. One had to maintain the spirit of what I have called the "Gregorian form," while the spirit and the letter of so many texts of Vatican II and the institutions postulated for the reform of the liturgy went more in the direction of a powerful retrieval.

Today, as well, we find ourselves in a precarious situation, one in which the intuitions and ambiguities of the council's texts are articulated with greater or less success, and the efforts at implementation and reforms arising from an ecclesiology dominated by the idea of the body of Christ and the People of God (together with the liturgy that corresponds to it), the institutions and theological presuppositions of the Gregorian form still dominate so many sectors of the Church's life. I hope that this situation, which is probably detrimental to the larger interests I spoke about in the introduction and at the beginning of this chapter, will not last much longer.

Under current circumstances, only the pope can initiate a solution. It will be necessary that he be more forceful than even the brilliant Pope Sixtus V (1585–90), who at the turn of the seventeenth century was responsible for systematically reorganizing the ecclesiastical government after the Council of Trent. It is not a question today of centralizing, but of diversifying, in such a way that responsibility will be more equitably shared among Christians. The proper authority of the Bishop of Rome over all the Churches will emerge stronger because it will be situated exclusively at those points where there is a need to intervene and preserve the churches in unity. This necessarily presupposes the establishing of Christian communities for education in spiritual freedom, done intelligently and with discernment—

---

4. Cardinal Rosalio I. Castillo-Lara mentioned this fact in a conference he gave. See "La communion ecclésiale dans le nouveau Code de droit canon," *Communicationes* 16 (1984) 242–66, at 244.

something still woefully lacking. A reformer pope would play a capital role in this regard.

Conditions

The conditions necessary for establishing such institutions are a renewing of faith in the Holy Spirit and the education in freedom I just spoke about. Concerning everything I've said and speaking about faith in the Holy Spirit, it is clear that I see no opposition between "spirit and institution," "life and structures," etc. Instead, I assume that the institutions Jesus Christ put in place by his word and example, or the spontaneous decisions of the group of disciples, arise out of the constant practical understanding which comes from an attention incessantly directed at the Spirit of creation and the covenant. Such an understanding finds a way to reorganize the essential institutions with a view toward different situations in time and space, whereas an inspiration also coming from the Spirit suggests the particular institutions that can be of service to those that are primary.[5] Faith in the Holy Spirit is particularly necessary when the Church is seen as a structured communion, because the ensemble of institutions is more diversified and more supple than in the Gregorian form of the Church. Such communion does not result in the *unicity* of a centralized authority (at least it is not apparent), but there is *unity* which comes essentially from the Spirit living in the Church and which is discretely sustained by the concerted action of various authorities. Thus, in case of necessity unity receives its ultimate support from the charism of primacy of the Bishop of Rome.

To say "faith in the Holy Spirit" is to speak of "education for freedom." Several times in the course of this book, I have distinguished between the idea and the practice of immediate obedience to such power and the evangelical docility that implies thinking, discerning, and taking responsibility. These three words spring from faith in the Holy Spirit, but they also signify an education, i.e., a formation of mind, a pedagogy of judgment, a training of the will, an apprenticeship in relationality. If the Holy Spirit is truly given to Christians at the moment of their baptism and confirmation, and if the Church is renewed by the Spirit's charismatic gifts, there is no reason to assume that every pedagogical activity of the Church in service of the formation of free men and women is ipso facto presumptuous or illusory. Such

---

5. For example, celibacy lived for the kingdom was instituted by Jesus Christ and belongs to the Church's constitution (see chapter 4, pp. 101–03); and the different orders, congregations, and institutes grow out of this institution by Christ and under the charismatic inspiration of their founders and then their members. Consequently, the life of celibacy will never be lacking in the Church, whereas the institutes mentioned are subject to reform and renewal; they can disappear when they no longer measure up to historical circumstances.

an education is profoundly evangelical and therefore supremely reasonable. That is the "gamble" the Church must take.

Abuses and Fear

I need to reply to several possible objections. Some will say that if we allow Christian communities greater diversity and freedom, there will be abuses, just as there were in the first days of the reform of the liturgy. In response, we can say that abuses are almost inevitable at the moment one breaks out of an extremely authoritarian system of doing things, precisely because one has not been formed to exercise one's freedom. If before the council there was, in certain influential but limited circles, a liturgical movement, the liturgical practice was entirely in the hands of the Congregation for Rites to which one had to turn for solutions even on the most minor ceremonial points or to obtain an indult for the tiniest variation. In seminaries, liturgy was (and unfortunately still is) a secondary area of theology (as was pastoral formation), and not the heart of a priest's formation. Right after the council, priests were caught off guard and whatever resources were made available to them were strictly limited to particular practices. They had no chance to imbibe a "liturgical sense" which could come only from years of training. It was inevitable that they did not immediately understand the meaning of the reforms and that, faced with ritual and theological novelties, they sometimes were tempted to do whatever came along. *The possibility of abuse came from the abrupt passing from a marked authoritarian regime to one characterized by immature freedom.*

Rather than dramatizing the abuses that some were guilty of, we can rejoice in the fact that on the whole the reform was well implemented because the Spirit was with it. Both the Christian people and its priests soon found their way, simply because it corresponded best to the truth of Christian worship in our world today. As far as important institutional reform is concerned (the kind I am considering here), the question should be how to define and manage it, so that there will be a minimum number of mistakes during the short period of transition. But to the extent that such a reform is genuinely anticipated by the Christian people and the churches—a waiting that is profoundly spiritual and not simply humanly endured—we can reckon that these mistakes will not be too numerous, just as was the case during the reform of the liturgy.[6]

---

6. Along this same line of thought, one could bring up the specter of schism connected with such reform. To tell the truth, I do not think that such a schism will be able to be avoided. Since its inception, the Church knows that as soon as it does something particularly important, some Christians leave it. This sad fact stands and has not failed to happen during the past two centuries also. Examples include the "small churches"

In a more general way, it could be objected that if the intensity and the scope of centralized power were diminished, we would run the risk of fractures, discord, and errors in matters of faith as well as in morals in the Church, and therefore we would risk being unfaithful to the gospel. On the contrary, I reply that though the risk is real, the moment is now auspicious, since the world today needs to know how to live in unity while respecting diversity. The Church today is ready to test the possibility of how we can live as one in diversity. We have recently witnessed the breakup of enormous and highly centralized political institutions. Now it seems to me that this dissolution has given rise to a resurgence of nationalisms, of opposition between cultures, of religious conflicts. This is only normal, even if it is painful, since living together in mutual respect for differences demands a long period of apprenticeship, especially when peoples' memories are burdened with injuries inflicted over a long history of oppression. But precisely because it is animated by the Spirit of God, informed by the Lord's commandments, solicitous of pluralities that are not anarchic or antagonistic, and the home where mercy and forgiveness are found, it is incumbent on the Church precisely for all these reasons to show that the gospel invites harmonious and tranquil diversity. *Now is the moment for the Church to give the witness of the gospel to the world precisely in this concrete way,* and not, as John XXIII said, issue warnings to it but shed the light of this marvelous example of a universal society that, thanks to faith and its charisms, can live in diversity *and* unity.

To surmount these final fears that might emerge, we can remark in passing that the way of managing the Church in the way of the "Gregorian form" has not delivered the expected results, viz., safeguarding Christendom. Even though the "Gregorian form" of administration aspired to keep Christendom intact, it crumbled. Heresies, schisms, religious indifference, the massive exodus of its members—all occurred even though the official Church had hoped to avoid these tragedies. In the face of such failure met by this institutional form, and not withstanding what it yearned to pre-

---

that were formed after the concordat of 1801 and the "Old Catholics" following Vatican I. More recently, after Vatican II, and despite unprecedented efforts made to offer explanations and take precautions so as not to disturb learned habits, the followers of Bishop Lefebvre started their own little church. As John Paul II stressed, the Church suffers from this action and is deeply saddened. Nevertheless, it cannot be paralyzed by the pretext that some people refuse to make the journey. All that one can do is to conduct such a journey with discernment, accepting in particular that there is a place reserved for those who walk slower or who want to take only the strictly necessary steps. If we continue to move forward hesitantly, it will be the forces that are alive in the Church that will depart, not by declaring a formal schism, but simply because they will not be able to breathe the gospel there any more.

serve and promote, and given the enormous generosity poured out in every epoch and in particular during these last two centuries, it would seem wise that the Church hand itself over to the Spirit, the one who works unity in the Church, and try another way of managing the Church, one whose objectives will be less ambitious and less monolithic. The attacks of the Enemy will be the same, no doubt, but the battle strategy will be better adapted, and will perhaps elicit better service of the gospel and a speedier advance of the kingdom. Stronger than the spirit of evil, the Spirit of God will lead the Church with greater surety, because the People of God as a whole will be more attentive to the Spirit.

Theological Foundations

I would like to conclude with several theological proposals. Behind the appeal for reform underlying the convening of the Second Vatican Council, behind the urgency of new forms of evangelization, behind the silent but pressing demand of a world in crisis and in search of forms and institutions that permit it to live in reconciled diversity, there is a new revelation of God, of the world, and of humanity.

I highlighted above how the medieval idea and the modern idea of God were marked by attributes of unity and unicity, immutability and omnipotence, and I presented the general notion of truth connected with them.[7] I do not believe that the relevance of these divine attributes is up for discussion and I remain reserved vis-à-vis efforts to do so. I have in mind certain recent attempts to be content with simply reversing our language and speaking about God exclusively in terms of vulnerability, suffering, and humility, and at the same time presupposing that the Trinity adequately provides the framework for understanding all of these rather unusual "divine" attributes. Since they can all be found in the Scriptures, it cannot be a question of substituting certain attributes for others, but of reconciling these contrary ideas as much as we can in order to keep them together in their vitality. Without contesting what classical theology has said of God's being and unity, it is necessary to do something similar concerning God's love, in the strongest sense of the term. What are we saying when we say "God is love"? How is it possible to attribute to God not only perfect identity of self to self, but the "otherness" needed for exchange, communion, gift, and welcome? How can we articulate at this level of communion what is innermost to God in God's very self, and what exists between God and what is not God? At an even prior level of reflection, what is *the first thing* we must say about God? What is the *order* of our language about God, i.e., what is the proper succession of the divine names? This is

7. See chapter 2, pp. 37–38.

not the place to take up these theological issues which are at the very center of theological study today. However, it is evident that if there is a development in our way of speaking about God, this includes a development in our way of speaking about Christ, the Spirit, and the Church. But it also implies a more nuanced understanding of truth and its modes of expression. Conversely, a change in our *practice* vis-à-vis creation and the Church is pregnant with a different perception of God. Consequently, at the heart of our discussion and ecclesiological research, the confession of our faith in God is what is at stake.

A notion of God dominated by the almost exclusive attributes of immutability and omnipotence leads in its turn to an idea of humanity in terms of perfection, whether at the first moment of its creation or at the end of its existence, perfection that has its origin in the divine idea, in the natural law, and in the gift of grace. Consequently, every fall from this perfection leads to loss, punishment, and (just as mercy is stronger than justice) to redemption, ultimately in the incarnation of the Son of God. Out of this flows the idea of the Church as the unique and perfect state of salvation, and a certain vision of heaven and hell, the latter, given the weakness and the wickedness of men and women, clearly more populated than the former. Here, as above with respect to the divine attributes, simply reversing our concepts will not do. We must learn to respect other parameters tied to human historicity, viz., time, discourse, being tested, gift, which implies that we will need to discover other accents in our way of understanding perfection, the law, and sin. Behind these different accents will be slightly different ideas of beatitude, vision, and love, but also—or maybe primarily—of communion and giving. The understanding of the Church as structured communion that I have tried to outline here springs from a theological anthropology that does not ignore nature and creation but articulates them in terms of the parameters of history, and which leads to our rethinking the theme of judgment. Consequently, the mission of the Church is not primarily to snatch men and women from the clutches of sin, original and personal, by means of institutions that afford them the greatest safety, but with infinite patience to introduce them into trinitarian love by means of flexible structures of communion that will be able to play here, as much as necessary, the role of the Good Samaritan.

Pope Paul VI thought that "in certain respects, the Second Vatican Council was more important even than the Council of Nicaea."[8] The importance of Nicaea (325) comes from the fact that it endorsed the encounter of the gospel with the Greco-Roman culture of its day. In giving definite

---

8. In a letter to Bishop Marcel Lefebvre dated June 25, 1975. See *La Documentation catholique* 58 (1976) 34.

precision to the vocabulary of the procession of the eternal Word, it opened the way for the formation of the Church's language for the ensemble of revealed aspects of the Mystery of God in God's very self, of the redemptive incarnation of the Son, and the sanctifying mission of the Spirit. This opening is not limited to the Mystery of God, but extends to humanity as well. Thus, an anthropology took shape that greatly expanded and refined the notions of antiquity, in particular concerning the question of freedom.

Perhaps, because it is not possible to hold together all the aspects of revelation, this necessary work of dogmatic precision toned down somewhat the dynamism of the history of salvation. At the risk of simplifying matters, we could say that the doxological formula "Glory to the Father and to the Son and to the Holy Spirit" supplanted the formula "Glory to the Father, through the Son, in the Spirit and the Church." This could not be without consequences for the doctrine and the practice of the Church, and of the authority exercised in it. The Second Vatican Council takes up the entire dogmatic and spiritual effort accomplished in past centuries in the wake of Nicaea, but it reintegrates it in a consideration of the economy of salvation moving toward the parousia of the Lord, and which it establishes on the experience of time that the Bible reveals to us. It seems that there we have a new point of departure in history, one that leads to another way of thinking in the Church and a new way of structuring itself. Nicaea and Vatican II were two major poles of the history of revelation and the Church. That is why it is important that we not miss the turning point[9] that Vatican II represents.

My wish is that in some modest way my effort in this book to present a synthesis of "imagination" will help us seize the *kairos* of the moment and hasten the day when the Lord will return.

---

9. When I wrote the word "turning point" I could not help but think of Heidegger's use of the word *Kehre*. My context is completely different from Heidegger's (or is it really?), but the dramatic intensity of the word is the same.

Index